Blind Bitter Happiness is a collection of acute, irreverent essays and reviews by one of our most candid and intelligent critics and novelists. It includes pieces on the evolution of gay politics in the UK, an essay on disability in film, interviews with sexually ambivalent pop stars (Boy George, Marc Almond), a bitingly perceptive review of Gore Vidal's memoirs and a brilliant polemic, published originally as a Chatto Counter-Blast, on Martin Amis and Ian McEwan, and their strategic use of feminist and anti-nuclear issues.

Alongside lucid cultural criticism there are more personal pieces: a eulogy to a lover, and a portrait of his mother, 'Blind Bitter Happiness', which was described by Penelope Lively in the *Daily Telegraph* as 'a wonderful piece of writing – humane, witty and perceptive.'

ADAM MARS-JONES was born in London in 1954 and educated at the Universities of Cambridge and Virginia. He has written three books of fiction, *Lantern Lecture*, *Monopolies of Loss* and *The Waters of Thirst*. In 1983 and 1993 he was selected as one of *Granta*'s Best of Young British Novelists. He is film critic of the *Independent* and writes regularly for *The London Review of Books*. He lives in London.

BY THE SAME AUTHOR

Lantern Lecture

Monopolies of Loss

The Waters of Thirst

Blind Bitter Happiness

Adam Mars-Jones

Chatto & Windus
LONDON

First published in 1997

1 3 5 7 9 10 8 6 4 2

First published in Great Britain in 1997 by
Chatto & Windus Limited
Random House, 20 Vauxhall Bridge Road,
London SW1V 2SA

Random House Australia (Pty) Limited
20 Alfred Street, Milsons Point, Sydney
New South Wales 2061, Australia

Random House New Zealand Limited
18 Poland Road, Glenfield
Auckland 10, New Zealand

Random House South Africa (Pty) Limited
Endulini, 5a Jubilee Road, Parktown 2193, South Africa

Random House UK Limited Reg. No. 954009

A CIP catalogue record for this book
is available from the British Library

ISBN : 0 7011 6617 7

Typeset by Deltatype Ltd, Birkenhead, Merseyside

Printed in Great Britain by
Mackay's of Chatham PLC, Chatham, Kent.

Contents

This book is for Christopher
Pratt and Frances Coady,
in memory of friendship

I

Gore Vidal/Regal Void

Palimpsest, his extraordinary memoir, if widely read, will do the sort of damage to Gore Vidal's reputation that would normally require a biography of great and subtle hostility. After many years of cultivating a persona, Vidal now tries to articulate a self, apparently not realising that the skills required are the opposite of the ones he has practised for so long. He comes out of the exercise almost unimaginably diminished.

Weary patrician cruelty; erudite negativity propounded with a paradoxical relish. These may not seem liberating characteristics in themselves, but in context they have been so. For decades now Gore Vidal has been an inspirational deflater of reputations – patron saint of the undeceived. Now he comes down among us and shows that he knows himself as little as anyone else. He has delusions of candour.

The first, and enduring, shock of *Palimpsest* is that it should be so slackly constructed and written. Almost nothing is told in sequence, and connections are arbitrary: 'Now you have just read a free-association attempt at writing a theatrical memoir' sums up a passage that was also a brief history of the author's pet dogs.

Meanwhile the epigram factory has fallen on hard times: no self-respecting parodist would dream of passing off most of the book as Vidal's work. Sample: 'It was as if literature, in its last act, decided to have one final great Paris season and we Americans – British, Italians too – came dutifully to Paris to see the gods in what proved to be their twilight, though none of us

suspected that we had come to the end of the day and that the horses of the night were, contrary to Faust's prayer, running very fast indeed.' Gore Vidal without the crispness is hardly recognisable as himself.

Cultivating a persona means suppressing your first reaction and substituting something that is more effective in a given context. In Vidal's case, this has meant aspiring never to be surprised or taken in. If there was, for instance, a subjective gap between his hearing of Truman Capote's death and his comment on it ('good career move'), a moment that predates heartless wit, then it has been purposefully erased.

Writing your memoirs, though, requires some investigation of sensations before they were modified, of the raw as opposed to the cooked. This doesn't fit with Vidal's chosen self-image of the man who's seen it all before. Describing his stepfather's house, Merrywood, he writes: 'I recall . . . the rich supper prepared by a Russian chef from the czar's Winter Palace. Where else? – all Russian cooks of that day were so billed.' He was ten at the time. His actual impressions of the event have been replaced by the commentary of his future self, connoisseur of prestige and pretension.

Autobiography is pre-eminently the genre of having it both ways, and sophisticated consumers demand a certain amount in this line. Vidal duly presents the writing of *The City and the Pillar* as a sort of sacred duty, since to write about homosexual acts in the late 1940s was to guarantee internal exile from respectability and reviewing slots, while also glorying in the book's commercial success. Later, he stoically describes the novel as an art-form that has long been 'of no great interest to the public at large', then casually reproduces as an illustration a list of bestsellers from the summer of 1964 featuring *Julian* at number one, ahead of *The Spy Who Came in from the Cold*.

Perhaps in a book that quotes extensively from other people's descriptions of the author at various stages of his career it would be best not to make excessive claims to modesty.

Certainly Vidal should have selected a pose and stuck to it, making a definite choice between the graciously worldly 'There does come a time when one stops reading about oneself' (p.213) and the more hard-line 'my lifelong reluctance to read anything about myself' (p.125).

Anyone who thinks that Gore Vidal is indifferent to the social world must be thinking of someone else. Indifference to the social world is in any case not a virtue. So who is Vidal thinking of when he observes that 'wherever I live, I seem to know only four or five people who happen to be at hand'? After all, when he mentions in passing seeing Orson Welles eating breakfast at Doney's in Rome, Welles is described as 'my future lunch companion'. In a book where much is shapeless and inattentive, care has been taken to let us know that Orson Welles in 1948 had *something* to look forward to.

When Vidal says, 'I am not social; I also like giving up things, letting go', he illustrates the point by mentioning that he has turned down an invitation to dine with Princess Margaret ('I wonder if I am a bad friend'). In this particular hermit's grotto, there is no shortage of embossed invitations on the rough-hewn mantelpiece.

If Gore Vidal was truly not a social creature, we would expect more in the way of an intimate register, but this is his single weakest area. He can describe routines of gardening or travelling, but he shies away from describing life with his partner, Howard Austen, with whom he has lived in sexless companionship for half a century (Austen gets fewer references in the index than Capote or Paul Bowles).

There are many possible reasons for discretion, the obvious one being that the partner has no wish to be written about, but it's not that he's excluded, exactly. In the course of a chat, Kinsey speculates that Vidal, if extrapolated from his sexual profile, would plausibly be ' "a lower-middle-class Jew, with more heterosexual than homosexual interests" ', and Vidal adds, 'Curiously, I have spent most of my life with such a person' (sometimes in *Palimpsest* it seems that basic information, like a satellite signal, has to be bounced off some orbiting celebrity).

The relationship with Austen has a beginning – the two met at a gay baths – and an anticipated ending, a plot in Rock Creek Cemetery next to Vidal's own, but he is very much a sleeping partner in *Palimpsest*, a trace element in the book's 'we' and 'our'. The only gratuitous biography of Austen ('born in the Bronx, worked at Walgreen's drugstore to put himself through New York University . . .') comes in the caption to a photograph.

It isn't with Austen, in any case, that Vidal dreams of being reunited, but with his first and only love Jimmie Trimble, 'the half of me that never lived to grow up', killed at Iwo Jima and waiting in Rock Creek Cemetery since 1945.

With the parts of *Palimpsest* that deal with Jimmie Trimble, Gore Vidal explores an uncharacteristically sincere and passionate persona. It is still a persona, though, since he describes his relationship with Jimmie in terms derived from Aristophanes' contribution to the *Symposium*. His relationship with Jimmie, though it involved (non-penetrative) sex, was Platonic in that sense. It has to be said, though, that if vengeful Zeus really did punish mankind in its original spherical form by bisecting people, it was sporting of him to instal the halves of one particular bisected sphere in the same Washington school, in easy reach of each other.

Vidal admits that at the time he spoke to Kinsey in 1948, he had yet to read Plato ('I had no theory'). Vidal is not someone who values theory in literature or politics, so why does he need an amorous one? Why does he need to borrow a vocabulary, to describe pre-war experiences he sees as formative?

Certainly the Trimble material feels studied and pseudo-classical, full of references to Achilles and Patroclus, and so forth. Jimmie's sweat 'smelled of honey, like that of Alexander the Great'. When exactly did Vidal pick up this piece of olfactory-historical information?

Even in the Trimble parts of the book, Gore Vidal seems to be less than fully attentive. He passes on two different accounts of Jimmie's death – one witness says he was killed by a grenade (p.38), another that he was shot and bayoneted (p.76) – without seeming to notice the discrepancies. Vidal compares the part that Jimmie Trimble plays in *Palimpsest* with 'Rosebud' in *Citizen Kane*, the secret that explains everything. But is he thinking of true personal obsession, or a writer's device for structuring a piece of work?

In the course of writing *Palimpsest*, Gore Vidal sent off for transcripts of a court case from 1915, in which his grandfather was charged with indecent assault. The accusation was false, and politically motivated, but along with the transcript came some much more substantial dirt, dating from an earlier period, 1895, in Texas. A blind girl claimed that she had been engaged to T. P. Gore, who raped her, impregnated her, tried to secure an abortion with medicine and finally with the aid of a small instrument, and then persuaded her to keep silence on the grounds that exposure would hurt his career and his blameless parents.

Gore Vidal describes this testimony as 'hair-raising', but points out that he's not in a position to establish its truth or otherwise. Then he blithely mentions that his great-uncle, Ellis, acknowledged his brother's guilt in the matter in 1960, immediately after the broadcast of Vidal's television play *The Indestructible Mr Gore*, which followed the family line in assuming his innocence.

It can't be a common experience to discover that your beloved grandfather, whom you have just celebrated on television, was in point of fact a liar, manipulator, rapist and forcible abortionist. It would seem likely to be rather disillusioning. Yet the eulogies of T. P. resume as if nothing had happened ('I always found him noblest when he put his career at risk for some overriding principle', 'Courage was Gore's most notable trait'). Vidal gives us no hint of what he felt when

Great-Uncle Ellis dropped his little bombshell in 1960, though he doesn't seem like someone who would enjoy being deceived.

The most puzzling parts of *Palimpsest*, though, are not the parts where Gore Vidal is telling an old-established story, and can't fit troubling material into it, but those parts where he seems not to have a story at all. One of his special disadvantages as an autobiographer is that he has been famous for a long time. Many writers have passed judgement on his various past selves, and the urge to set them straight is powerful – in the case of Anaïs Nin downright irresistible.

He is definite that they met at a lecture by Kimon Friar on his 'Medusa theory of poetry', while her version is that the lecture was on love. But when she elaborates ('Kimon was lecturing on Plato's symposium of love'), he seizes the chance to mock her lack of classical learning: 'I have forgotten that detail, which sounds true, since she had not read Plato's *Symposium*'. Does that mean that the lecture was about love after all?

These squabbles bring an incongruous note of lovers' tiff to what is already an unlikely friendship. What was it that drew Gore Vidal to Anaïs Nin, since as he puts it, this was a case of 'chicken hawk meets chicken hawk'? The only elements surplus to her account, and present in *Palimpsest*, are: (1) in being a bloodsucker who saw herself as nurturing the victims she drained, she resembled his hated mother Nina, and (2) both women were born in 1903. The reader is under strict instructions from Vidal to ignore these delusive correspondences ('no, Freudians, *forget it*'), and Anaïs Nin would be in agreement, since she hardly advertised the age gap. (No one mentions the similarity of name between Nin and Nina.)

Yet apart from squabbling over the details, Vidal seems unable to account for the friendship, though Nin even visited him in Guatemala. Vidal doesn't say so in so many words, but she was presumably invited: he would hardly pass up the chance of denouncing her as an intercontinental gatecrasher. All he can say is 'I find it impossible to believe that I once listened to all this with perfect seriousness', or 'I, too, was ensorceled – a favorite Nin verb – by her for a time', where the sneer at vocabulary doesn't exactly compensate for the gap in his emotional memory.

It turns out that Gore Vidal finds his behaviour towards Nina herself, the hated mother, equally baffling. If she was so hated, why did he invite her to stay with him in London? 'Why? I don't know.' Even Howard breaks silence to ask why he bothered with her at all: 'I don't really know. But I am beginning to think that she knew how to play on a sadistic streak in me that would, once awakened, impel me to detonate the Queen Lear of the Lobby in order to revel in her howlings.' *I don't really know* seems closer to the mark.

Even supremely sophisticated people are entitled to their ignorance about themselves, but perhaps less so in a book that includes this piece of suavity in its mission statement: 'Of course, I am not so sure that I have known even one person well, but, as the Greeks sensibly believed, should you get to know yourself, you will have penetrated as much of the human mystery as anyone need ever know.'

Summing his mother up, Vidal remarks: '. . . today I feel nothing other than curiosity that I should have remained on the case for as long as I did in actual time and now in surprised retrospect'. In its untroubled flatness this comes close to being a sin against autobiography. His 'curiosity' is hardly intense, since it asks no questions.

If with Nina and Anaïs Nin Gore Vidal is emotionally blank, there are two figures who always bring a charge into the book, sometimes a disproportionate charge: Jackie Kennedy and JFK. He broke off with Jackie in 1963, though he doesn't go into detail (the underlying reason being his dislike, and her love, of Bobby Kennedy). Still she brings out some of his most elaborate games of denigration. In a passage where he is supposedly describing his sex life, he mentions once being offered $10 after the act, which he accepted. 'As a result I, alone in the family, did not condemn Jackie's marriage to Onassis, since I, too, had once been a small player in the commodities' exchange market.'

Vidal must have considered the possibility that he will enter history, not as planned, but as a footnote to the Kennedy story. But perhaps it's better to enter history on those terms than not at all (later in the book he takes credit for having introduced Jackie to dark glasses). Perhaps that's the reason for this particularly intricate manoeuvre – spitting on someone's back without actually dismounting from her coat-tails.

JFK turns up in even more unexpected places. Vidal is struck by the similarities 'between my youthful self and his, particularly in sexual matters', before adding that 'unlike Jack, I had once been . . . in love'. Still, the promiscuity contest must go on: 'I was setting world records for encounters with anonymous youths, nicely matching busy Jack Kennedy's girl-a-day routine'.

Even describing what must have been the worst moment of his life, hearing the news of Jimmie's death, Vidal can't leave Kennedy alone: 'I think my first reaction must have been somewhat like that when I heard Jack Kennedy had been shot.' He digresses on to Kennedy's posthumous fame, 'a great media monster, now wreathed in garlands of paranoia of a most unpleasant sort'. It seems to be an actual effort to get back to Jimmie Trimble: 'Jimmie was no media monster, but he was already vivid in his own right and, thus, no candidate for death.'

Cheap psychological explanations in *Palimpsest* are for other people – in fact they are specifically for Kennedys. JFK's promiscuity, superficially so like Vidal's, turns out to be based on the need to outdo his father ('the object of the exercise'), just as Bobby's large family undermines rather than confirms his claims to heterosexuality: 'anyone who has eleven children must be trying to prove – disprove? – something other than the ability to surpass his father as incontinent breeder'.

But if we readers are allowed a little speculation of our own, we're likely to think that Jack Kennedy is Vidal's dark twin – the person he wanted to replace – as Jimmie Trimble is his light one. Each twin haunts him with what might have been.

Reading *Palimpsest* is a bizarre experience, since memoirs don't usually include such major lapses of curiosity alternating with episodes of distorted preening. It's like being the weekend guest of someone who makes a great point of not having any mirrors in the house, but whom you then come across peering at his reflection in the back of a spoon. A spoon with the JFK monogram.

Guardian, 1995. Anyone who has ever written mean-spirited prose owes a debt of honour to Gore Vidal. It's only fair to say that *Palimpsest* was generally well received – but I saved him from the fate of being the wasp none dare sting.

Taking the Yellow View

Cyril Connolly in 1938 pinpointed the advantages enjoyed by the homosexual writer: combativeness, curiosity, egotism, intuition and adaptability, 'equipment', as he put it, 'greatly to be envied'.

At the same time Connolly assumed that homosexual writers would always, 'until we can change society', have to avoid certain subjects and substitute others, just as stammerers learn to avoid the syllables that give them trouble.

This was, for its time, and despite its tacit omission of women, a distinctly enlightened opinion; in practice Connolly was offended when Isherwood implied that his feelings for a lover were comparable to Connolly's own feelings for his wife. But that time is in any case past; for the past fifteen years homosexual men in Britain have been accorded a lavish fraction of civil rights. Homosexuals are, intermittently, freer than ever before.

The result has not been an explosion of unleashed sensibility and the instant integration of the minority (perhaps only Leo Abse, MP, expected these things); it takes people a while to get over the shock of decriminalisation. The result has been an assortment of improvised moralities combining in various proportions reaction against, and imitation of, heterosexual precedents. By and large, they resemble the provisional motorised vehicles which appeared before someone realised that a horseless carriage need not look like a carriage without a horse.

America, where social change is chronic as well as epidemic, has played a large part in the shaping of gay attitudes in Britain. Whereas in Britain an urban area needs to have several years of solid gentrification behind it before it becomes possible to buy food there after 6 p.m., in America a neighbourhood (whatever its previous reputation) can be transformed by a single newspaper article in the right place; at the end of a week the streets will reliably bristle with roller-skate hire firms and exotic-pet shops.

Gay Americans have been quick to exercise their rights in the marketplace; for years now it has been possible for a gay man in America to live entirely in a subculture of bars, baths and gay-owned businesses.

Such concentrations of gay men may or may not have political power, but they certainly have bright green dollars in their faded-denim pockets. So it shouldn't be surprising that Avon Books (a division of the Hearst Corporation), publishers of Bard, Camelot and Discus Books, should have had spectacular success with titles aimed specifically at this market.

Gay women present a less susceptible marketing profile than gay men. Their lower income prevents them (as a group) from affording a high turnover of attitudes and accessories, and if they do mobilise their resources they are as likely as not to move away from a city. Feminism, moreover, gives them a certain immunity to the siren voices of the marketplace.

Gay men's periodicals tend to be weekly, fortnightly or monthly (the *New York Native*, the *Advocate*, *Christopher Street*) and to be based in a traditional gay stronghold. Women's magazines are more likely to be quarterlies put together in provincial cities; *Common Lives/Lesbian Lives* in Iowa City, for instance, *Sinister Wisdom* in Amherst, Massachusetts.

Avon's gay-targeted books are available mainly in gay areas, and are imported into this country only by specialist bookshops; they tend not to be reviewed in newspapers with cultural pretensions. Some, like the novels of Gordon Merrick (*The Lord Won't Mind*, *Perfect Freedom*, *Now Let's Talk About*

Music), dispense frank pulp; others have a certain sophistication.

My plan is to dissect a sophisticated example of Avon's output, to see what it has to say about the way men and women behave. This isn't a matter of a highbrow beating hell out of an unliterary text; it's actually an advantage that Avon Books don't represent any sort of personal vision. In any case, gay liberation doesn't need to have literary pretensions to be largely a verbal matter; its first products, after all, were slogans, and it sets out to construct a new rhetoric to neutralise the prevailing one. Twenty years ago, to use an uncontroversial analogy, it was possible to hate your job, to go through your working days in a trance of boredom and misery, but it wasn't possible to have a 'mid-life crisis'; this term solves no problems, but by providing a category for experience it asserts that certain underprivileged emotions are real. The rhetoric of gay liberation has become very various and sophisticated, but it is still a set of manoeuvres which responds to the techniques of literary criticism.

Nathan Aldyne's *Vermilion*, a detective novel set in Boston, was published by Avon Books, as a paperback original, in October 1980. It was successful enough to spawn a sequel, *Cobalt*, in 1982. It received enthusiastic reviews in magazines that are either gay (*Alternate Magazine*, the *Advocate*, *Numbers*, *Drummer*), Boston-based (the *Boston Phoenix*), or both (*Gay Community News*).

You are only likely to get a negative review in the *Boston Phoenix* of a novel set in Boston if you get the bus routes wrong, and the same general rule applies to the other publications. The view of gay life in *Vermilion* is either authentic, or plausible enough for its inaccuracy not to be noticed by experts in the field; it is true at least on the level of myth.

Vermilion so successfully represents the mainstream of gay fiction that the reviews of it concentrate on its genre ('a first-rate mystery', 'a classic whodunit', 'a wonderful detective novel') and treat its gay setting as an utterly neutral medium. Is this the atmosphere that gay men breathe? What is its composition?

A gay detective novel is certainly a variant with possibilities. Homosexuals, after all, have little excuse for being in love with the police, while the police traditionally regard homosexuals, not as an especially vulnerable group, but as trouble-making degenerates. So there are at first sight better reasons for a homosexual to be dissatisfied with conventional criminal enquiries than for a vain little Belgian with an egg-shaped head and luxuriant moustaches to give a little help to his old friend Inspector Japp.

The victim of the murder, moreover, is a young hustler called Billy Golacinsky, whose death the police would normally regard as uninteresting.

The reason for the police's abnormal interest is the location of the corpse: the body was dumped on the lawn of Representative Mario Scarpetti, 'an ignorant, loudmouthed, and powerful enemy of Boston's gay community'. This is the excuse for the selling line on the book's cover: *The murderer had a weakness for boys . . . and dirty politics.*

Scarpetti wants a scapegoat.

As things turn out, the dumping of the body on Scarpetti's lawn had no significance and was purely a matter of chance; Scarpetti's home was simply a house on a dark street in a quiet suburb. In this respect, *Vermilion* breaks the rules of the classic detective novel, where apparently neutral details can turn out to be unnoticed oddities, but where the reverse never happens: flagrantly unusual events cannot simply be ascribed to chance. Any misleading impression must be due to a human agency; red herrings may very likely clutter the landscape, but they must have been planted by a person with something to gain from every intricate deception.

Thrillers, after all, deal in reassurance as well as fear (both in homoeopathic doses), and people who say they like a good mystery usually mean they like a seamless solution. It isn't only Representative Scarpetti that wants a scapegoat, and a book that fails to tie up loose ends fails to resolve the emotions that it trades in.

The murder of a hustler is likely to trigger two orders of fear in a gay reader: the generalised fear that gay sexuality is by definition destructive, and the more circumstantial fear that a life of urban anonymity, with the sexual instinct hived off from all others and expressed in isolation, brings with it a massive vulnerability. Gay men living in urban ghettos distance themselves still further than other Americans from the privilege enjoyed by more settled communities, of being killed by people they know.

Vermilion can counteract the first fear only if the killer turns out not to be homosexual, so that the murder has no actual connection with gay sexuality. It is in any case unthinkable that a book so accurately targeted on a gay readership would preach damnation to the converted by revealing a homosexual as the murderer.

Things have changed a great deal in ten years. In 1970 Ellery Queen, winner of five Edgars (including the Grand Master award of 1960) and both the silver and gold Gertrudes awarded by Pocket Books, Inc., published a detective novel called *The Last Woman in His Life*.

A millionaire playboy is murdered in his bedroom. Near the body lie an evening gown, a wig, and a pair of long white gloves, belonging (one item each) to the playboy's three ex-wives. And here is an excerpt from the killer's confessional monologue:

> From the start of the weekend I felt a kind of crisis in identity that turned physiological with great rapidity. It sapped my usual control. That Friday night, when Audrey, Marcia and Alice came downstairs all dressed up, something happened to me. Audrey's stunning evening gown with the sequins, Marcia's silly 'fun' wig, Alice's elbow-length gloves . . . all of a sudden I was wildly attracted to them. I had to have them . . . put them on . . . parade around in them. If we'd been in the city I could

> have used one of my own drag outfits, but we were in that damned backwoods town . . . And there was my beloved Johnny – the unsatisfied passion of my life – practically in my arms . . . signaling to me, as I thought, giving me the come-on . . .

I can forgive the murders. I can forgive the lifetime of deceit. But what kind of monster would steal Marcia's fun wig?

It does seem a bit hard, though, not that a homosexual should be revealed as a murderer, nor that a murderer should be revealed to be a homosexual, but that someone should be unveiled all at once as a cross-dressed murdering invert, as if these elements had a natural affinity. Many homicidal transvestites, of course, are heterosexual, and would bitterly resent the imputation of abnormality.

There is no question in the book of analysis in depth; you don't win Edgars and Gertrudes for your sympathetic portrayal of minority groups. Homosexuality in *The Last Woman in His Life* (guess who?) is used purely as a thriller prop. The fact that no one detects the killer as homosexual is not a piece of social comment ('they're not so different from us'), but assimilates homosexuality to the status of an untraceable poison; the crucial point here is simply absence-of-clues.

In the same way, the victim's dying words (on the phone) are carefully contrived:

> 'J-J-J . . .'
> 'Johnny? Is this Johnny?'
> 'Yes. El . . .'
> 'Yes, yes, what's wrong?'
> 'Dying.'
> 'You? Wait! I mean, I'll be right over.'
> 'No . . . time.'
> 'Hang on –'
> 'M-m-m . . . Murder.'
> 'Who, Johnny? Tell me. Who did it?'

'Home.'

'I mean, who attacked you? . . . Hold on, Johnny, hold on! Who did it? . . . Try to tell me.'

'Home . . . Home . . . Home.'

Johnny refrains from naming his killer, or from describing him explicitly ('It was a queen, Ellery . . . a goddamned cross-dressed kleptomaniac homicidal queen'), for no human reason, but because for the purposes of the novel it is necessary that he be misunderstood. Johnny uses (but is unable to finish) the word 'homosexual', apparently with a long first syllable, not because it is a neutral term, but because there can be no equivocation with the more likely words 'fruit' or 'faggot'. 'Home' as the unsuspected first syllable of 'homosexual' admirably obeys the detective-story rule that apparently neutral details may turn out to be unnoticed oddities; but that's about all that can be said for it.

The Last Woman in His Life, remember, appears the year after the Stonewall Riots and the beginnings of gay liberation, and the terms 'gay' and 'cruising' are used by the killer in his monologue of confession. There is even a wistful plea for understanding ('If only people stopped regarding us as some sort of monsters . . .'), though the fact that these sentiments are voiced by someone who steals Marcia's fun wig and kills people may lessen the impact of his message on society.

The assumption made by *The Last Woman in His Life* is not in any case that homosexuals are not people, but that people in any given group are not homosexual. From Ellery Queen's point of view (or points of view, since 'Ellery Queen' is in fact two people who pretend to be one in order to write about violent death) it is about as likely that a homosexual should read detective novels as that a native of Borneo should write a letter of protest to the author of a detective story about his use of untraceable poisons, pointing out that the tribesmen use them only for executions, a method infinitely superior in humane terms to such barbarous devices as the gallows or the guillotine.

Nathan Aldyne is on much firmer ground with the assumption that very few more heterosexuals or women than murderers will read *Vermilion*; the novel's scapegoat will hardly be gay. At an early stage of the book, we are told that the Boston *Globe* would like to see it turn out that Billy Golacinsky was murdered 'by a straight couple out for sleazy thrills'. By implication this is a reactionary theory, determined solely by Representative Scarpetti's denunciations of a gay conspiracy.

But the *Globe*'s wishful thinking is not so very different from the novel's. Billy was indeed killed by a straight couple out for sleazy thrills, with the extra twist that they were commercial purveyors of sleazy thrills; one of their clients was a policeman ashamed of his sexual nature, and Billy, having witnessed their goings-on, was blackmailing him. The conspiracy, in fact, was between 'a straight couple and a Boston cop'.

Hidden homosexuality, responsible in *The Last Woman in His Life* for the murder and all its consequences, plays a surprisingly similar role in *Vermilion*, since Lieutenant Searcy's inability to accept his attraction to men sets the plot in motion; but all the stigma has been transferred from the homosexuality to the hiding of it. Don't blame the skeleton, blame the closet that has kept it out of circulation for so long.

A novel whose denouement exonerates healthy homosexuals and incriminates hypocritical self-described heterosexuals might be felt to have done its bit for the peace of mind of gay readers, but *Vermilion* has more reassurance to offer.

Its hero, Daniel Valentine, is presented as the sum of all gay virtues; it would be an understatement to describe him as an idealised role-model. The reader is simply denied any opportunity to question the values he represents.

In the first scene of the novel Daniel Valentine meets Billy Golacinsky, the hustler; it is a bitterly cold first of January, the last night of Billy's life. Billy is trying to pick someone up; he's broke, and was thrown out of his lodgings earlier in the day. Daniel, who is out walking a dog, is described from Billy's point of view:

> The tall slender man appeared well built beneath his black pea coat. Sandy blond hair showing beneath his black knit watch cap matched the color of his well-trimmed beard. His features were not exceptional, but his expression was one of self-confident easeful strength . . .

Billy finds Daniel attractive, but the feeling is apparently not reciprocated. Daniel offers only advice:

> 'Listen, kid, nobody's out tonight. Nobody's playing. Nobody's buying. Everybody shot his wad last night. Remember? New Year's Eve. John is home with his wife, John is home with his lover, John couldn't get his car started in the cold. John is not going to show up on the Block tonight. Your timing's bad, kid. Go home and get warm.'

This sets the pattern for the rest of the book. Daniel is more desired than desiring; and he has an inordinate amount of worldly knowledge. He has never been so poor as to have to sell his body, nor so unattractive as to have to buy someone else's; yet he knows more about hustling than a hustler does.

Daniel goes home, and Billy gets killed; Daniel has no alibi for the murder.

Daniel works as a bartender in a gay bar called Bonaparte's; he is thus placed squarely in the middle of the subculture. There is already an element of exoneration in this: Daniel can spend a great deal of time in a sexually charged atmosphere without choosing to do so. His is a privileged access to sexual attention.

But Daniel has multiple exemptions. We learn that he tends bar as a stopgap, until he can return to his real job. He lost his 'real' job, as a prison counsellor, when he exposed corruption in the prison service, by reporting a superior who had used $10,000 of taxpayers' money to buy curtains for his living room. He must now wait for a change of administration before he can be reinstated.

There are three levels of exoneration present in this piece of background information. For a start, it establishes Daniel Valentine as an exile from the dominant culture, making a casual living in the gay subculture through no wish of his own. His values, moreover, are actually superior to those of the dominant culture, since his reward for a public-spirited action is dismissal from his socially useful job; and still he retains his idealism, waiting patiently until he can take a salary cut and resume his career. Then, too, in his capacity as a prison counsellor he spent his working life trying to rescue people from a (criminal) subculture. How many jobs fit this description?

Daniel Valentine, in fact, may have no alibi for Billy Golacinsky's death, but he is given an impressive set of alibis for his own daily life. He may look as if he is leading an entirely subcultural existence, but he is in some important sense somewhere else, doing something quite different.

Daniel's self-confident easeful strength seems to need quite a lot of propping up.

Daniel doesn't actually do anything in the course of the book to distinguish him from stereotypical inhabitants of the subculture, but evidence is constantly being offered of his unfettered access to people of all sorts and conditions.

The bartender Mack, for instance, has only one big speech, which runs as follows:

> 'I tell you, Lieutenant: twenty-five years ago it was straight men got me in trouble, and ten years ago it was straight men that got me put in jail. It was a *fag* that got me out of jail, and it was a *fag* that made sure I got a decent job. I got *nothing* against 'em. I'm not a fag, but I know what they know . . . that straight men are just trouble.'

Sixty pages later, we learn from Daniel the identity of his helper: 'Mack's one of my success stories.'

Another of Daniel's success stories (Silber, breaking and entering, three-to-five, now working as a florist) makes an appearance in Chapter 16 to offer thanks. His only function in the novel is to endorse Daniel's value as a human being, and since Silber is an old man, he might just as well come out and say: 'This boy doesn't just care for the young 'uns.'

The relationship of Daniel's that we see most of, though, is his friendship with Clarisse Lovelace, Nora Charles to his Nick. Clarisse is a successful estate agent, in spite of her somewhat cavalier attitude to her employers. In Bermuda, at an unspecified date in the past, Clarisse and Daniel had something that was almost an affair:

> 'Those happy days when I fell in love with you by the pool, those happy nights in my cabana, and those happy mornings that you spent in bed with the assistant manager –'
>
> 'I didn't know quite how to break it to you . . .'
>
> 'I thought your impotence was *my* fault – but by the time you got around to me in the evening, you were just worn out. God was I upset when I found out!'
>
> 'I would have been impotent *without* the assistant manager,' smiled Valentine, consolingly.
>
> 'So why did you even try?'
>
> 'Because you were in love with me, and I was in love with your tits. I still am.'

Notice that in this penultimate sentence a woman who wants to have a sexual relationship with a man is described as being 'in love with him', whereas a man who doesn't want a sexual relationship with a woman is described as being 'in love with her tits'. Even in contemporary Boston, and no matter what anybody actually wants, women are emotional creatures, while men by their nature deal in sexual objectification.

Not that Clarisse is consistently characterised. In a curious way she is called upon to be both a woman and an honorary homosexual.

Clarisse is an honorary homosexual in the sense that she lives a largely subcultural existence; her clients at the estate agent's are predominantly gay, and she spends much of her leisure time in bars like Bonaparte's or Nexus. She has adopted a milieu that doesn't cater to her, and she has also adopted its values.

In this context she is perfectly well able to treat men as sexual objects; when at a late stage of the investigation she spies on an orgy from a balcony, she comments approvingly on the muscular 'definition' of one man, and disparagingly on another, who 'doesn't work out' and should join a gym. Although as a woman she carries a torch for Daniel Valentine, as an honorary homosexual she rates casual sexual encounters above relationships. She prescribes a week of debauchery in San Francisco to a client whose lover has left him: 'Believe me,' she says, 'after a week . . . you won't even remember who George was.'

Nowhere in the book does she diverge, in her assessment of a man, from the gay men around her; and they for their part show an astonishing unanimity of taste.

Clarisse has achieved her emancipation from conventional lifestyles without benefit of feminism. She sees no conflict between being a career girl and being a sex object; for her, they are different terms for the same thing. 'I rent more flats,' she says at one point, 'if I don't wear a bra.' But then the gay men in the book don't refer to social movements of the sixties either; they may be proud that there are no more 'squishy faggots' in Boston, but they show no sign of knowing that gay liberation was started by a riot and not by an article in *Uomo Vogue*.

Although in theory Clarisse is a solitary heterosexual surrounded by gays, in practice she is the character who resorts most readily to camp. Camp, with its brittleness and insistent triviality, is a conversational style that is perceived as compromising, however enjoyable, by contemporary gays; overindulgence in camp is felt somehow to be letting the side down.

Clarisse, feminine already, has nothing to fear from the stigma of effeminacy. She can get away with the occasional brutally bitchy remark, which would corrode the masculinity of any man who uttered it: 'Maybe now you can pass for butch,' she says to Daniel when a lover gives him a leather jacket.

Most of the time, though, she is content to embody Hollywood's imagery of women for the benefit of the men around her. 'Oh, God, I feel like Joan Crawford in *Rain*,' she says at one point; she does dinner-table impersonations of the stars for Daniel's entertainment (notably Ida Lupino in *They Drive by Night*), and even her Afghan hound is called Veronica Lake. She delivers the final line of the book: 'In the immortal words of Mildred Pierce, "let's get stinko!" '

Clarisse has a certain amount to gain from moving in a gay milieu; she has plenty of social life, and some of the social skills rub off on her. When two men renting a flat from her talk about their girlfriends, she knows when they're actually gay.

Her sensitivity to the bush telegraph, though, is less than perfect, since she is, after all, only a hanger-on. She is attracted to Lieutenant Searcy, whom all the bona fide homosexuals in the book spot as a closet case, busily denying his nature. Once and once only does she compete with Daniel for the attention of a man, and then Daniel gets the date.

Clarisse's sex life takes place out of the confines of the book. 'Last week', apparently, she went off with an insurance agent she met at the Laundromat; at an unspecified period in the past she had a short affair with a wholesale florist. In Chapter 6 she has coffee with a 'cute fireman' and they arrange a date, but it doesn't take place in the timespan of the book.

Clarisse's sex life in fact follows a gay model of casual pick-ups and short liaisons, although she doesn't have to cope with the social disapproval which generated that model in the first place. Are there experiences in her past which determine her behaviour in the present, or is she issued by her author with a standard model of consumerist urban lifestyle, as a matter of routine?

Only in one respect is Clarisse treated differently from the men.

On her first appearance she is described, like Daniel on his, from a stranger's point of view, in this case Lieutenant Searcy:

> His gaze went no further than the foyer, trapped by the woman he saw there. She was tall and leggy beneath a mahogany-brown fur coat. The garment was cut in the 1940s style, with padded shoulders and wide cuffs . . . She snatched off her fur skullcap; a great mane of hair cascaded in soft black waves beneath the dull red light of the foyer . . . Her cheeks were flushed with cold. She had strong, even features, large dark blue eyes accented with blue eye shadow, and a full sensual mouth softly tinted with pale coral lipstick . . . The fur fell open to reveal large breasts beneath a tailored, expensive blue work shirt, blue jeans tight-belted around a slender waist and hips. The jeans were tucked into knee-high brown leather riding-boots.

Clarisse is clearly an object of value, just like Daniel, but she is described much more in terms of her clothes. Daniel wears 'boots'. Clarisse wears 'knee-high brown leather riding-boots'. If a man was wearing her shirt, it wouldn't be described as 'tailored' or 'expensive', however much it cost, however artfully it was cut.

Clarisse's outfits are described in some detail over the five days of the book's action. On Wednesday she wears 'full-cut black corduroy slacks and a white silk blouse opened one button too many'. On Friday she wears 'a gray silk dress with wide padded shoulders, black seamed hose and matching gray heels'. On Saturday she wears 'new denim jeans and a western shirt with a flowered yoke'.

If a man was wearing those jeans, they would just be 'jeans'; their material would be taken for granted, and their newness tactfully passed over. This doesn't mean, though, that Clarisse's specifications for jeans are likely to be more stringent than a man's; rather the reverse. On the streets of a subcultural America, if you aren't wearing faded Levi's 501s (new if necessary, but never looking it), you might as well be wearing bombazine for all the good it will do you. Gay men's dress is subject to laws of some rigour.

But *Vermilion* presents men as natural, women as artificial. Men are somehow nouns, and unadorned; women are encrusted with adjectives.

Take hair, for instance. One evening Clarisse asks Daniel for advice about her hair: what style would suit her? Would short hair make her look like Faye Dunaway or Diana Dors, Glenda Jackson or Marjorie Main? The next day, although in the end she doesn't have her hair cut, an important scene is laid at her coiffeur's, Chez Marcel.

Women are composite references to other women; men are originals.

So where does Daniel get his hair cut? The subject isn't raised. As far as hair goes, he resembles that quintessential sixties person, the Tressy Doll (Her Hair Grows). Tressy's hair grew only in the sense that nylon fibres could be pulled through a sort of sieve on her scalp, and winched back by way of a plastic key in her back. Daniel's hair grows just like Tressy's does, when there's no one around.

Part of the point here is presumably to clear gay men of any taint of narcissism, but the end result portrays Clarisse as a consumer on a grand scale (buying $200 worth of perfume at one point), while Daniel's lifestyle verges on the austere.

Vermilion proposes women as the sum of a series of decorative decisions, men (in the teeth of the evidence) as creatures of a substantial solidity, requiring no explanation.

Daniel changes his clothes very little in the course of the book. After a visit to the International Health Spa on the Thursday he keeps on a red sweatshirt under his coat, but that's about it.

Clarisse seems to do his washing for him. Certainly she goes to the Laundromat, where 'last week' she met that insurance man; Daniel complains that she went off with her new friend, and let his underwear melt in the drier.

Only one garment of Daniel's is described in real detail: 'a waist-length jacket. It was of shiny dark-brown leather, had zippered pockets, a wide collar, and dark-fur lining.' This orgy of description is excused by the fact that the jacket is a present to Daniel, and so doesn't represent any incriminating choice on his part.

Mark, who gives Daniel the jacket, is a lumberjack from New Hampshire who had a two-week affair with him the previous August, and fell in love. In the course of the book he returns to Boston, hoping to continue the relationship.

Daniel has other ideas.

It isn't that Mark is short of attractions. As he puts it: 'Mark is hot, Mark has the body of death, Mark is just about the handsomest most rugged man I've ever come across in my life, and he'll make somebody a great wife, but not me!' Nor is it that Mark's personal qualities lag behind his appearance; *Vermilion* doesn't acknowledge the existence of qualities as opposed to attributes, those fractional selves that the men in the book project towards each other.

It's just that Mark's clinging to the outmoded notion that experience is not infinitely interchangeable, that it is possible to prefer one person to another, even in bed, makes him an embarrassment.

He doesn't even have the excuse of isolation; true, he is up there in the wilds of New Hampshire, but he is surrounded by 300 lumberjacks, so his feeling for someone less available can only be perverse.

In the course of the book Mark is led gently from a romantic late adolescence to a casually exploitative maturity; and though this plot-strand is entirely unconnected with the murder story, it is in many ways much more neatly constructed.

The world of *Vermilion* is threatened, after all, by monogamy or any approach to it, not by hustling; a mutual prostitution (with money changing hands only to remedy a gross disparity in the attractiveness of the partners) is in fact the book's model for sexual encounters.

What would happen if gay men formed relationships? They would stop frequenting Bonaparte's, for one thing, and they might stop renting an apartment from Clarisse. They might move out of the subculture, to the suburbs even.

They must be saved from themselves.

Both Clarisse and Daniel have a vested interest in a system of sexual exchange. A gay bar may be a subcultural meeting place, but it is first and foremost a commercial establishment, and the sexual possibilities, like the bowls of peanuts so freely offered, are there only to make you drink more.

All the energies of *Vermilion* are devoted to removing sex from the realm of the personal, the emotional, the subjective, and establishing it firmly in the marketplace. At the same time, the book is too canny to make this process explicit; the element of choice in the lives of gay men is downplayed to the point of extinction, since otherwise the marketplace might be called on to justify itself. This might not make pretty reading.

So monogamy is presented as a matter of bad taste, as a gaffe like drinking white wine with steak, rather than an immoral option.

Monogamy is only one form of bad taste, but it is linked with others more obviously pernicious, just as soft drugs are linked with heroin. So when Clarisse and Daniel let themselves into an apartment, using Clarisse's keys, so as to spy on the next building, they are confronted with an appalling vista of flocked wallpaper, plush velvet, veneer, chandeliers and crystal frogs, all in clashing colours.

The lovers who live there have forfeited the privilege of having their interior resemble an illustration from a recent magazine; they no longer listen to the voices which tell them what to buy, and (just as important) what to discard. Consequently their apartment fails to impress those who break and enter in their absence.

Mark's bad taste is much less entrenched; there is hope for him. But he does turn up at Bonaparte's on Thursday bearing 'an enormous package, done up in bright red foil paper and wide gold ribbon tied in a grotesquely large bow', which he gives to Daniel. The package contains the leather jacket.

This is the beginning of Mark's redemption from bad taste; the packaging may be tacky, but the choice of gift is astute. Although Clarisse describes the jacket as a wedding ring ('most beautiful wedding ring I've ever seen'), it has none of the disadvantages of one; it doesn't remove Daniel from the sexual marketplace (rather the reverse) and it embodies no private message. Moreover, it immediately declares its value on the open market (Clarisse estimates it at $175), while a wedding ring's worth can only be guessed at by those not in the know.

Mark's emancipation from romance takes great strides later that night; he has agreed to meet Daniel at midnight, for what Daniel privately terms their 'divorce', at a bar called the Eagle. Daniel is late for the rendezvous, and by the time he arrives Mark is dancing with another man; Boston has wrought in thirty minutes what New Hampshire couldn't manage in five months, and Mark has woken up to reality.

So in the end the dreaded confrontation with Mark is less like a showdown than a Platonic dialogue, with Daniel as Socrates gently prompting a newcomer to logic:

> For a moment, Mark said nothing, thinking hard. Then he smiled. 'I know,' he said at last. 'I guess I expected more, but I'm glad to see you again too. I guess when I was up in New Hampshire, I had some funny ideas. I was thinking about you all the time, I was always thinking about coming down here to see you in Boston . . .'
>
> 'You weren't thinking about *me*,' said Valentine, 'you were just thinking about *men*.'
>
> Mark nodded. 'I guess so . . .'

So that's all right then.

Mark gets his reward that very night for the progress he's made. His new friend, Joseph, is also from out of town, and they have nowhere to stay. What to do?

Daniel is only too pleased to help; Mark already has the keys to the apartment (he left his luggage there earlier in the day), and Daniel himself will crash at Clarisse's. 'Crisco's under the sink,' he says, 'poppers are in the freezer.'

Mark in fact gets every element but one of the fantasy he cherished up there in the wilds of New Hampshire: Daniel's address, Daniel's furniture, Daniel's bed, Daniel's drugs, even Daniel's lubricant. The fact that he isn't sharing these facilities with Daniel is a minor matter; the body of the loved one becomes the most easily substituted element, in this version of gay life, an accessory to all the accessories he owns.

Mark has learned his lesson, although he does show signs of wanting with Joseph the relationship he wanted with Daniel. But perhaps there's nothing better available in the provinces.

Mark has come to realise the limitations of provincial morals. As he asks Daniel despairingly, 'Is everybody from New Hampshire as much of a hick as I am?' Tactful Daniel makes no answer.

There is a certain selectiveness, though, in this matter of backgrounds. Minor or unappealing characters tend to have their roots exposed; so Lieutenant Searcy, we are told, was brought up on the South Side of Chicago, and Billy Golacinsky comes from Harrisburg, Pa., though he claims (without knowing that San Francisco is north of Los Angeles) to come from California. A pair of lovers is given, crushingly, an origin in Ohio.

None of the other characters comes from anywhere. Daniel has a father (he and Clarisse are the only people to know Daniel's phone number; we are told nothing else), but no other means of arriving on the planet. But if *pretending to come from California* is an embarrassing piece of pretension, what sort of manoeuvre is *not coming from anywhere*?

It may be that the principals are left blank in this respect so that they are easy to identify with; *Vermilion* is certainly anxious that its major figures be liked. But there's another set of reasons.

Vermilion presents an urban life of casual sexual exchange as the only option for a male homosexual; but at the same time it doesn't present this lifestyle as a matter of choice. Consequently the book must exclude all other possibilities.

First to go is any whiff of the counterculture; and so, although Boston is the single American city with the strongest radical tradition, you would be hard put to deduce that from the book. Reference is made to the gay papers *Esplanade* and *Gay Community News*, but Boston as presented in *Vermilion* is essentially a subcultural city, a string of bars and baths where there isn't even a bookshop where you could buy *Vermilion*. Otherwise Boston exists purely for local colour.

Hence too the disappearance of any lingering subjectivity in sexual matters. Only if there is total agreement about the attractiveness of a man, expressed as an absolute and not a relative value, can a system of sexual exchange emerge as an ideal, with any sustained relationship incurring the disapproval reserved for those who hoard a commodity and thus create an artificial shortage. Why would you want to sleep with someone on a regular basis, any more than you would want to read a detective novel more than once? It's a good read, and that's all there is to say about it. Read another one.

Backgrounds are the next to go. If Daniel Valentine has a background he also has a past, in which he quite possibly collected crystal frogs and had a crush on his best friend. No one is born, after all, with a subscription to *Architectural Digest* and a membership card for the Club Bath chain. If *Vermilion* acknowledges any such previous state of affairs, it must also acknowledge the series of choices which have led to the current Daniel. This would run counter to the whole spirit of the book.

Luckily a novel, unlike a repressive government, isn't forced to rewrite the history books; it can simply omit them. So Daniel Valentine has no place of birth, no childhood experience, no existence on the planet prior to his time at university (he was a history major at Tufts, where he shared a room with one of the book's minor characters).

These are trifling omissions; it's not as if sexuality has anything to do with early experience.

Another conspicuous absentee is Christmas. Although the novel's timespan runs from the first of January to the sixth, and there is still a Christmas tree in Valentine's apartment, not to mention a massive blue spruce in Prudential Plaza, Christmas as a family ritual is never mentioned, even to be dismissed. When Daniel says, 'I hate Christmas,' he means that he abhors the bad taste of disco carols and seasonal tat, not that he resents the continuing tidal pull of a family which can be ignored for most of the year. But perhaps his father phoned, from out there in the void, for a festive chat.

Vermilion's strategy throughout is to associate a certain style of sexuality (any approach towards monogamy) with a sort of civic bad faith, like hanging on to an overdue library book, without ever admitting the existence of a library, which might have dues or restrictions on membership.

It's quite a *tour de force*, to describe a gay urban lifestyle on its own terms without acknowledging the forces which have created it. On occasions a different tone of voice can't help but creep in, as in this description of the gym that Daniel frequents:

> Though set a little to one side, the bench press was the 'center ring' of the place. For the straight men who visited the International Health Spa it was the essential element in foundation building, and they employed it to develop bulky, rounded upper bodies which, according to heterosexual lore, was the universal turn-on to beautiful women. Gay men, on the other hand, flocked to the defining equipment, the barbells and the UGMs, after a short while on the bench press, to carve out their muscles, until, ideally, they resembled a page out of Gray's *Anatomy*.

Here at least is a suggestion that gay men make choices; the existence of 'heterosexual lore' at least implies the possibility of a gay equivalent.

Except that *Vermilion* needs to protect Daniel from the appalling possibility of choice. So exercise becomes something that Daniel hates, a duty that he fulfils with resignation rather than eagerness, something that is somehow imposed on him from outside. Once again, he is elsewhere at the time.

He isn't allowed, though, whatever his feelings about exercise, to perform at less than an Olympic level. On the Thursday, although he is a smoker, has let himself slide over the holidays, and wore himself out with exercise only the day before, he manages (in his second hour at the gym, mind) a hundred of those fancy press-ups where you clap your hands in self-applause at the top of each push.

It isn't that he's not allowed to win. It's just that he mustn't be seen competing.

His sex life follows the same pattern. On Wednesday morning he wakes up with the feeling that someone 'ought to have been lying on the other half of the bed, although he had no idea who'.

Perhaps it was only a dream.

But no, it turns out that last night's man has had to go to work early. Sex in *Vermilion* is a supremely efficient transaction, so he has left no involuntary trace, but he has left a flattering note on the coffee table ('Thanks for a great time. Call me soon.') and signs himself Gary. He leaves his phone number.

It isn't likely that Daniel will phone him, since he can't remember what Gary looks like. Nor can Gary contact him in order to remind him, since only Clarisse and Mr Valentine, Senior, know the phone number. Daniel has taken the precaution of removing the number from the phone itself, in case an early-rising trick gets presumptuous. Some people have no taste.

This is, of course, 'only a dream' in a different sense, a dream in which you make a much stronger impression on other people than they do on you, in which they endorse your sexual status without your needing to remember their names or faces, and in which the phone doesn't ring only because no one knows the number. There's an army of men out there pining for it. But you have to be firm.

Can you help it if you're an *homme fatal*? Well, yes, actually. A sexually attractive person isn't a person without needs, simply a person whose needs are appetising to others. At best, and with a lot of help, a sexually attractive person can dodge the unrewarding task of examining those needs. So what if he's worn quite smooth by the need to be desired?

Daniel doesn't even need to make breakfast, since Clarisse arrives freighted with pastries; she has catered for three, but nothing goes to waste.

Daniel's kitchen window is brightened by three Boston ferns, but these again are gifts from Clarisse (short affair with wholesale florist) rather than tell-tale signs of domestic aesthetics on his part. Daniel in fact resents 'the demands put upon him by green plants', and declines to water them. Clarisse sees to their needs behind his back.

This is the life.

The apartment, too, though it has only three rooms, makes demands on Daniel that he resents. Housework depresses him, but he doesn't like to see other people clean up either. So a maid comes in three nights a week, while he's at work.

In Quentin Crisp's philosophy of dust, you resist any temptation to clean up, since after three or four years it doesn't get any worse. In Daniel Valentine's, you have the dust invisibly removed, so that you see neither the dirt nor the cleaner. Gay men living alone seem to theorise about housework, either reconciling themselves to the reality of dirt or denying its existence.

So how does Daniel express his personality, in an apartment full of magically surviving plants, where the ringing of the phone can never announce an unexpected caller, where the build-up of dirt can never announce the passage of time, where the murmuring fridge keeps the stimulants in tip-top condition, and the vegetable shortening waits under the spotless sink for the next successful applicant? He collects playing cards.

Daniel's collecting urge verges on the obsessive; it leads him to break hygienic taboos (picking up a torn and filthy ten of spades from a storm drain) and even infringe property laws (stealing the joker from a Monte Carlo casino pack in a bedside table drawer). He has his choicest examples framed or embedded in a coffee table.

He hates card games, and never plays them.

For a card-player, cards are symbols; for Daniel, they are fetishes. He has removed cards from a realm of play into a realm of repetitive possession, fixated on differences between packs which would make no difference to someone who actually used them.

In a book like *Vermilion*, any single detail may be accidental; but every element is characteristic.

Daniel's relationships with objects and institutions are in fact warmer than his relationships with living things, excepting Clarisse, who combines heterosexual status (when the two of them walk arm in arm they look 'like an affianced couple in the "Living" section of the Sunday *Globe*') with a blessed immunity to heterosexual lore, who wants him but doesn't blame him for not wanting her.

Since he has no sexual responsibilities towards Clarisse, he can be her friend; and since Veronica Lake is not his dog, he can take her for walkies.

True, when Clarisse embraces Daniel so as to escape detection by someone they are following (Clarisse's obscuring mane of hair coming in handy), Daniel bites at her tongue, just to remind her that this isn't the real thing; and when Searcy beats him up, he prefers to lick his wounds in private rather than go to Clarisse's for comfort. But perhaps someone who was born as a university student doesn't associate physical contact between friends with warmth and consolation. To be physically intimate with a friend would break the rules of *Vermilion* just as profoundly as treating a sexual partner as a friend: these are the little sacrifices tht city life demands.

Daniel's relationship with his new jacket, since it was never human and is no longer alive, is distinctly tender and expressive. Teasingly he fingers its zip. He takes great care to hang it up; even if the phone is ringing when he enters his apartment, the jacket must come first.

The jacket, after all, as he says in his speech of thanks to Mark, will mean an improvement in his love life. The library book has a new cover, and will circulate more smoothly than ever before.

It shouldn't surprise the reader of *Vermilion* that an article of clothing should be perceived as part of a person's attractiveness; the book consistently blurs the distinction between qualities and attributes, essences and labels. Daniel himself once followed Ms Winifred 'Boots' Slater, who always wears leather, for three blocks, thinking she was 'a hot new man in town'.

Apart from this momentary lapse, Daniel is spared the stigma of trouser-chasing. In the course of the book he makes no sexual overtures; he goes to bed with two men (unmemorable Gary and an unnamed taxi-driver), but in neither case does he make the first move. He is given one moment of pathos, when late one night he almost regrets refusing two offers of intimacy, but that is as close as he comes to expressing desire.

This is in a sense oddly passive behaviour, though it accords well with the book's presentation of sex as performance, sex as marketing, sex as status, sex as anything but need.

But how does Daniel actually express himself, with Gary, with the taxi-driver, when at last he takes up the burden of pleasure? Daniel's sexual practices aren't specified, any more than a general level of desire is admitted, although in effect we are told that they are specific (nothing wishy-washy about Daniel): when he lends Mark his apartment keys he detaches them 'from his back belt loop', and when Clarisse wants to borrow a bandanna he gives her a blue one 'from his back pocket'. In the context of an urban subculture, this means he is giving clear sexual signals, but without being told which side he wears these accessories, a gay reader can't work out exactly what they are.

For a gay reader, the hero of a novel can just as easily be a role-model or a pin-up, a subject of identification or an object of desire. But he can be both these things only if his behaviour remains studiedly vague. Someone who is giving clear sexual signals by implication narrows his market, while increasing his chances of success within it; but *Vermilion* is anxious to hang on to every scrap of approval from its audience, and so must leave its hero an all-powerful blank, perfectly full of status, perfectly free of role-playing.

There are other ways of writing about roles than pretending they don't exist. The system of sexuality which *Vermilion* advocates makes demands on those who enter it; it makes some transactions possible and others impossible. But it can't indefinitely pose as natural.

Consider for contrast this passage by the estimable Merril Mushroom, which focuses on the actual moment of entering a subculture:

> When Buddy came into my room and announced that these two women we knew who were twenty-one years old would loan us their proof of age so that we could finally go to the bars, I was ready. My first lesbian affair was behind me, and I'd been hanging out with the gay kids for the past year. At seventeen, I was a hot-shot dyke, ripe for the bar scene.
>
> Buddy and I spent the rest of the week preparing for our big debut. We went shopping for men's trousers and shirts. We bought a large bottle of Vitalis 'greasy'. Buddy decided that she would be a butch. I was not sure if I wanted to be butch or fem – it was important to be one or the other – so I decided to go out butch Friday night and fem Saturday night and see which role I felt most comfortable with.
>
> On Friday evening Buddy and I showered and dressed in our new clothes, then spent an hour doing our hair, slicking it back just so neatly, spreading on more Vitalis and wiping it off, making sure the one casual curl hanging

> down in front was just casual enough, making doubly certain that the duck's ass in back creased perfectly straight and that it was the only straight thing about us. At last, clutching our borrowed proof of age, bearing phony nicknames to match, we left for the bar . . .
>
> That first butch night out, Buddy and I were the objects of a lot of cruising, since we were new dykes on the scene. Invariably we were asked if we were butch or fem, and I answered that I was butch; and if the woman said something like, 'Oh, that's too bad,' I'd respond with something like, 'Well, I'm coming back tomorrow night fem.'
>
> The next night I met Sharon and was smitten. Sharon wasn't sure if she was butch or fem either, but since I was fem that night, she decided that she'd be butch for me. We made a date to honeymoon the following weekend.

This passage makes no bones about the artificiality of the system it describes, but once that is confronted it becomes possible for a person to express herself through it. When, a few pages later, one woman is described as a 'butchy-looking fem' and another as a 'femmy-looking butch', it's hard to feel that the forms are constricting; the system has been transformed, without being denied, by a sense of play and of adventure.

Perhaps women are better able to work this transformation than men, since for them being allowed to choose between roles in itself represents an intoxicating freedom. Men have rather more to lose from acknowledging the artificiality of social arrangements.

Vermilion, though, is solicitous about men and their claims to status. It embodies a scale of values on which men who define themselves by their relationships with other men enjoy a clear superiority over their fellows. Straight women come next in the hierarchy (best of a bad job), then straight men (sad waste) and finally gay women (wilful abandonment of status).

Not that lesbians abound in the world of *Vermilion*. No

declared gay woman inhabits these pages, but on the Thursday evening Daniel Valentine practises his powers of observation:

> Valentine watched carefully the dismay of two young women who had stopped in front of the window. *Students*, thought Valentine. *Boston University, School of Applied Music, 700 Commonwealth Avenue, one has a boyfriend who's a trumpet player, the other is a closet lesbian*. They moved on before he could delve any deeper into their obvious lives.

Or before he can find out that they are attached to one of the Boston area's 400 other colleges, if they are students at all.

Gay men in *Vermilion* not only have all the status, they have all the knowledge. Daniel knows something about a woman, at first sight and without benefit of conversation, that she imagines she is hiding even from her intimates.

The tone of this passage is startlingly dismissive, and the overcompensation involved fairly astounding. If a friend whose sight seems to be failing reads a number-plate at the end of the street, you are likely to be reassured. But if he offers to read a number-plate in Tokyo, your doubts will actually increase.

Clarisse lags behind in the intuition stakes until the end of *Vermilion*, when she solves the murder. The ability to do so is entirely at odds with her other characteristics, but she is already such a compound of contradictory elements that the reader may not notice. In the course of the book she has shown herself unable to organise so much as a handbag or a bunch of keys, constantly cutting herself in a lovably feminine manner, losing her contact lenses, getting on the wrong train, but she ends the novel in a blaze of analytical cunning, working out all those ticklish details about the angle of the fatal blow which vain little Belgians dispose of in Chapter 3.

Clarisse's solution doesn't in fact stand up to examination. A handkerchief smeared with vermilion lipstick was found on the body of Billy Golacinsky. In the book's overall structure this clue leads unmistakably to a female impersonator ('Trudy') who works at Bonaparte's as a cabaret artiste and did, as it turns out, pick Billy up on the night of the murder: this is the book's first false solution.

But Clarisse's eventual solution requires Billy to have been given the hanky, or else the lipstick, by a woman whose invariable costume is black leather, and who would hardly have a tube of vermilion lipstick tucked away in a pocket of her motorcycle jacket. The circumstances are never explained.

If Clarisse's solution had incriminated a gay man, it would have had to resist a much closer scrutiny; but readers of *Vermilion* will have no particular objection to the guilt of a straight couple and a Boston cop. The actual mechanics of the solution are of little consequence, as long as the presumed reader's group is cleared of blame.

If, as Confucius suggested, nothing is more obvious than what a man seeks to hide, the most obvious characteristic of the community which produced and consumes *Vermilion* is fear: fear of isolation and fear of dependence.

These are legitimate fears in a community which is constantly being reminded of its provisional status, but they are never expressed directly by the book. They are denied without ever being mentioned, just as Daniel Valentine's dust is cleared away without his having to admit its existence. An artificial state of affairs passes itself off as natural. If this is the atmosphere that gay men breathe, why does it contain no oxygen or nitrogen?

Some less defensible fears, fears of pleasure, fears of responsibility, fear of choice and fear of need, are attemptedly exorcised by *Vermilion*'s propagandist version of gay life in the city. The book's genre, comedy-thriller, makes no promise of realism, but how many casual readers of *Vermilion* appreciate the wildness of its wish-fulfilment? Gay Boston in *Vermilion* is an idealised version of gay life in a subculture, in the same way that levitation is an idealised version of gravity.

My analysis of *Vermilion* is necessarily a jaundiced account of an unexceptional piece of work, but there's a lot to be said for taking the yellow view.

Vermilion contains no more silly lies about human behaviour per hundred words than, say, *Doctor No*, but its position in the marketplace is different. There was not, when Ian Fleming embarked on his literary production, a thriving community of secret agents longing to be told how to treat their women and their enemies, desperate to keep up with the latest styles in Lugers and martinis. The fantasy dispensed by *Doctor No* and by books like it was frankly distant from the daily lives of its readers, and made only a small contribution to the formation of their ideas about sex and power. They could draw their worldly knowledge and their sexual lore from many other sources.

Readers of *Vermilion*, by contrast, are likely to be hungry for roles and codes of conduct, grateful for any image that presents gays as people of importance and interest. *Vermilion* provides them with a good read. It also provides them (in a sort of ideological version of subliminal advertising) with a series of attitudes which they are invited to take for granted. Because the book is a comedy-thriller and innocent of any claims to literary stature, it is assumed by its readers to be telling them nothing new. In this way, and thanks to a generalised air of sophistication, a number of dubious propositions can be sneaked past the reader's peripheral vision, which he might view very differently if he was invited to consider them on their own merits.

How much damage is actually done by what people believe, and how much by what people assume other people believe? If you take a group of people and tell them, 'A person under hypnosis (as I'm sure you know) is unable to move his or her dominant hand', your statement will become true of members of that group, if you then hypnotise them. The crucial point is placed in parentheses (I'm telling you nothing new) as if it was unimportant, and manages to trigger uncritical acceptance rather than scrutiny.

The ghetto sets you free. Men are monoliths, women are mosaics. Politics is irrelevant. It's tasteless to mix your sex life and your social life. Nothing is subjective. Gay men and gay women have nothing in common; lesbianism doesn't exist anyway. Only in the city is gayness possible. Sexuality is determined by market forces. Experience is interchangeable. These ideas, though not mentioned in the blurb, are in a real sense what *Vermilion* is about.

Few of these ideas stand up to analysis when their air of self-evidence is taken from them. The book's suggestion, for one, that membership of a subculture involves no separation from the dominant culture, is as good as disproved by the book's own marketing strategy; exquisitely it homes in on urban gays, and receives reviews only from partisan journals. Its sequels are likely to go on reassuring a commercialised ghetto that there is nothing outside it.

People at least have the choice of whether to betray you or not; institutions can't help it.

If Nathan Aldyne's future books stop advocating a system of casual sexual exchange, the 1982 epidemic of panic and sexual fear will probably be responsible. This epidemic has already changed attitudes almost as much as the decade did that separates *Vermilion* from *The Last Woman in His Life*. In time, the level of perceived realism in *Vermilion* is likely to dwindle to nothing.

In the meantime, between one backlash and the next, with the appropriate fears and the appropriate confidence, this collection of lesbian and gay fiction sets itself as much against the expectations of subcultural commerce, as against the studied indifference of the dominant culture.

Introduction to *Mae West Is Dead* (Faber, 1983)

Gay London 1984

1983 was the year that *Gay News*, the single unifying institution for gay people in this country, collapsed. Gay women thought it was male-dominated, hedonists that it was boringly political, Londoners that it tried too hard to cover the whole country; gays outside London resented its metropolitan bias, politicos disliked its lists of commercial establishments, and a number of men objected to the prominence it gave to women. *Gay News*, in other words, received the normal accolade of peace-keeping forces, of being shot by all sides, and then resented for dying.

The new *Gay News*, which retained only the name of its predecessor, offered proof of the theory that a gay periodical that avoids politics rapidly becomes a sportswear catalogue.

But 1983 was also the year that Edmund White's *A Boy's Own Story*, an exquisite account of growing up American and gay in the 1950s, sold over 80,000 copies in Picador paperback after numerous rejections from hardback houses. An earlier book of Edmund White's, *The Joy of Gay Sex*, has made such an impression on H.M. Customs that they keep every copy they can lay their hands on.

1983 was the year that AIDS-obsessiveness reached London in a big way, so that an American just off the plane (and unwise enough to betray his origins by tipping the bartender and wearing a sweatshirt decorated with little scampering lambdas and the logo *FrontRunners, New York*) could be shunned by a roomful of people dressed exclusively from the imagined wardrobes of American cowboys, soldiers and motorcyclists.

But it was also the year that the GLC promised (and almost delivered) extensive support for a gay arts festival – which surprised the gay population almost as much as it surprised the ratepayers, where the two groups didn't overlap.

Gay London, in other words, is in the usual placid turmoil, and the only workable way of describing it without falling back on a list of personal prejudices, is to examine one of the institutions that serve it. A bar, then, inevitably, since gay people (in spite of the efforts made on their behalf) haven't grown out of their desire to meet each other.

The expert witness on 'Homosexual London', necessarily anonymous, in *The New London Spy* (1966) refers to 'a few people with business acumen realising that a cellar room, sparsely furnished but equipped with a juke-box and fruit machine, and serving coffee and Coke will be a lucrative means of attracting quite a lot of queers who want to continue the hunt after the bars have closed'.

Even those visionary entrepreneurs of the sixties might be a little startled by the London Apprentice on one of its late-licence nights. There's a fruit machine just inside the door, but no juke-box. There's a disco sound-system instead, with a digital display by the DJ's booth, dispensing information. WELCOME TO THE 'L.A.', it says, A BAR FOR GAY MEN (the last two words flash wickedly as they move across the screen) RUN BY GAY MEN (another flash of wickedness) . . . YOUR DJ TONIGHT IS 'GARETH'. People's eyes stray to the readout from time to time, as if it were the departures board in an airport.

The London apprentices in the seventeenth century, who were virtually owned by their masters, were in effect the first subculture. They developed a slang and a camaraderie, and they resorted on occasion to street violence that would make the Stonewall riots in 1969 (the beginning of gay liberation) look tame; the butchers' apprentices tended to hang their rivals from hooks.

For the last two years the London Apprentice has been catering to a freer subculture, though the author of the gay section of *Alternative London* (2nd edition, 1971) would not describe it in those terms: 'Homosexual freaks in GLF [Gay Liberation Front],' he wrote, 'do not use the usual pubs and clubs that straight homosexuals use, simply because they refuse to subscribe to the plastic exploitative scene created and perpetuated there.' Only five years separate the self-lacerating 'queers' of *The New London Spy* from the contemptuous 'straight homosexuals' of *Alternative London*, and much more has changed since then. It is of course money, and the respect due to those who dispose of it, which has worked the transformation. Even the agreed age of sexual attractiveness has risen over the last decade and a half, so that the prime object is more likely to be a man of thirty-five than a boy of twenty.

He is also likely, at the L.A. at least, to be stereotypically masculine. All but one of the barmen have hairy faces of some description, and many cows have died to provide the customers with their jackets and accessories. The dress code, though, is self-enforcing, and women are admitted, without being welcome.

This is a ticklish issue. At first blush you might think a gay bar was just like any other pub, except for its customers – the social equivalent of the Left Handed Shop in Beak Street. Why should right-handers be a threat? But there's more to it than that.

A bar isn't the same thing as a pub, for one thing: a pub offers public space, while a bar offers shared private space. The London Apprentice is a bar *par excellence*; it opens at lunchtimes for a different clientele, with maids instead of men behind the bar, but its priorities are clear. The gay posters on the walls (for Le Sling in Paris, for Steps in Amsterdam) outnumber the horse brasses, and they don't do much for the lunchtime trade.

In the evenings, the lighting is intentionally dramatic; spotlights create tight shafts of brightness, leaving other areas dark. A black-light generator dramatises the lint on your shoulders (I hope it's lint). There isn't a lot of seating, since gay bars work better without; people need to be able to shift about, to find their individual balance between mysteriousness and accessibility.

But the London Apprentice has a number of overlapping functions: it's a community centre as well as a pick-up joint, and like any other multi-purpose device (an ugly sofa, say, that takes twenty minutes to convert into a lumpy bed), it can only achieve flexibility at a cost. It would be unreasonable to expect your sofa-bed to double as a cocktail shaker, and it would be unreasonable to expect the pick-up-joint-cum-community-centre to be a good place to bring your girlfriends.

The atmosphere of the L.A. is only intermittently oppressive, in spite of the absence of women. The bartenders are light on their feet (they tend to wear running shoes, not work shoes or boots like the customers) and quick to spot an empty glass. They often socialise in the bar on their nights off, so there are usually reserves to be drawn on if there's an unexpected crowd, or if a jacket goes astray at the coat check (which is likely enough, since novelty in costume wins no prizes here, except at Hallowe'en).

Beer is the basic drink, and the real ale is well looked after; but you aren't made to feel a fool for ordering something else. In butch bars in the States, the bartender won't insult your virility by offering you a glass for your Perrier water, and he'll ram a wedge of lime down the neck of the bottle with his thumb – but that particular affectation has yet to cross the Atlantic.

The barmen are flirtatious, and customers are likely to assume they're on the make, but most of them have lovers. Nobody wants to wait until three in the morning for a date, particularly when there's no lack of competition; so the barmen's base relationships get quietly refreshed by the surf of sexual attention that comes their way from the customers.

The bar staff know exactly how much backchat and gossip they can get away with under cover of the music. A lip-reader from Brothers and Sisters, the gay deaf group, would soon see the word 'queen' formed under a stylised moustache – though in fact the music at the London Apprentice is too quiet for Brothers and Sisters. If you're deaf the music is never too loud to stop you talking, and if you want to dance it's best to have it so loud it reaches you through the soles of your feet. Heaven is a better bet.

The barmen go on chatting and serving. The landlord, Michael Glover, still does his turns of duty, though he certainly doesn't need to. He set up the London Apprentice because he was disgusted by the bashed-down beer (mentioning no names) and the surly service (mentioning no names) that straight landlords of gay pubs thought was good enough for their customers. The site he chose isn't in a residential area, which made it easier to get the late licence.

The London Apprentice represents a new breed of gay bar, because it can't rely on a natural catchment area (like Earls Court or theatreland); gentrification may be on its way, but it hasn't hit Hoxton yet. The L.A. isn't the most extreme case (the Ship and Whale in Dockland is served by two reluctant buses), but it still has to work hard to keep people coming.

Michael Glover takes good care to keep the customers happy. He organises parties from time to time; once he had the staff frying fish and chips in the upstairs bar, and doling it out to the customers. One punter complained about the size of his portion of fish, and for once Michael lost his temper. '*Give it back here*,' he bellowed. 'Now go down the Black Cap, go down the Vauxhall Tavern, and ask *them* for your free fish and chips. See what you get . . .'

Michael Glover is also on the steering committee of the Terrence Higgins Trust, which campaigns for research into AIDS. Terrence Higgins was the first English casualty of the disease; the trust was set up by his lover and friends. It's a somewhat amateurish organisation, as compared with Gay Men's Health Crisis in New York, but it can still just about afford to be. Gay Men's Health Crisis is the largest gay organisation in America, with a thousand volunteer workers and a massive fund-raising drive.

The Los Angeles *Advocate* reckons that the BBC Horizon programme on AIDS (*Killer in the Village*) is the best TV programme on the subject, which gives you some idea of the competition. The gay press in America generally handles the issue better than ours does; there should be AIDS-coverage awards for Paranoia (nominees: everyone except *Gay Scotland*) and Smugness (nominee: *Gay Scotland* for the phrase 'since AIDS can't climb Hadrian's Wall . . .').

The coat check at the London Apprentice is free, but there's a collecting box nearby for the Terrence Higgins Trust, and most people take the hint. The biggest donation the trust has received to date was raised at the L.A., by the MSC (Motor Sports Club), who use the upstairs bar as their regular meeting place. It may seem strange that the MSC, the oldest leather club in the country, should show so much *esprit de corps* and organisational flair; but leather clubs are by definition hidebound, and fond of structure.

Ten years ago, when the MSC was founded, the leather scene was assumed by most people to be marginal; but since then it has moved a lot nearer to the mainstream. The digital readout at the London Apprentice regularly recommends the services of a late-opening leather shop called Expectations, round the corner in Hoxton Square. This is somehow both convenient and uncomfortable, like having an abattoir and a restaurant in the same block. It reminds people of sexuality as a system, something they are normally encouraged to forget.

But that seems to be the function of leather in a gay subculture: to enable people to construct a sexuality instead of experiencing one, to promote intensity at the expense of expressiveness. And there also seems to be, hidden away at the heart of the leather cult, a desire not to be sexual except in response to pre-set stimuli. That way you can't be attracted to someone who can't be attracted to you (at one time the great disadvantage of homosexuality), and you can take off the essence of sexuality along with the accessories.

There is even a guide to gay-bar etiquette and the proper

projection of virility; inevitably, it's imported from America, and it's stocked by Gay's The Word bookshop in Bloomsbury, where they would rather you read politically sound material, but they aren't going to get nasty about it. *The Butch Manual* assesses your butchness quotient according to whether 'Nancy' to you suggests Sluggo's girlfriend in the comic strip, or the underground stop in Paris. *The Butch Manual*, in what I suppose is one of the great traditions of homosexuality, parodies masculinity while taking it very seriously indeed.

There's a lot of that at the London Apprentice. I remember telling a friend, who claims to have been rescued from shyness by a sexual code that rewards silence and immobility accompanied by the appropriate moustache, that his shoes were not butchly laced. He had laced them $\overset{\mathrm{x}}{\mathrm{x}}$, not $\equiv$. 'Don't you know anything?' I asked him. 'People will see at once that you want a string of tender kisses on your instep.' I thought I was joking, but when I saw him next, his laces were obeying house rules.

Early in the evening at the London Apprentice, when there are only forty people in the place, the effect is definitely oppressive. Everyone seems to be expressing sexual contempt for everyone else. They might just as well economise on leather, and wear T-shirts that say KEEP YOUR DISTANCE or THINK OF ME AS SHEER ALIENATING RAUNCH. But later on, when the crowd is four hundred strong, the feeling is very different, and this I think is what keeps people coming back.

No one can move, to go to the Gents, to get another drink, to get a better look, without touching people; and the contact is quite surprisingly affectionate. You're a lot more likely to get patted than groped. The costumes continue to insist that human warmth is at the bottom of their wearers' list of priorities; and the people inside the costumes are thereby freed to express something they claim not to want. It takes hours of hierarchy, mind you, to achieve minutes of community, but that may always be true. People who start off by defining themselves as very separate slowly, quietly, provisionally, and without much wanting to be reminded of what they are doing, allow themselves to be reabsorbed. And if you want a one-sentence history of the gay movement in this country over the last fifteen years, you missed it. That was it.

Tatler, 1984. The magazine's 'gay issue' was highly provocative, right down to the slogan on its spine, which read *Right Up Your Straight*. Advertisers like Tampax were huffy, and the magazine's next issue was not much thicker than a restaurant menu. The editor, Tina Brown, has since gone on to greater things, but the gay issue of *Tatler* must be reckoned one of Queen Midas's off days.

Gay Rights and Wrongs

These three books show some of the range of contemporary gay thinking in Britain and America, and also manifest a clear hierarchy of intellectual ambition. Here are gay Studies Advanced, Intermediate and also Rudimentary.

Colin Spencer's *Homosexuality: A History*, for instance, is the work of a hobbyist, who offers what is essentially a scrap-book of the various ways that homosexuality has been inflected in different periods and cultures. Spencer leaves 'Analysis and Reflections' for his final section, which occupies less than twenty pages of a 450-page volume. Certainly the previous thirteen chapters of the book have been unanalytical and unreflective, but Chapter 14 doesn't do a lot to buck the trend.

Here for instance is an analytical reflection, as well as a fair sample of the book's prose style:

> In human society it is apparent that, depending on the cultural context, at different times both the male and the female have made the final choice. Enormous emphasis is placed on the beauty and accoutrements of the other, for wealth and social position will influence offspring. Yet throughout history there have been non-procreative partnerships, the choice of which cannot be based upon selection of genes. Some of these partnerships are alternative arrangements continuing while the procreation is committed elsewhere, but some are not. Because the

> evidence of a definite refusal to procreate is so overwhelming, because there are many who opt out of the stud competition, we have to conclude that in many men and women this amounts to a definite choice. The choice may exist on an unconscious level, but nevertheless it is still there. Why some people but not others are obsessed with the survival of their species is a fascinating question. I would suggest that it may be that, in times like the present, this is an instinctive but nevertheless responsible reaction to an over-populated planet which needs, if it is to survive, either to stabilise its birth-rate or to engineer a decline.

Did anyone spot the 'overwhelming' evidence on offer in this passage? Or were you distracted by New Age thoughts of the Earth's preoccupation with its birthrate and survival?

Here is Spencer's credo as spelled out in his Foreword: 'I believe that sexuality exists in all its depths and complexity, regardless of how society tries to control or guide it.' This would be a nice thing for a sixteen-year-old to hear from Mum or Dad on the night of his or her coming-out. It has a nice accepting sound; it bleats of good intentions. But as a serious statement it's a joke. If the depths and complexity of sexuality are not affected by social forces, then sex expresses itself identically in all societies at all periods, and *Homosexuality: A History* has no material to work with – not a scrap. A book for which the publishers expect to get £20 is a mirage in prose.

And so it is, a mirage in bad prose. A writer who sets himself up as some sort of authority on sexuality can barely deploy the basic descriptive vocabulary: 'By the third stage of initiation, the boys [of the Sambia people of New Guinea] changed roles and began to fellate the new, younger initiates.' As the context makes very clear ('the younger boy was always placed in the passive position'), that's *fellate* in its less common sense of *be fellated by*.

If there are limits, strict limits, on Colin Spencer's knowledge, there are none on his willingness to go beyond them.

Everyone, as Oscar Wilde never said, should know something about love and history – except, of course, the historians of love. This is a relatively modest imputation of sentiments to Wilde, as *Homosexuality: A History* makes clear: 'he opened his evening paper to discover that Queensberry's eldest son had committed suicide . . . Wilde reading the report felt all his hatred for Bosie melt away to be replaced by infinite pity. He telegraphed him at once. They were back together again.'

If Oscar Wilde's heart and mind hold no secrets from Colin Spencer, the same turns out to be true of his trousers: 'Bisexual men who are happily married – and Wilde was before Bosie appeared in his life – generally do not commit sodomy on youths (for they prefer to penetrate their wives), but have a strong desire to fellate them.' (It is even possible in this passage that *fellate* is used in the sense of *fellate*.) This sentence is offered as evidence of Wilde's sexual character, but no evidence is offered for the evidence. Is bisexuality a stable category, or does it change from time to time and place to place? Are sexual acts fixed in their patterns and their meanings? These are questions you might expect a history of sexuality to address, or at least to regard as open. Instead Colin Spencer introduces his assumptions at every point.

Things don't improve when we enter a century where Colin Spencer might allow the sheer volume of testimony to interrupt the flow of what he perhaps imagines is common sense – neutral knowing that laughs at mere documentation.

Here for instance is his description of American clone culture in the 1970s:

> Sex was rough, uninhibited and phallocentric. Tricking involved 'deep-throating', 'hard fucking' and 'heavy tit work'. Drugs were usually used to alleviate the pain of these sexual experiences: pot, poppers and Quaaludes were the most popular. Deep-throating involved the penis being rammed down the other's throat in such a way that there was a chance of choking. Fucking meant slapping the

buttocks while ramming the whole penis into the other's anus, and the tit work involved heavy biting, sucking and pinching of the nipples.

This strenuous giving and receiving of sado-masochistic sex was surely only another form of self-punishment. It was the gay aping the worst excesses of the chauvinistic sexist male, treating his sexual partner with insensitivity and cruelty. What is more, the receiver fully colluded with the act. Both the gays in the partnership were as fully locked in to the heterosexual structure as they had been when they played at domesticity and keeping house together. Further, the butch imagery and the semblance of masculine normality was as artificial a pose as the frock that had been worn before. But trying to create a social niche in a society which still negates you forces caricatures of that society upon you.

It takes some nerve on Spencer's part to use that word 'caricature', seeing that he has himself just reduced an entire subculture to the level of snuff porn. What is his evidence? Was he there? Presumably not – he was off somewhere else, being non-phallocentric. But even if he was there, he wasn't everywhere, and should speak only for himself.

To fantasise the private actions of a whole group of people and pronounce definitively on the moral worth of what you have invented, to claim simultaneously the authority of knowing and the respectability of not being there – it's hard to find a better word for these procedures than homophobic. With 'gay historians' like these, who needs bigots?

In fact clone culture, if we can so specify gay men in 1970s San Francisco, had interest beyond the sexual. (Things are getting pretty bad when you find yourself thinking that there is more history in *Tales of the City* than in *Homosexuality: A History*.) Clone culture was preoccupied also with brunch, and with political action. Perhaps it's too much to expect the brunch aspect to be explored in Colin Spencer's scrap-book, but mightn't he have found space for the name of Harvey Milk? For the first openly gay elected public official? Clone culture voted him in, and clone culture rioted when his murder was condoned by the courts. But these trivia fail to turn our author on. They seem not to fit his definition of historical material, unlike his moralising dreams of punitive sex wall-to-wall.

Do you remember Colin Spencer's credo? ('I believe that sexuality exists in all its depths and complexity, regardless of how society tries to control or guide it.') If so, you have the advantage over Colin Spencer, who 390 pages later writes: 'How a society expresses its sexuality is a direct result of its political structure and ideology.' It's not uncommon for people to end up rather awkwardly divided in their allegiances between essentialism (sexuality is an unmediated biological drive) and constructionism (sexuality is socially manufactured), but it's a distinct novelty to be a hardliner in both camps, at different ends of your book.

Another novelty of *Homosexuality: A History* is that though a book of non-fiction, it begins with a lie. In the first sentence of his Foreword Colin Spencer writes: 'Throughout my life I have been shocked by homophobia.' *Throughout your life*? As a 1970s vintage Castro clone might say, in a moment of leisure from aping the worst excesses of the chauvinistic sexist male: *Please*, Mary.

Homophobia is resilient as a system because of a quirk of its chronology: even those individuals who will suffer in time profit from it before it works against them. Any child, any male child at least, has disparaged gay people, or been party to such disparagement, long before he realises that this joke category is one that has claims on him. Homophobia is a bribe whose first instalments are spent in ignorance of where the money comes from.

When Colin Spencer says 'Throughout my life I have been shocked by homophobia' he means something like 'Ever since I accepted myself as a gay person I have been . . .' – but with this emendation *shocked* is revealed as a weasel word. You can't be shocked by something you're familiar with from the inside. More to the point, homophobia would not be a problem if it was possible to step outside it so easily, with no memory of collusion.

Some gay people, of course, never step out of it at all, and when he has to report on such cases Colin Spencer is shocked all over again:

> What is so deeply shocking that it veers almost upon the unbelievable, is that the architects of this oppression, McCarthy, Cohn and Hoover were all homosexual themselves, contriving to hide their natures from the general public until after they were dead. Here again, society colluded with them, for among their inner circle it was public knowledge. As ever, the great and the powerful were indulged while the nameless suffered.

Isn't it time that gay studies – if that umbrella can be extended to shelter Colin Spencer – took gay complicity more seriously? Spencer's analysis ('society colluded with them') misses the point, which is that these men colluded with society. They didn't invent the system, they just played it. The best thing about Tony Kushner's baggy monster of a play, *Angels in America*, staged so successfully at the National a few years ago, was that it took Ray Cohn seriously, as a representative of Us as well as of Them. To demonise homophobic gay men, or to keep on saying how shocked you are by what they did and do, is a failure of imagination, and it ignores the fact that homophobia, then and now, is a system of rewards as well as punishments.

At the end of his Foreword, Colin Spencer looks back on his project: 'What we now call homosexuality has been a constant theme in the sexuality of all societies. Sadly, I have had to conclude that our Western societies have lately grown more homophobic than before, not perhaps in legislation but in moral attitudes. It was with great relief that I discovered many societies of the past entirely free of such a taint.'

Sadly, the material Spencer has thrown so nonchalantly together can be described quite differently. He has not come across a society where homosexuality is non-existent, but nor has he come across one where it isn't controlled.

Suppose for instance that Colin Spencer was a young member of the Sambia people of Papua New Guinea, and made in the flesh the blunder that he makes in language when he describes them: of confusing active and passive in an oral act of sex. Suppose to be brutally frank that he blew when the cultural imperative was for being blown. He would find himself at the sharp end not of a code of manners, which might judge his action as on a par with drinking the fingerbowl or using the wrong fork, but of a fixed set of religious meanings. He would be guilty not of committing a gaffe, but of breaking a taboo, and would be lucky not to become an object of horror in consequence.

In other words, it's not that other cultures are more casual about homosexual acts, merely that they police them differently. Other cultures provide formal contexts where homosexual acts are expected, and ours does not; that's all. Or perhaps that should be *formally labelled* contexts, since in a single-sex dormitory, ship, prison or cloister expectations have always been high.

But even if it was true that 'many societies of the past' were free of the 'taint' of homophobia, there would still be a gap in the argument: homophobia not being cross-culturally necessary wouldn't make it an optional part of *our* culture.

Andrew Sullivan is considerably more honest about homophobia in the autobiographical fragment with which he starts *Virtually Normal*, a book rather bizarrely oversold by its publishers. You'd better be pretty confident about the ballsiness of your product before you promote it as the same-sex *Female Eunuch*.

Sullivan remembers making an anti-gay joke in a school debate at the age of twelve, and remarks: 'We had learned the social levers of hostility to homosexuals before we had even the foggiest clue what they referred to.' Nevertheless, he presents this as an incidental irony of his experience rather than a defining characteristic of homophobia: that it is ignorantly reinforced by the mimicry of each young generation – a percentage of whom will later be obliged to occupy the category they have helped to sustain.

Isn't there a case for thinking that homophobia *is* a system of social levers rather than a mysteriously widespread personal pathology? Because homophobia is authentically present in the culture, we assume that it is an authentic impulse in some individuals, but it doesn't need to be so. Homophobia can be real in the culture without being personally real. Perhaps there is no distinction between the 'innocent' homophobia whose levers lie so readily at hand for twelve-year-olds, and the guilty kind which they deplore when they grow up and feel the pinching of the levers.

Andrew Sullivan is hardly a Freudian, but in passing he invokes a tidy little package of Freudian concepts (basic bisexuality, disavowal) to account for homophobia: 'There is something of both attractions in all of us, to begin with . . . Sometimes, the strength of the other attraction requires such a forceful suppression that it resonates much later in life. How else to explain the sometimes violent fear and hostility to homosexuals that a few heterosexual males feel?' Certainly some such speculation is needed to entrench a distinction between true homophobia (a perverse passion), and counterfeit homophobia, a mere social reflex.

Sullivan's autobiographical sketch contains some evidence to suggest that homophobia runs a little deeper, even in the innocent, than he likes to think. He considers his generation at school: some, 'sensing their difference, flaunted it. At my high school, an older boy insisted on wearing full makeup to class; and he was accepted in a patronizing kind of way, his brazen otherness putting others at ease. They knew where they were with him; and he felt at least comfortable with their stable contempt. The rest of us who lived in a netherworld of sexual insecurity were not so lucky.'

This gives us information about what was going on in the older boy's head (his sense of comfort), but not what was going on in Andrew Sullivan's. The dubious observation that the boy was 'lucky' to have a fixed identity, even a contemptible one, is presumably a product of hindsight: it's self-pitying, but rather too sophisticated to convince as adolescent self-pity.

Isn't it likely (at the risk of turning this essay into Therapy Corner) that Sullivan's emotion at the time was not envy at the luck of the boy's comfort, but relief that here at last was someone who could be safely despised? Someone who fully fitted the hated stereotype, and made it less likely that Sullivan himself would suffer from the contempt of his world.

The four core chapters of *Virtually Normal*, after the more personal Prologue, are devoted to representing and criticising four schools of thought about homosexuality, schools which Andrew Sullivan describes under the headings Prohibitionist, Liberationist, Conservative and Liberal. To condense still further his condensations of them: Don't Do It It's a Sin (prohibitionism), Human Sexuality is a Project Not a Fact (liberationism), Don't Frighten the Horses (conservatism) and You Have a Right to Love (liberalism). In his view each tradition has something to contribute, but none can claim to offer an adequate politics. This he puts right in a further short chapter.

The attempt at fair-mindedness, though, has definite limitations, and *Virtually Normal* has its fair share of black holes and whitewash. Arguably Andrew Sullivan, as an openly gay man with Catholic allegiances who edits a conservative American journal (*The New Republic*), is more interesting in his contradictions than his attempts to transcend them. Certainly the determined evenness of tone in his book gives way fairly regularly to more jagged opinions. The reader of *Virtually Normal* must become accustomed to some strange sights on the battlefield of ideas: barricades manned in the middle of peacefully bustling streets, much sniping under a flag of truce.

Andrew Sullivan defines conservatism and liberalism with some care, and his account of these ideologies is relatively lucid. Still, it can only be a strain, if not actually an impossibility, to describe different value-systems both objectively and consistently, and there are bound to be lapses. It must come as a surprise on page 147 that liberalism 'became wedded to a confusion of public and private realms that gave an ideological opening to conservatives, who had always disputed the distinction', since on page 97 it was axiomatic that 'Conservatives combine a private tolerance of homosexuals with public disapproval of homosexuality.'

It is in his chapters on prohibitionists and liberationists, though, that Sullivan tips the scales with a fist rather than a finger. With the prohibitionists the problem is essentially one of tone; with liberationists it is also one of definition, of intellectual integrity as well as emotional investment.

When he deals with the prohibitionists, after all, Sullivan is talking about a tradition with any amount of blood on its hands. Yet his tone is never less than conciliatory, and often craven. It would be a different matter if he was explicitly writing from a Catholic point of view, addressing an audience of co-religionists and opting for a softly-softly approach as a matter of prudence in tactics. The result would not be a book published by Picador and claiming kinship with *The Female Eunuch*.

In context, however, the chapter on prohibitionists offers a simply grotesque reading experience, with Sullivan apparently fighting the urge to genuflect. He presents a slowly crumbling orthodoxy of intolerance as a fearless advance into the light. After a while, it's like reading a code, and while your eyes are traversing a formula like 'the Catholic Church doggedly refused to budge from its assertion of the natural occurrence of constitutive homosexuals' your brain effortlessly supplies the gloss *wasn't able altogether to deny the existence of those it had persecuted for so long.*

In Cardinal Ratzinger's 1986 letter 'The Pastoral Care of Homosexual Persons', for instance, homosexuality is discussed 'with candor and subtlety' (*sophistry and fudging*), and the letter contains 'a stunning passage of concession' (*breathtaking piece of hypocrisy*) in which homosexual dignity is defended. Even Sullivan admits that Ratzinger guided the Church 'into two simultaneous and opposite directions: a deeper respect for and understanding of homosexual persons and a sterner rejection of almost anything those persons might do to express themselves sexually'. It's quite a shock when Sullivan's prose dares a little independence of mind, after so long spent at hassock level.

With his chapter on the liberationists Andrew Sullivan goes in for sophistry and fudging on his own account. You might think – in fact you are entitled to think – that 'liberationism' would have something to do with the gay liberation movement, which from 1969, on the analogy of the civil rights movement, sought to advance the cause of a different disadvantaged group. Andrew Sullivan can hardly be ignorant of this piece of social history, but he chooses to ignore it and instead to discuss under the rubric of 'liberationism' two later and very ill-assorted manifestations of radical thought: Michel Foucault's theory of sexuality (elaborated in books published from 1977 onwards) and the controversial practice of 'outing', which has been an issue only in the last few years.

The irony is that Foucault's writing about homosexuality was roundly attacked at the time for its failures of liberationism: for its questioning of the philosophical validity of the category of the homosexual, and for its warnings against the pitfalls of identity politics.

Andrew Sullivan must certainly know that gay liberation in the 1970s was not based on a constructionist analysis of sexuality (an analysis, incidentally, which Sullivan caricatures). The slogans chanted at Gay Pride marches of the period did not go *2–4–6–8, Gay Is No More Real Than Straight, 3–5–7–9, Constructionism's Mighty Fine*. Even if it is only Picador hype that presents *Virtually Normal* as the only book you need to read about homosexuality, it's absurd that *any* book addressing the subject should ignore the actual history of a specifically homosexual politics.

When he comes to discussing 'outing' Sullivan misleads by suggestion rather than omission:

> To be sure, there was no direct link between this tactic and the philosophical structure I have just been describing. The ad hoc political movements of the 1990s did not spring into action bearing Michel Foucault's latest tome on the history of prisons. It is doubtful whether many recent gay activists have ever heard of Foucault, let alone read him. But indirectly, 'outing' follows the logic of liberationist politics.

The next page contains five uses of the words *Foucault* or *Foucauldean*. This is less like objective argument than the establishment of guilt by association.

'Outing' isn't even an orthodoxy among self-described gay radicals, and Foucault of course was long dead by the time outing hit the headlines. But it isn't easy to see how someone who resisted homosexuality as a valid category would throw his weight behind the enforced disclosure of preference.

By the time Sullivan sums up his chapter on the liberationists there isn't a lot of objectivity left: 'Insofar, then, as liberationist politics is cultural, it is extremely vulnerable; and insofar as it is really political, it is almost always authoritarian. Which is to say it isn't really a politics at all. It's a strange confluence of political abdication and psychological violence.'

'Liberationism' abdicates from politics because it follows Foucault (supposedly) in refusing to engage with the status quo: 'To achieve actual results, to end persecution of homosexuals in the military, to allow gay parents to keep their children, to provide basic education about homosexuality in high schools, to prevent murderers of homosexuals from getting lenient treatment, it is necessary to work through the very channels Foucault and his followers revile.' In fact classical gay liberation of the 1970s addressed this agenda, with the partial exception of the first (since gay servicepeople were regarded as first and foremost self-oppressive, they commanded no high priority).

As for 'psychological violence': there is something weirdly dissociated about someone who can accuse a political movement he has essentially invented of this unattractive characteristic, while in the same book rather smarmily lamenting that the Catholic Church 'has still not fully absorbed its own teachings about the dignity and worth of homosexual persons'.

Do you want to talk about power, Andrew? How much power is a frustrated gay journalist in a position to abuse, if he is tempted to expose the hypocrisy of a film star, as opposed to a member of the Catholic hierarchy, say, authorising a payment that will hush up an accusation of sexual abuse in the choir? The discrepancy of tone in *Virtually Normal*, stern with mavericks, soft on institutions, is not normal but virtually pathological.

It should go without saying that after the null bumblings of Colin Spencer's prose Andrew Sullivan comes dangerously close to looking like a master stylist. He turns the occasional neat phrase, and can mount a lucid argument as long as he keeps his sentences short.

Perhaps it's a mistake, though, for someone who suffers from a certain amount of preposition dysfunction (*in* a rubric? *at* a prerogative?), to refer to gay people's 'sharp alertness to language and discourse . . . shaped by generations of concealment and code'. The reader's response is likely to be: *shape* that sharp alertness. Shape it some more.

The trouble really starts when Sullivan tries to construct a substantial piece of rhetoric (figurative language and complex syntax not being strong points): 'It is surely possible to concur with these sentiments, even to appreciate their insight, while also conceding that it is nevertheless also true that nature seems to have provided a jagged lining to this homogenous cloud, a spontaneously occurring contrast that could conceivably be understood to complement – even dramatize – the central male–female order.'

As the book moves into its last chapter (as distinct from the Epilogue – 'What Are Homosexuals For?'), where Sullivan advances his personal political agenda, the element of rhetoric increases. His proposals are simple, or rather dual: the admission to the military of open homosexuals, the extension to homosexuals of marriage rights. Nothing less is due, but nothing more is needed. The question is, are these proposals either cogent or practicable?

Classical gay liberation disregarded the situation of gays in the military because of a feeling that homosexuals already in the Services were denying their natures and were committed to playing a part. War was getting a bad press at the time, appropriately enough in a period dominated by Vietnam. Surely self-accepting gay people would somehow hex the imperialistic war machine by their very presence?

This is undoubtedly a simple-minded critique of the Services, but still it is a critique of sorts. Some of those who argue for the right of gays to serve in the military, like the late Randy Shilts in his vast book *Conduct Unbecoming*, seem willing to endorse absolutely everything about the military and the policies it is called upon to enforce, *except* its refusal to admit gay people. This may not be a good bargain.

Sullivan decries the failure of President Clinton's efforts to force gay equality on the Armed Services. In his view, liberals 'fumbled the issue . . . largely due to the flaccidity of liberalism today, by the fact that its heirs do not even understand its fundamental principles and arguments'. You may feel rather that liberalism has still not fully absorbed its own teachings.

But if Clinton underestimated the opposition to what may have been the single issue most personally important to him (and a political posture that might reward some of his supporters, but would certainly cost votes overall), might not Andrew Sullivan be doing the same? When he writes about things he knows directly, after all, he has a very clear sense of gay people's exclusion from full participation in apparently neutral social situations:

> I remember . . . that around the age of eight, I joined a gang of four boys . . . and developed a crush on one of them . . . I felt the first strains of that homosexual hurt that is the accompaniment of most homosexual lives. It was not so much the rejection; it was the combination of acceptance and rejection. It was feeling that that part of the male–male bond that worked – the part that works with most heterosexual male–male friendships – was also the part that destroyed the possibility of another, as yet opaque but far more complete longing that for me, but not for him, was inextricable from the relationship.

If Sullivan can see (despite this last sentence's incoherence) that informal social interaction among eight-year-olds resists the possibility of same-sex love, then why should the same not apply to an institution that sets out to produce a specific pattern of masculine behaviour?

With the Armed Services too, you might say that it isn't the rejection so much as the combination of acceptance and rejection that is so hurtful. Welcome to fight and die, not allowed to be yourself. Sullivan is unimpressed with the 'Don't Ask, Don't Tell' compromise that currently applies in the American military, saying it 'formally introduced hypocrisy as a rule of combat'. (*A rule of combat* puts it a bit high, surely: *the requirement of an institution* would be more accurate.) In any case, Sullivan has no objection to hypocrisy as such, as he indicated in his chapter on conservatism. It's just that he feels it can only work when there is a culturally accepted distinction between public and private – and the preconditions for stable hypocrisy no longer apply.

When it comes to marriage, though, hypocrisy seems to be the prescription all over again. Sullivan is too honest to pretend that monogamy particularly suits gay people, and goes so far as to say that 'there is something baleful about the attempt of some gay conservatives to educate homosexuals and lesbians into an uncritical acceptance of a stifling model of heterosexual normality'. It's all very well to say that within marriage there is 'plenty of scope for cultural difference', but if one of the things he champions about gay relationships is that 'there is more likely to be greater understanding of the need for extramarital outlets between two men than between a man and a woman', then what does marriage mean? Isn't he really saying that gay couples are not so much qualified for marriage as skilled in coping with adultery?

The objections to Sullivan's two-point programme, then, like the book, are partly ideological and partly practical. It isn't simply a matter of hacking into the statute book's data base and making two little amendments. A form of marriage that welcomed gay people would be very different from marriage today: a form of the military that welcomed gay people would be very different from the US military today. Those changes would certainly be fought every step of the way. Should they really represent the whole of the agenda for gay politics?

But in fact, despite the way he announces it, this is not a two-point plan. Andrew Sullivan spells out the small print: 'an end to sodomy laws . . . recourse to the courts if there is not equal protection of heterosexuals and homosexuals in law enforcement . . . an equal legal age of consent . . . inclusion of the facts about homosexuality in the curriculum of every government-funded school', and 'recourse to the courts if any government body or agency can be proven to be engaged in discrimination against homosexual employees'. Put this way, without the rhetorical concentration on uniforms and wedding rings, this begins to sound like a promising broad agenda. What it doesn't sound is new. None of these ideas is a novelty in the politics of gay liberation. But then it's a characteristic of *Virtually Normal* that when its author doesn't like a proposal or piece of analysis he firmly attaches it to one of his four groups, but when he does like it, he tends not to mention its provenance.

Andrew Sullivan ends the book with his most sustained piece of rhetoric, in the Epilogue, 'What Are Homosexuals For?' It's as if he knows that he must end on a note of uplift, the way *Gone With the Wind* ends with 'Tomorrow is another day.' He writes: 'the seeds of homosexual wisdom are the seeds of human wisdom. They contain the truth that order is in fact a euphemism for disorder; that problems are often more sanely enjoyed than solved; that there is reason in mystery; that there is beauty in the wild flowers that grow randomly among our wheat.'

This rather feverish botanical moment, like so much of *Virtually Normal*, is just good enough to be a letdown. Figurative language needs to be approached with more care, handled with a greater tact. After all, if the seeds of homosexual wisdom are the seeds of human wisdom, why do the gay seeds grow up as wild flowers and the straight seeds as wheat? Then again, if you're growing wheat, presumably as a food crop rather than a decoration, how pleased are you, actually, when wild flowers spring up in it? Above all, someone with Andrew Sullivan's religious education should be more sensitive to the biblical text that haunts his peroration, the hellfire sermon under his mystical-cheerful homily. The ur-text mentions *tares* rather than wild flowers among the wheat, and it isn't part of a Patience Strong nature ramble, but a terrible warning from Jehovah, gardener with a rare love of bonfires.

Religious language with a different resonance is deployed by David Halperin in his *Saint Foucault*, which bears the subtitle 'Towards a Gay Hagiography'. Halperin is well aware of the dangerous echo of *Saint Genet*, Sartre's overbearing and invasive gloss on another writer's life and work, but appropriates another famous French formulation to convey his sense of the proper distance, in this particular case, between himself and his subject: '*Foucault, c'est moi.*' Fair warning. This is academic criticism at its most impassioned.

Saint Foucault contains many less telling phrases and coinages – 'credentializing the disempowered', for instance, and 'heteronormativity' – but also a freshness, even a crudity of expression unusual in a book published by Oxford University Press (and no worse for that): '. . . let me make it official. I may not have worshipped Foucault at the time I wrote *One Hundred Years of Homosexuality*, but I do worship him now. As far as I'm concerned, the guy was a fucking saint.' The change in Halperin's outlook must be considerable, if it allows him to substitute for a previous watchword ('no orgasm without ideology') the phrase of Foucault's which he uses in the book's dedication, 'Pleasure has no passport', but he doesn't go into the details of his conversion.

Foucault is a saint whose books are his miracles, and whose martyrdom was paradoxically posthumous, in the form of the various biographies which have appeared since his death in 1984. Those biographies (by Didier Erebon, James Miller and David Macey), which Halperin discusses in some detail, take very different approaches, but are vulnerable to the same objection. Foucault was not in the business of leading an exemplary life, merely of advancing useful ideas, but the objection is more agonised than that: Foucault's entire intellectual project was to open inspection hatches on to the machinery that produces our culture's truths. Not to list lies, but to show how the gears mesh – and whose lives are disengaged or broken when they do.

Foucault's martyrdom by biography is specifically a kind of flaying: the skin of a life is peeled off and displayed. The biographers compete over the completeness of the hide, and point to the flattened-out fingerprints to prove that no mistake has been made in identification, that this is truly Foucault. It hardly matters whether the caption of the exhibit is *Nihilism: A Cautionary Tale* or *Propagandist for Perversion* or even *Hero of Modern Thought*. Even a well-meaning biography of Foucault is somehow an act of revenge, a closing down and rendering personal of what he sought to open up and make available to others.

But David Halperin's book doesn't set out to defend Foucault merely from his biographers, but also from an earlier generation of gay critics, who regarded his work on sexuality as unhelpful. Poor show to undermine the struggle from within, by remaining sceptical about the existence of 'the homosexual' as a species.

Halperin rejects the term 'irony' when describing Foucault's ordeals at the hands of his biographers: it isn't *ironical* but punitive when the procedures someone has opposed throughout his career are instantly used against him once dead. Yet there is an irony to Foucault's being subjected to such a definitively gay experience without having assented to that category.

Homosexuals are routinely expected to be discreet about their private lives, but when they submit to this expectation their discretion is taken as proof of hypocrisy or secret shame. Polarities of secrecy and exposure, without a defensible middle ground. *Consigned to the shadows or the accusing spotlight*, as an Uranian might put it on an off day, *begrudged the ordinary day*. The way Foucault's ideas are reductively reattached to his life by the operations of biography repeats on a huge scale one of the routine double-binds of gay life.

But the irony doesn't diminish Foucault. Despite his being unconvinced about the validity of the category *homosexual*, Foucault and Foucauldian criticism provide the most significant account of the paradoxes attendant on 'coming out' – that odd business of going public with what is unlikely to have been altogether unknown in the first place, relinquishing the convenience of the open secret.

In Colin Spencer's world, coming out is as inescapable an obligation as breathing. Andrew Sullivan sees it rather as an act of personal clarity and social virtue, though he does admit that at an earlier stage of his evolution he felt that 'the closeted homosexual was a useful social creature . . . possibly happier than those immersed in what sometimes seems like a merciless and shallow subculture'. Yet if many gay people find that in practice coming out changes life less than they had expected, perhaps the subculture is not the guilty party.

As Halperin puts it:

> If to come out is to release oneself from a state of unfreedom, that is not because coming out constitutes an escape from the reach of power to a place outside of power: rather, coming out puts into play a different set of power relations and alters the dynamics of personal and political struggle. *Coming out is an act of freedom, then, not in the sense of liberation but in the sense of resistance.*

This distinction is crucial to *Saint Foucault*, but might it not be applied to Foucault's own position on the category of the homosexual? *Liberation* from the category assumes, again, a position outside the system that is hard to imagine, whereas *resistance* to the category of sexual orientation is a meaningful idea, and even a salutary one. (Those are the contagious italics of academic prose.) It could even be said that those who live by a politics of identity may die by one.

After all, when Hitler wished to extinguish the German homophile movement, at that time the most highly organised in the world, he didn't have to do a lot more than buy a box of matches and ask for directions to the Magnus Hirschfeld Institute.

The writers of both *Homosexuality: A History* and *Virtually Normal* assume that if every gay person in the world came out, bigotry would wither away. Homophobia by this account cannot exist in the presence of large numbers of self-affirming gay people. This idea has been around since at least the early 1970s, when it was sometimes expressed in terms of 'If only gay people were all purple, so everyone could see them . . .' (purple was a fashion colour just then, and the idea of a gay black person was perhaps as remote as the idea of a purple black one). But the very best that could be hoped for in those circumstances was that gay politics would become a racial politics – and life is not easy for racial minorities, as members of those minorities will willingly tell you.

One thing that can be said with certainty about Michel Foucault is that he did not underestimate homophobia. While Colin Spencer seeks to dismiss hostility to homosexuals by showing that it varies from time to time and place to place, and Andrew Sullivan tries to refute its arguments, David Halperin's point is that homophobia is not susceptible of refutation. As he puts it: 'Homophobic discourses ... are composed of a potentially infinite number of different but functionally interchangeable assertions, such that whenever any one assertion is falsified or disqualified another one – even one with a content exactly contrary to the original one – can be neatly and effectively substituted for it.' Homophobia is a premiss masquerading as a conclusion.

An exquisite example comes from the American legal system's treatment of a teacher called Acanfora (Halperin quotes Eve Kosofsky Sedgwick's account) who was transferred to a non-teaching position when the Maryland board of education found out he was gay. He spoke about this injustice on television, and was refused a new contract altogether. He sued. The federal district court held that he had brought undue attention to his sexuality by appearing on television. An appeal court overruled this argument, and accepted Acanfora's right to free speech. However ... the overruling of this argument did not mean that he won the appeal. In fact the appeal court affirmed the lower court's decision, this time on the grounds that Acanfora was not in a position to sue in the first place, since he had not mentioned on his original application for the job that he had been, in college, an officer of a student homophile organisation. (It was admitted that if he had done so he would not have been given the job.)

As Sedgwick puts it: 'The rationale for keeping Acanfora out of his classroom was thus no longer that he had disclosed too much about his homosexuality, but quite the opposite, that he had not disclosed enough.' Each of the two rulings in the case emphasised that the teacher's homosexuality 'itself' would not have provided an acceptable argument for denying him employment. Everyone agreed that he had rights: it's simply that in order to defend them he was required to walk a legal tightrope, and when against the odds he kept his balance there he was made to jump from one tightrope to another, until eventually, to no one's surprise, he fell off. His rights were unimpaired; it was only his life that had been rendered impossible.

Saint Foucault proposes that refuting homophobia, dismantling its routine slanders and fantasies, is ultimately a mug's game and a poor use of personal and political resources. What to do instead, then? Foucault characterised desirable interventions as marginal and strategic, but was notably reluctant to recommend specific courses of action: 'I absolutely will not play the part of one who prescribes solutions'. Nor did he endorse any existing social group as a political vanguard.

David Halperin feels, though, that one set of groups and actions since Foucault's death have earned the designation *Foucauldian* (he prefers this form of the adjective over Andrew Sullivan's *Foucauldean*, which has subtly sulphurous overtones of *Sadean*). He means the AIDS Coalition To Unleash Power, or ACT-UP, which even Sullivan credits with 'some brilliant tactical victories in the very practical area of accelerating AIDS research, reducing prices for certain drugs, and putting pressure on local and federal governments to take the epidemic more seriously'.

Halperin's first argument is his weakest: his subjective feeling that Foucault's *History of Sexuality, Volume 1* was the indispensable jacket-pocket book of the ACT-UP generation – as books by Marcuse or Norman O. Brown would have been for equivalent radicals in the 1960s – as if that, even if true, would establish a chain of political connection. But gradually he builds his case, that ACT-UP in some way fulfilled

Foucault's requirements for effective action – or rather, cunning and tantalising phrase, that Foucault 'produced the non-theory of which ACT-UP is the practice'.

ACT-UP, though, has had its day, and it doesn't seem to be asking too much to expect some hint of what lessons might be learned from it and more widely applied. One answer seems to be appropriation and theatricalisation.

Halperin's example is a response to a notorious issue of *Newsweek* from 1993 which treated lesbianism as a problematic phenomenon which should be tolerated only up to a point. Ten days later, the *Bay Times* in San Francisco appeared with a cover (HETEROSEXUALS – WHAT ARE THE LIMITS OF TOLERANCE?) exactly mirroring the tone and arguments of the original, complete with helpful glossary:

> WIFE Traditionally the 'feminine' partner; responsible for domestic tasks and child care. HUSBAND Wears suit or other 'manly gear'. Watches sports on TV. Performs heavy lifting, household repairs and yard work. MARRIAGE Ancient quaint custom in which males and females pair up, supposedly for life. 50 per cent failure rate. SEX POSITIVE He sleeps with his secretary. She sleeps with her priest. VANILLA He comes in five minutes. She just likes to be held . . .

The truth-value of the two articles is identical, but only one represents the norm. Only one is common sense, true without having to mount an argument. It's true, moreover, because of where you read it: it's not because it's authoritative that it appears in *Newsweek*. It's authoritative because it appears in *Newsweek*.

The radical use of parody is an attractive idea, but even in this case parody doesn't seem to change anything. It's marginal, but hardly strategic. The overlap in readership between a local radical newspaper and a national glossy is insignificant, and there's nothing particularly subversive about preaching to the converted. The objection to *Newsweek*'s 'coverage', after all, was that it told a straight readership what that readership thought it knew already – preaching to the converted, but to a rather larger constituency of the converted.

The other side of a reluctance to prescribe courses of action is an unwillingness to stigmatise any mode of life or self-description that gay people may choose for themselves. If you can't say in advance which approaches will be fruitful, nor can you rule anything out.

In this way Foucauldian politics tries to avoid the trap of subcultural scapegoating. One of the most touching passages in *Saint Foucault* is one where Halperin sets out to muffle the snarl of his own critical sensibility, and makes a case despite his reservations for what he calls 'the gay male gym body', on the grounds that '[gay muscles] are explicitly designed to be an erotic turn-on, and in their very solicitation of desire they deliberately flaunt the visual norms of straight masculinity, which impose discretion on masculine self-display and require that straight male beauty exhibit itself only casually or inadvertently, that it refuse to acknowledge its own strategies'.

The temptation to carp is a little stronger with the vexed question of the word 'queer'. David Halperin can see that Foucault is in some way a prophet of this new style of self-description, but regards the term as dangerously susceptible to nullification by co-opting:

> Lesbians and gay men can now look forward to a new round of condescension and dismissal at the hands of the trendy and glamorously unspecified sexual outlaws who call themselves 'queer' and who can claim the radical chic attached to a sexually transgressive identity without, of course, having to do anything icky with their bodies in order to earn it. There is nothing enviable about the lot of lesbians and gay men who wind up living in the sort of queer world where, as a friend of mine reports from a certain New England women's college, all the women

who are sleeping with men identify themselves as lesbians and all the women who are sleeping with women identify themselves as bisexuals.

It's clearly in its way a relishable moment, when a follower of Foucault ends up defending the fixed category of sexual orientation against those who would blur it. But one of the valuable things about *Saint Foucault* is that it shows us a Foucault who was, particularly in interviews, anything but stringently Foucauldian. A man who could say (speaking to Gilles Barbedette), 'I think we should consider the battle for gay rights as an episode that cannot be the final stage', was someone for whom *gay rights* was not a category mistake but an insufficient agenda.

The sense in which Foucault can be claimed as a prophet of queer theory is exemplified in this passage from the same interview, with its extraordinarily relaxed and inclusive use of the first person plural: 'Rather than saying what we said at one time: "Let's try to re-introduce homosexuality into the general norm of social relations," let's say the reverse: "No! Let's escape as much as possible from the type of relations which society proposes for us and try to create in the empty space where we are new relational possibilities." By proposing a new relational *right*, we will see that non-homosexual people can enrich their lives by changing their own schema of relations.'

This idea of the empty space has a metaphysical ring to it, but there is also a potential aspect of political pragmatism: it's clearly a better use of resources to claim an ignored or disparaged space than to lay siege to an esteemed and well-defended one.

One of Foucault's nominations for a disparaged and available space, famously, was sadomasochism, and an eroticism based on fist-fucking. Halperin discusses these matters without apology, acknowledging that Foucault's championing of them made him particularly vulnerable to calumny after his death, but properly refusing to be swayed by that.

In fact Foucault seems naive rather than demonically sophisticated on these subjects. The idea that fist-fucking would necessarily generate modes of relation more radical than those created by, say, stamp-collecting seems distinctly wishful. When Foucault, describing bath-house sex, states that 'It's not the affirmation of identity that's important, it's the affirmation of non-identity', it's hard to suppress the heretical thought that perhaps Foucault spent more nights at home reading than his biographers have dared to suggest. Sexual scripts are not so easily abandoned. The anonymity of a bath-house is theatrical, allowing for much mutual projection of fantasy, rather than existential, as Foucault has it.

There's a moment in *Saint Foucault* when the politics of the empty space suddenly comes into focus as an idea. The subject is marriage, which Foucault at one stage considered an important objective, going so far as to say, over dinner at Lacan's house in 1963, that 'there will be no civilisation as long as marriage between men is not accepted'. But that was table talk, not strategy.

Foucault's later thinking on the subject is fascinatingly lateral. He has second thoughts about frontal assault on the central institution of heterosexuality, not because marriage is a worthless goal or even a bourgeois concern but because it is heavily defended, impregnable. Luckily there is another way of conferring rights on a chosen person that is much less regarded, that doesn't even begin to compete with the sacred tedium of marriage. It is a procedure moreover that is exempt from the spurious equality of the marriage bond, so that relationships can be formalised without needing to be symmetrical.

Foucault proposes that gay people should seek to legitimise their arrangements by extending the mechanism of adoption rather than trying to appropriate marriage: 'Why shouldn't I adopt a friend who's ten years younger than I am? And even if he's ten years older? Rather than arguing that rights are fundamental and natural to the individual, we should try to imagine and create a new relational right which permits all possible types of relation to exist and not be prevented, blocked or annulled by impoverished relational institutions.' This customising of adoption would work by multiplying the meanings of the existing institution, rather than conforming however hypocritically, as in the case of marriage, to a pattern that was hardly designed to be flexible. In this case Foucault's agenda seems not only more genial but also more practical than Andrew Sullivan's.

The three books considered here vary enormously in method and ambition, from incoherent scissors-and-paste job to passionate engagement with difficult but rewarding texts. David Halperin's book is far and away the richest, the most honest and profound. He manages to rehabilitate his hero ('our Marx . . . our Freud') in exactly that area where, in life and after it, he has been felt to be most wanting, as a political thinker who wanted to be useful, to offer not counsels of despair but strategies of resistance.

Yet Halperin's book is shot through with an anxiety that is sometimes plaintive, more often paranoiac. His Acknowledgements thank someone for 'his unswerving loyalty and friendship during the composition of this book – a period in my life during which such items were otherwise in short supply'. Asked to contribute a paper on a biography for a magazine, he experienced a severe case of critic's block: 'under the circumstances, I couldn't *not* defend Foucault, but I couldn't defend him either'. He has eventually produced that defence as part of this volume, but he still has a sense of its futility, with the damage long done.

In the introductory section of *Saint Foucault* he describes the incident that partly explains this feeling of embattlement, a lawsuit brought by a female colleague against their employer (the Massachusetts Institute of Technology) alleging 'professional, political and sexual harassment', and implicating Halperin. The case was settled out of court by MIT, and Halperin himself eventually decided not to undertake retaliatory litigation against his colleague, instead accepting what was presumably a goodwill package from MIT: two years' leave on favourable terms and a hefty research budget.

As he puts it:

> what the affair brought home to me is the very real vulnerability which until that moment, I hadn't realized I shared with all other lesbian and gay people in our society, a vulnerability I foolishly thought I had managed to escape *by coming out* . . . it turns out that if you are known to be lesbian or gay your very openness . . . simply exposes you to the possibility that . . . people can say absolutely whatever they like about you in the well-grounded confidence that it will be credited. (And since there is very little you can do about it, you might as well not try to ingratiate yourself by means of 'good behaviour'.)

This would be an understandable reaction from almost anyone in the world *except* a radical gay professor who had been teaching Foucault's work for years by this point. You can't take seriously Foucault's political critique of institutionalised rationality, and then expect it not to apply to the institution that happens to employ you. You can't talk about the importance of strategic work on the margins and also rely on smooth professional advancement. (Forget for a moment that Foucault himself enjoyed a level of academic security from which mere humdrum tenure must have looked like vagrancy.) If *Saint Foucault* was a less impressive piece of work, Halperin might almost be suspected of wanting to claim the radical chic attached to an intellectually transgressive identity, without having to do anything icky with his career in order to earn it.

The current turmoil of the academy is general and not confined to gay teachers. When Halperin writes, 'The incident has come to represent for me an object lesson in the institutional crisis of gay authority', he relies on a formula – 'gay authority' –

hardly sanctioned by Foucault. Foucault seems to have spent quite a lot of time and energy, by Halperin's own account, trying to avoid being an authority.

It's natural that David Halperin should be marked by a painful experience, but surprising that he should foreground his feelings in the book. A little further reflection would have led him to remove the disastrous nihilistic flourish with which he ends *Saint Foucault*: 'whenever those of us who feel ourselves to be in Foucault's embattled position, or who share his political vision, hear those who aren't, or who don't, invoke the notion of "truth", we reach for our revolvers'.

For someone who has been telling us, at some length and with great eloquence, of how monstrous it is for Foucault's analysis of power relations and interest in sadomasochism to be presented as a sort of Nazism, then to appropriate a saying attributed to Goering is neither clever nor funny. And of course it's not true: when he hears the word 'truth', David Halperin reaches for his word processor. To strike a rather Pollyanna-ish note, 'If everything is dangerous, then we always have something to do.' Except that it wasn't Pollyanna who said that, it was Michel Foucault.

London Review of Books, 1995

Survivor Art

The Christmas and New Year double issue of the *New Yorker* carried an article under the rubric A CRITIC AT BAY – the regular heading being the less embattled 'A Critic At Large' – by the magazine's dance critic, Arlene Croce, with a forthright title, 'Discussing the Undiscussable', and a grievance to match: the replacement of a viable dance culture by special-interests posturing – what Croce calls 'victim art' – as exemplified by a piece of work, 'Still/Here', by the dancer/choreographer Bill T. Jones, which she has chosen not to see. She argues her case at length, but the essential point is that 'Still/Here' cannot be art because of its subject matter (terminal illness in general, HIV in particular). Jones makes no secret of his antibody-positive status, and this new piece incorporates video testimony from terminally ill people.

Under Tina Brown, the *New Yorker* has lost a lot of its shyness. It's nice to know that even the most sedate institution, given a little assertiveness training, can pick an occasional genteel fight.

This particular fight is partly about art, partly about criticism, and mainly, I feel, about AIDS. AIDS is a new subject, one that people find it easier to deal with, in some curious way, by treating it as if it had nothing in common with anything else in the world.

If there is a divide between those who produce art work and those who judge it in the marketplace, then I have been on both sides of it, but I'm only on one side of this argument. I've written fiction about AIDS that has been dismissed, on occasion, *a priori* on the basis that AIDS cannot be the subject of art (a point of view you hear less often these days in literary circles). Those reviews seemed to me to be indefensible: if you exclude in advance the possibility of a book succeeding, you have no business pretending to assess it. If I have also been the beneficiary of imperceptive favourable notices, prompted by the supposed virtue of the attempt rather than by anything I actually brought off, those were only routinely inadequate reviews – they weren't corrupt.

But I have also reviewed films – usually Queer with a capital Q – that set out to overturn my assumptions and change my fuddy-duddy life, but which only reminded me of Godard films I hadn't enjoyed in the first place. On those occasions it wasn't unreasonably hard to detect the lousy film underneath the right-on sweetie-paper.

What is art? That's a big question. Let's discuss that another day. What is a critic? That's much more tractable. Here's where we scale down from philosophy to ethics. We can settle that now if you like.

There are times when everyone wants to stay home, with a strippagram and a risotto, and the good news is that everybody can, except for critics. Art is optional for everyone, always, who isn't a critic. Anyone but a critic can avoid the theatre, shun the cinema, boycott the music superstores and the bookshops, and not owe the world a policy statement. A critic, though, is obliged to experience art on a regular basis, in the mood or out of it, or else find another line of work.

Most art has designs on us – moral, political, sentimental. Most art is also bad (just as most time is wasted and most love lost) and it follows that much bad art has designs on us. Isn't it the critic's job to point us away from bad art, and if there is reviewing space left over, to analyse its failed designs?

It would be unfair to characterise Arlene Croce simply as conservative in her tastes. Some years ago, for instance, she wrote an extraordinarily exciting account of Karole Armitage's

'Drastic Classicism', one of those rare pieces of critical writing that make you forget you missed the actual event, as if it was you personally that was in rapid succession deafened, baffled, and elated. But as a dance critic she has a technical vocabulary of description – very precious in an art-form so impermanent – which is routinely violated or ignored by much modern work, and that seems to be the heart of her grievance. In other words, much of her animus against Bill T. Jones and 'Still/Here' is not that he and it are drastic, but that they aren't classical.

One of the phrases coined by Arlene Croce in her article is 'victim art', which I confess I find offensive. If an exhibition was mounted of art produced by inmates of concentration camps who had subsequently died there, no one would dream of referring to it as 'victim art', even though the artists were in a very real sense victims. In that context it would be clear that the phrase denies even the possibility of generalising from a place of suffering. We would find terms like *testimony* to describe such an exhibition, or even *survivor art*, on the grounds that victims don't make art. (I apologise for the hackneyed AIDS/Holocaust analogy, bane of the partisan think-piece. It's not that I think the two subjects are deeply linked, only that people are more lucid about the supposedly unthinkable in the older context, where they've had more mental practice.)

Reviewing such an exhibition would not be easy, but that it would not be impossible is shown by the careful analytical responses to the recently opened Holocaust Museum carried by, for instance, the *New Yorker*. What is it about AIDS that provokes a fiercer recoil? If we can imagine an AIDS Museum of the future, why is it hard to accept AIDS-informed art now? And more crucially, what is an artist personally affected by HIV to do, if not include it in his or her working practice?

Bill T. Jones's dance life and *life* life were shared with Arnie Zane, who died of AIDS. Jones himself is antibody positive. That's an awfully large chunk of his existence to expect an artist to rise above: to rise above and have the good taste or manners not to mention. AIDS by its nature gives people a good long time to think about endings. Why should it not bring on a late style (a subject explored in different contexts by Edward Said): late Jones on the analogy of late Beethoven, late Strauss? A dancer's working life is so short in any case that a performer/choreographer of Jones's age would need to be thinking of a change of direction anyway.

AIDS-informed art need not be frightening, but it seems likely that people will go on being frightened of it anyway. The most revealing sentence in the whole of Arlene Croce's article is this one: 'I can't review someone I feel sorry for or hopeless about.' For one thing: sorry and hopeless. Tweak those terms a little and you have pity and terror, not emotions which art should exclude but actually the emotions that tragic art depends on, according to one of the oldest definitions we have.

For another: if you look at that sentence, you'll see that Croce sees herself as reviewing a person. (If you do see yourself as reviewing people rather than what they make, then a stroppy gay black man with HIV may well be a tough assignment.) If there is a breaching of the proprieties in modern art, and that is the substance of her complaint, then it is one which she herself insists on.

To go back to the question of what an artist affected by HIV should actually do: there are two exemplary paths. One is to restrict information about your health as much as you can, and to carry on as you did before. By the time you lose control of the information you will probably be too ill to work anyway. This is the choice made typically by interpretative or non-autobiographical artists, for whom art is a way of not being themselves, and we can call it the Freddie Mercury Defence.

The other option is to include HIV in a working practice already in some degree autobiographical. This will tend to suit those for whom art is a way of being themselves, and we can call it the Derek Jarman Option.

Both of these choices are brave, and neither of them amounts to being a victim. The great drawback of Freddie Mercury Defence is that when the facts become known the art changes in retrospect. If you look now at the video for the Queen song 'I'm Going Slightly Mad', for instance, it's impossible not to think that Freddie Mercury, prancing dutifully in a top hat, was preoccupied with the likelihood of AIDS-related dementia, rather than English eccentricity, however marketable. With Freddie Mercury Defence, the pity that the artist refused comes back to haunt the work.

The dance world already has one towering example of Freddie Mercury Defence, in Nureyev. The pathos inherent in a great dancer refusing to retire when well past his prime, already almost overwhelming, is many times magnified when we understand how much he was denying. And now the dance world has, in Bill T. Jones, someone who is trying the other option. He is entitled to bad reviews, but at least he should be spared non-reviews, either from critics who turn up knowing that nothing of what he wants to achieve can be done, or from those who stay at home.

Independent, 1995

II

Mr Philips

Ask at the desk for Mr Philips.

The desk is tucked away, less impressive than I'd expected. The porters absurdly young. 'I have a seven o'clock appointment with Mr Philips.'

Narrowed eyes from the absurdly young porters. 'Is that Mr Philips in 312?' I don't know. 'What's his first name?'

I go to pieces; don't know that, either. So what do I do? Mime someone licking a microphone? 'I'm sorry. I wasn't told.'

Porter to bell-boy: 'I'll try Mr Andrew Philips first . . . Oh, Mr Philips, are you expecting someone? . . . No, a man . . . Yes, I see. I'm sorry.'

Clever Mr Andrew Philips. This has happened before, and he has learned to ask, 'Is it a girl?'

The porter dials again. 'Are you expecting a visitor, sir? . . . Right, I'll send him up.'

At last the porter looks at me differently. An early-teenager takes me upstairs, knocks at the door of 312, and disconcertingly walks away. I had expected to be ushered in, I don't know why, and feel deserted.

A pause. Giggles.

A girl lets me in, short hair, metallic pumps, ra-ra skirt. It's a large suite. Jagger is wearing a big-cat-stippled T-shirt, tight white trousers (slightly flared?) and no shoes. Charlie Watts wears a brown and pink shirt, beige pleated pants and golfing shoes with a touch of the co-respondent.

They are both sprawling on a sofa. There is champagne on the table. The TV is on.

I had been told that a day watching cricket made Jagger relaxed and amenable, but Pakistan (quite without meaning to offend) have been making a lot of runs, and something a little different has happened. They are teasing the girl, and they are talking sport, which is not something I'm good at.

Are they on the ball? These are people who encourage you to underestimate them.

Jagger crouches before me on the carpet (I suddenly realise that his shoes – white Puma runners with Velcro-fastened straps – are by my feet) pointing to a card.

'Charlie 'n' me are fixin' up an England team, but we've only four names we're sure of. What d'you suggest?'

Nothing.

I am wearing a bandage round a cut elbow (eight stitches) which catches Charlie's eye. 'Naaaasty. Bill Graham had something like that, just like that . . . you 'member, Mick?'

'Yeah . . .'

'. . . it blew up and blew up and they had to keep puncturing it and puncturing it and it just kept blowing up, for *four months* . . .'

Won't happen to me.

'Nasty, though. Nasty. Really freaked me out, seeing that.'

Jagger has spotted Paul Jones on the TV, and gestures wildly for me to turn the volume up.

'Christ almighty, look at this cunt,' he says.

For a while we watch Paul Jones on the TV. 'There but for the grace . . .' says Charlie. He tries to explain why Mick Jagger isn't Paul Jones, but doesn't quite get there.

'He's selling summink, the dirty bugger,' says Jagger. 'Wonder what he's selling.'

'I think he's in a musical,' I tell him.

'Maybe that's it. Oh and look, here's Eric Morecambe joining him. Wonder what *he's* selling.'

The compere says, '. . . novel *Mr Lonely*, done very well,' and Jagger and I say 'paperback' together.

Paul Jones reads aloud from a children's book about a toothless vampire who could only give you a good suck. This is cute. Then he sings a song with the Blues Band. 'It's called "So Bad",' he tells us.

'There but for the grace . . .' says Charlie.

We turn the TV sound down. 'Wasser time?' asks Jagger. Seven-thirty, we tell him. 'Is that your VCR or mine?' asks Charlie. 'Mine,' says Jagger. 'What would *your* VCR be doing in *my* room?'

The girl is making her departure. She just grins when Jagger tells her what time she should get up the next morning. She can cope. She leaves.

I'm supposed to be making an impression, on Jagger at least, so when one of the Stones stares, I stare right back. 'What are you staring at?' says Charlie.

The phone rings. Charlie shouts, '*Hollywood* at last it's Hollywood. At last my big break.' He does this every time the phone rings; for the next three hours.

But this time it *is* Hollywood. The Stones have had a film made – each putting up half a million – and Mick discusses it on the phone for a while. Overdubs and stuff.

When he rings off, Charlie says, 'When I first saw that movie I thought it was the worst fucking film I'd ever seen. Just fucking awful. And now it's really good. Maybe he did what you do, Mick, you know, turn in the out-takes and hang on to the masters.'

At some stage I realise that Charlie thinks I'm a film-maker of some kind.

'Well,' says Jagger. 'I've seen it on a big screen and it's fucking great. But some of the early . . . montages were crap.'

'That one . . . montage of you peering through some railings was crap anyway. We soon got rid of that.'

I like '. . . montage'. I like '. . . montage' very much. It's the little lurch I like.

'Oh, I hate business,' says Jagger, picking up a telegram, which he reads out. 'BW and CW and KR . . . MJ. Fuck all this,' he says, 'I hate all these cables.'

'You love it all, Mick. Who wanted a dish installed outside his house, big fucking dish receive every signal in the world?'

Jagger isn't embarrassed. 'Then everybody did, remember? Remember me fixing you up with a fucking dish out in fucking Gloucestershire?'

'Oh, fuck, what a day,' says Charlie. He shows me an MCC cap and a fielding-positions tea-towel he bought at Lord's. 'With my own money, mind. One pound twenty and £1.40. And all for *his* fucking girlfriend.'

Mick says, 'Yeah, but can you imagine growing up in America, playing God knows what and not knowing how to play cricket?' He seems genuinely stricken.

The phone rings. 'Hollywood,' says Charlie, 'my big break.' But it's the porter announcing a visitor.

Meanwhile Mick is ordering smoked-salmon sandwiches and more champagne. I try to indicate I'd like some food, but the message falls short and I'm not confident enough to repeat it.

The visitor arrives, introduced as Steve, bringing a package. He hands it to Charlie, who hands it to Mick. 'It's for yer house-warming, Mick. The house in France.'

House in France equals château on Loire.

Mick unwraps it, apparently imitating Jerry Hall as he does so. It sounds like the cod falsetto on 'Dear Doctor' from *Beggars Banquet*. '*Oh* Ahm so tickled *Oh* Ahm so grateful Ya *know* ya shouldn't Oh Ahm so *tickled*.' Inside a corrugated cardboard wrapping is ribbon and paper; inside that, a painting.

Jagger sobers up in the presence of value. 'I'm most grateful, Charlie, really I am.'

'It's for the house in France.'

Micks looks at it; the painting is of a horse. 'I'm most grateful. Is it a Stubbs?'

'No it's not a fucking Stubbs. Fifteen thousand quid, though.'

It's hard to believe. The painting is dark and small. 'D'ya like it?' asks Mick.

'The light is bad in here,' I say.

Mick switches lights on.

Champagne arrives, and Mick is generous with it. 'And some for this gentleman too, please,' he says, indicating me.

The painting is left, partly wrapped, on the floor, where Charlie walks over it twice in the next ten minutes, on his way to the Room Service button. A little later he says, 'Fifteen thousand quid, just left on the floor, old man Jagger walking all over it . . .'

Steve is offered a smoked-salmon sandwich, and I am too shy to claim one. I can't see how many there are, from where I'm sitting.

Charlie is fascinated by the Savoy logo on the plates. It's a gondola, something to do with *The Gondoliers*, I guess, but I don't say anything.

Mick says, 'It's a Viking ship, Charlie. They dug it out of the Thames just here.'

Charlie says, 'Really?'

'No, you silly faggot, I'm joking. But I do know, Henry VIII, or Elizabeth, used to sail from here in their barges. Savoy. Sounds French, I dunno. But there's been a building here since 13-something.'

The phone rings. It isn't Hollywood, it's Jerry Hall. Mick says he's had a long day taking some kids to see the cricket. He'll phone back later.

By now Charlie is talking music to Steve, and Mick joins in. They all like Junior ('Mama Used To Say') and Jagger even sings a bit. 'Take your time young man . . .'

I try to remember more of the words. 'Don't be in a rush to grow old . . .' This is obviously wrong, but Jagger tries singing it anyway.

They all like Kid Creole, not 'Stool Pigeon' so much as the single before. 'The one about being wonderful,' says Mick.

It is my moment of glory. ' "I'm a Wonderful Thing, Baby".'

'That's it,' says Mick.

Mick claims to have four Kid Creole albums, and Charlie defies him to name them. I am getting above myself, and I say, 'Well there's *Fresh Fruit* and *Tropical Gangsters* . . .'

'Hey, shut up,' says Charlie. 'Who asked you?'

Then Charlie asks Steve about a record he's seen him carrying. 'What was it, Fashion? Are they any good?'

'Yeah. Two twelve-inches for £1.99. Bloody good.'

'What?'

'Two twelve-inch singles for £1.99. Good.'

'But the music?'

'Good.'

Mick turns to me. 'I read your book,' he tells me.

Charlie cuts in. 'Up to page 81.'

Charlie picks up the sunhat and tea-towel and does his fuck-what-a-day routine again, '. . . and all for *his* fucking girlfriend'.

The phone rings. It's someone called Ian, not from Hollywood. Jagger talks to him. 'Yeah . . . yeah. Come on over. Yeah. See ya.' He rings off.

'My God,' says Charlie. 'I. T. Botham. I. T. fucking Botham. He's like W. G. Grace, you know, fucking W. G. Grace. I've never met him.' Awe-struck.

'I have,' says Mick. 'Twice, three times.'

Steve leaves. As he goes, Charlie says, 'Fifteen thousand quid. Just lying on the floor.'

Charlie is less aggressive to me now that he knows I'm nothing to do with films. 'What sort of book you doing, Mick?' It's a good question, and my role is far from clear. Jagger is known to dislike the term ghost writer; so I have a phrase prepared to reassure him: Word Engineer.

'Memoirs sort of thing,' says Jagger.

'Yeah? . . . I. T. Botham. Shit.'

'I read your book,' Jagger tells me.

Charlie cuts in. 'Up to page 41.'

Botham arrives, with a team-mate, introduced as Vic. They order gin-and-tonics. Vic, like Charlie, smokes cigarettes, Botham smokes cigars. He wears a yellow sports shirt, jeans and blue and yellow Nikes without socks. Even through a shirt, his belly has pleats, like an accordion.

Jagger explains about his England team (four picked and eight to go) and about how Willis, who has a crick in his neck, talked to him earlier in the day. He mimes a cricked neck. 'Now if my drummer gets a crick in his neck, he plays the gig anyway.'

' "*My drummer*",' says Charlie. 'If I'm your drummer you're my singer. Hey I.T., would you say, "my bowler"? Course not.'

Mick asks Botham for confirmation of a famous story. 'Is it true that on tours the English team used not to be allowed to sleep with their wives? That true?'

'I dunno,' says Botham. 'But can you imagine those guys on the job? All that sweating and grunting?'

'Speak for yourself,' says Charlie.

'How do you mean?'

'I mean speak for yourself, you fat slob. How do you think you'd look yourself?'

'Come on now, Charlie, be fair. I take quite a pride in it.'

Very likely.

Charlie turns to Vic, and pretends to flirt. 'You and me, Vic, we're two of a kind. We're close. Come on down to the bar.'

Vic laughs.

Charlie reminisces about his love of cricket and music. Since the age of eight. Hutton. Bradman. Well, not Bradman in the flesh. 'I.T., it's the same as Coe and Ovett. Thirty thousand people'd come and see you any day of the week. But you belong to a club, to a load of old colonels, and what do *you* get out of it?'

Botham doesn't mind this line of argument. 'Appearance money, that's about it.'

'That's how it was for us when we started. It was 10–90. A

dollar for you, a few cents for us. Then we got a dollar each. And now it's 90–10. We hire a stadium – say, we hire Wembley for 15 per cent of the gate. Nobody hires *us*.'

'I know. So what do we do about it?'

'There must be something. Because fuck it, you're like W. G. Grace. You're one of the greats, I.T.'

'Right,' says Mick.

Charlie turns to Vic again. 'You and me, Vic, we're close. Can we be alone?'

Vic laughs.

Botham takes a deep breath. 'Well, there's one thing you *can* do, and that's play a gig for me in my benefit year, that's 1984. Say I put up the expenses, and we share the profits.'

'Where?' says Charlie, sarcastic. 'Taunton?'

'Glastonbury, more like,' says Botham. 'Do it proper. Make it a good show.'

'I dunno,' says Jagger. 'I dunno about that.' The atmosphere isn't what it was. 'I dunno about that, even in terms of the business.'

What can he mean? Surely he can't mean *Keith and me aren't what you could call chums and he thinks cricket's a joke, so why would he play guitar for you? Would I do a benefit for a retiring distiller?*

Botham cuts his losses. 'Anyway, you're going to play in a special match for me in 1984, aren't you?'

'Right,' says Charlie, clearly relieved, 'I'll face old man Jagger's bowling any day of the week. He's rubbish.'

They need to make plans for the evening. Charlie wants to go to Ronnie Scott's. Jagger is undecided.

A girl is shown up. It's ten o'clock. She isn't named, sits down and smiles. Charlie bullies her a bit, asking her why she's here. She smiles and smiles.

My own face aches from smiling, but only on seeing her do I at all dislike myself. I am also very hungry.

Mick sits next to the girl, which is tricky in her narrow chair. She smiles fit to bust.

Botham and Vic make excuses. I don't know if I'm expected to stick around. Somehow it seems unlikely.

I make excuses myself. 'See you 'round,' says Mick. Once out of the room I am much more at ease with the cricketers. They could almost be normal.

'Have those two had a tankful?' asks Botham. We laugh as we reach the foyer. The relief is overwhelming.

Tatler, 1982

Boy George

Over the last year or so, there has been a new costume in the dressing-up box for fashionable teenagers: black broad-brimmed hat, long hair in braids (real or false) tied up with strips of cloth, mask-like make-up, plucked eyebrows, bright lipstick, and a loose smock (sometimes with abstract and geometrical patterns resembling a patchwork Mondrian) worn over loose matching trousers. This ensemble minimises the differences between the sexes and is every bit as popular with girls as with boys; it rehabilitates the androgyny of the early 1970s, with touches borrowed from Third World styles and the *kabuki*, and its originator is a twenty-two-year-old pop star known as Boy George.

Last autumn the band he leads, Culture Club, released a single ('Do You Really Want to Hurt Me') in fifty-two countries which became the most popular song in fifty-one. In the fifty-second, the United States, where what Boy George describes as 'my gentle little song' was assumed in some quarters to be a subtle paean to sadomasochism, it only went to number two. George has since consolidated an impressive popularity with an age range that is unusual for an androgynous pop star. His appearance on *Jim'll Fix It* was certainly a turning point; Jim can fix anything.

Boy George has many advantages as a media figure, which he will list for you if you're interested. He is indefatigably chatty; in spite of the trouble he has taken to look like pop culture's answer to Greta Garbo, he shows no sign of wanting to be alone. His conversational skills would stand him in good stead as an airline steward or a manicurist. He is constantly mimicking people (*Coronation Street* characters, his mother, some 'old gyppo women' he knew when he was a fruit-packer in Birmingham) which isn't a virtue in itself but shows that he can listen as well as talk.

'I'm very photogenic,' he says, with a lack of embarrassment that makes you wonder why people bother with hiring press agents. 'I have a talent for dressing up. I do it properly.'

In person, Boy George is disconcertingly solid and definite; all the ambiguity goes into his appearance, leaving him free to have clear opinions about absolutely everything. His costume, like a traffic warden's or an archbishop's, sets him apart from social expectations, so that his good manners, which would be taken for granted in someone who looked more ordinary, come almost as a shock.

He is certainly properly dressed up, with black training shoes lending a sporty element to the collage. Although it's hot, he only checks his make-up with a fingertip very occasionally; about as often as a bank manager checks the closeness of his shave. 'Most people who dress up are really nervous,' he says. 'I'm not. I suppose I'm an old-timer.'

George admits, though, that in other respects he is letting himself run to seed. 'I'm a slob now,' he says, 'compared to how I used to be.' He no longer shaves his wrists, for one thing, which is sensible as his hands are low in ambiguity. They are masculine and his gestures are awkward, almost fumbling. He is not, he says, a very hairy person; he shaves his chin but doesn't need to anywhere else. He's not sure he'd shave elsewhere even if he was hairier. 'After about ten years,' he says, 'you look like a werewolf.'

Sexual ambiguity is obviously crucial to Boy George's image, but (as perhaps you'd expect) he is ambivalent about it. 'I trade in effeminacy but I don't think of myself as an effeminate person. A lot of things about me are masculine – my voice, some of my mannerisms.'

George is particularly anxious not to be identified as a gay hero, as has happened to some extent in America. 'I think gay people are nice, on the whole,' he says, 'nice to be with.' At the same time, he thinks it sad that people should limit themselves so much with stereotypes and exclusive categories. 'I don't want to fit into a gay scene,' he says, 'or any other. I've never had much trouble meeting people, in Tesco's, anywhere.' Mind you, an ethereally chunky androgyne has an altogether superior chance of being noticed, in Tesco's, anywhere.

Commercially, it's a bad idea for someone like George to be associated too closely with homosexuality; but there seems to be more naivety than calculation in his insistence on flying the pigeonholes. In terms of sophistication, even so, George towers over his colleagues in Culture Club; a band member who recently bought a house from a long-established gay couple was disconcerted that they seemed so much like ordinary people.

'I don't consider myself sexy,' says Boy George. 'I'm more like a statue than like Hot Gossip or Simon Le Bon [of Duran Duran].' He takes pains to make it clear that he wouldn't go home with someone he met at a club; he thinks of himself as 'attractive in a personality way'. Categories are meaningless, like Gents and Ladies. 'I use the first toilet I come across,' he says, 'as long as it has a mirror.'

America, where sexiness in a showbiz figure is not an optional requirement, came as a bit of a shock for George (though he enjoyed seeing himself described in print as a 'slinky songbird'); the persistence of groupies is a new phenomenon to him. One girl propositioned all the members of the band, asking anyone who would listen: 'What does George do? Would he come to stay with me?' George is of the opinion that 'there is nothing sacred in America'. One man in New York took one look at him and said: 'Hey man, LSD's for everyone.' Another followed him down the street asking endlessly, 'Are you in drag? Are you in drag?'

Boy George hasn't done so badly harnessing this sort of curiosity. He experienced it at first hand when he was fourteen

and met in Brighton someone he eventually realised was a pre-operative transsexual, male to female. 'I met her recently,' he says (she has now had the operation), 'and she told me, "When you met me all you would do was talk about it. Nothing else interested you." '

Boy George has something in common with transsexuals: he owns up to a degree of narcissism in the past though he says quite plainly that he has never wanted to be a woman. But his persona has everything to do with conventions of masculinity, and nothing to do with desire; his obsession is with gender rather than sex. Boy George has turned himself into an object: all the conflict and intensity you might associate with sexuality has been deflected into his appearance leaving a relatively calm subject enthroned in all the finery. Despite his cultivated air of oddity, his preference is for conventional romantic intimacy.

Perhaps this is the key to his popularity. Boy George and his imitators combine a maximum of display with an air of separateness from common humanity which could almost be construed as a fear of sex. Certainly the lyrics he writes for Culture Club are more reassuring than anything else. Even a song with a polemical title, 'Church of the Poison Mind', has a wistful little verse that goes:

> I'd be a fool to think
> You're being more than just kind,
> But in a life of maybe
> Love is hard to find.

In the early days of the band, George wrote song lyrics addressed to men ('Eyes of Medusa', 'Don't go Joe'). 'They had "he" all over them, and everybody explained that you can't do that.' He still doesn't see why you can't do a song from someone else's point of view but he's learning to live with it. 'I'd love to do "He Gives Me Love," ' he says, 'you know, the old Pearl Bailey tune, but I can't.'

There is nothing obviously evasive about Boy George. As a

teenager he felt betrayed when David Bowie claimed to hang up his various personas in the closet at the end of the day. 'That wasn't even a clever thing to say to the newspapers,' says George. He was surprised, just recently, to find that he still had all of Bowie's albums.

George's urge to turn his persona into a full-time job has had some odd effects. He's on duty all the time. 'I'm so used to meeting people I don't get on with. I just persevere,' he says. But no one is allowed to see him out of costume; there must be no one backstage but the star. If you ask him if he's lost weight he says, defensively: 'I change shape every day.' It's something of a *faux pas* to mention his body as distinct from the whole swathed ensemble. One of the virtues of the costume, from his point of view, is that it dramatises by hiding rather than revealing. 'People don't know,' says George, 'whether I have muscles or fat.'

Boy George tells a story that may be more revealing than he thinks. He once had a girlfriend who liked skinheads; he went over one morning to visit her and there she was in bed with one. 'He started talking about blacks and Jews, saying his father had been with Mosley. Then he started calling me queer and poof. And he had tattoos all over him, so I said, "You're more of a freak than I'll ever be. You're scarred for life." And he wanted to hit me, but he couldn't stand the thought of me seeing him without his clothes. Without his uniform he was nothing. So he waited till I'd gone and then asked my girlfriend where I lived. And he punched her, but she wouldn't tell.'

George's own image seems pretty fixed. Will he change it? 'People were asking me that about three weeks after the first single came out.' He's in no great hurry to move on. 'My face is exactly how I want it to be,' he says with the calm pride of someone who has grown a prize marrow at his first attempt. 'That won't change for a few years.'

At the moment, it certainly looks like a winning combination. George is writing songs for Musical Youth, for Joe Cocker, for Petula Clark. The second Culture Club album, due next month and supported by a national tour, contains two rather promising singles: 'Karma Chameleon', which George describes as a country-and-western campfire song, and 'Victims', a ballad which A&R men at Virgin (known for their psychic powers) predict will be *enormous.*

George's voice, which is strong and intermittently convincing, is improving all the time. 'I have a strong style, so I can afford to copy.' Helen Terry, who sang backing vocals on earlier Culture Club songs, is now a member of the band. She is in fact an almost overpowering singer, and George is brave to recruit her; but he is canny enough to know that contrasts of context work in his favour. He doesn't mind sharing the limelight if it gives him the durability he admires in, say, Churchill or Lulu. He would like Culture Club to be a family, the way the Mamas and the Papas were in the 1960s.

His relations with his own family are cordial. 'When my parents were younger,' he says, 'they were really very stupid. Now they've grown into people, they've become younger.'

'My mother just talks about herself,' he says. 'We're similar. And I love my father more than anyone. The thought of anything happening to him – he's been ill – is beyond fear for me.'

George doesn't seem to need a family for reasons of protection; he can look after himself. He had a running battle with a group of girls who would lie in wait for him outside the studio. 'They wore tweed skirts, Lacoste shirts and gold chains,' he says, as if he was listing the symptoms of a disease. 'When they started shouting I just held up a bottle and said, "This bottle of foundation cost more than you'll ever earn in your life." ' George believes in accelerating out of danger.

Boy George's style of repartee is modelled on Tallulah Bankhead's; he claims that *Tallulah Darling* is the only book he has ever read. He takes it for granted that you have big rows with people you love; a sharp tongue comes in handy. 'I'm one of those people who doesn't know how to stop.'

In spite of the occasional ambush, Boy George receives more

bouquets than brickbats. He was given so many presents by fans in Japan that he had to pay £600 excess baggage. He has a large collection of dolls; his bedroom, according to fellow band members, looks like a débutante's.

Success, by all accounts, has made Boy George nicer as well as richer (Somerset Maugham always said it did); all his gambles have paid off. Not for the first time, the public has been offered a two-stage pleasure; first of being shocked and scandalised, then of taking the outcast to its bosom. The Fabergé Easter egg turns out to contain (of all the decadent novelties) a yolk and some white; the sacred monster answers to the name of Rover.

Boy George arrives for the photo session with his father, his sister Siobhan, and a handful of young friends. He also brings some spare hats and some instant Boy George head-dresses: combs adorned with false braids.

George gets down to dressing his sister up; he borrows his father's belt, and makes a new hole in it. He cuts cloth into strips for her hair. George's father sits down, reads the *Mirror* and smokes his pipe. One of the girls asks him: 'How does George make those wigs?' 'I dunno, darlin',' he tells her, 'I'm not into all that. I hope I never need a wig.'

George is finishing work on Siobhan. 'Yesterday you were an ordinary suburban girl,' he tells her. 'A wally from Woolwich. Now look at you.'

Next in line for the beauty treatment is eight-year-old Samantha. Samantha screws her face up when George picks up the eyeliner. 'Don't worry,' he says, 'it doesn't hurt. Not like the doctor's.'

'I like the doctor's,' says Samantha. 'I like being ill.'

'You're mad,' says George. 'You're crazier than I am.' Samantha giggles.

'I bet you have natural rosy cheeks when you're happy,' George says. 'I have to put mine on. I'm never happy.' George is good with people.

George's father has brought his camera but he doesn't get a chance to use it until after the session. Everyone is tired; the amateurs find out what George has always known, that posing is hard work.

There is a knock at the door. A woman appears with baskets of sandwiches and crisps. 'The Milky Bars are on me,' says George. 'Ooh,' says the sandwich lady, 'who are they filming?'

George holds his tongue until she's gone. 'There's always one wally who says she's not heard of you. "What you do then?" ' he mimics, ' "Roadsweeper?" This one was quite convincing though. In a Pam Ayresish sort of way.'

George's father finishes with his camera and asks for his belt back. George helps Samantha take off her make-up. 'Let's take all that slap off,' he says. George, of course, will keep his slap on.

George phones for taxis for the kids. George kisses his father goodbye, leaving a mark. Mr O'Dowd steps back and rubs his cheek, like any shy man at a party, kissed without warning by the office bombshell.

Sunday Times, 1983

Marc Almond

Twinky the Senegal parrot thrusts a stiff grey tongue into my cup of tea. Marc Almond says, 'Don't worry, it'll be too hot for him,' but for the time being Twinky seems content. Marc offers to put both parrots back in their cage, but we haven't begun to talk, and rapport is a delicate furtive thing in these early stages. I say: 'I'm not bothered a bit. Why should the humans have all the fun?' I think: *Oh God, I'm about to become the first journalist to contract psittacosis from a rock-star interview.*

There is a slight haze of joss-stick smoke in the room. The décor is scrupulously tacky-exotic – wooden tigers, fake-fur cushions, Indian religious tat. A glitterball of the sort associated with 1970s discos hangs in one corner. The room is being encouraged to forget that it is part of a mansion block in Earls Court.

A Peggy Lee record (*Latin à la Lee*) is playing when I arrive. While Marc is out of the room making me a cup of tea I settle cross-legged on the floor, so that my tape recorder can pick up what he says even over Miss Lee's sly vocal stylings. But then he comes back in with the tea, in what he claims is his only matching cup and saucer – which turns out, rather touchingly, to have been inherited from his gran (he can remember drinking from it as a child). He turns the music off as he comes back in, which means that my posture, down there on the floor, becomes mildly enigmatic.

Marc Almond is a slight figure, who brings out almost a protective instinct in this hardened reporter, and on the day of our interview he is getting over flu. He wears a black shirt with panels of a leopardskin print, and little boots with side zips that refer knowingly to the naff 1960s. The cuffs of the shirt are rolled back to reveal a few inches of the tattoos that he talks about in every interview he's done for years. He likes to think they're like the tattoos of *yakuza* gangsters – thrillingly transgressive markings. But there is something stubbornly polite and English about him, which makes him find himself a posture that will harmonise with mine. He sits propped up with a cushion on the downward slope of a large sofa, so that he won't loom unduly over me.

Twinky's beak clacks against the ceramic rim of my, of Marc's, of Marc's gran's cup. Then he moves to my pen and takes firm hold of its tapered tip. Finally, with an unnerving flurry of wing-blurt, he flies back to the cage. He perches on the outside, while his grey companion Jacko remains inside, though the door is open.

Over the hour or so that the interview takes, my tape recorder picks up not only the words spoken but Twinky's non-verbal contributions. Almost every noise a parrot makes has a sardonic edge to it – the dry rasp of a beak against nut, for instance, or the fierce occasional plucking at the cage bars – and the tape when played back seems full of commentary.

We begin to talk. To start with, Marc's answers have the nervous fullness of a shy man professionally accustomed to performing for journalists. He sprinkles his sentences with artificially tentative 'for me's and 'in a way's, presumably used to being asked personal questions and then to being dismissed as self-absorbed for answering them.

He offers some astrological self-analysis – he is a Cancer with Leo rising, apparently, which accounts for his loving the spotlight but not the limelight, returning to the concert hall every now and then for a fix of live excitement and then retiring for long periods.

Marc Almond has been a sort of pop star for ten years or so now. His first hit, as part of the duo Soft Cell, was an obscure cover version, 'Tainted Love'. The self-disgust and self-pity of that song gave fair warning of a lugubrious musical persona, relieved by flashes of a wry and campy humour, that has proved surprisingly durable. Several generations of listeners – by the foreshortened reckoning of popular music – have turned to Marc Almond for a bracing wallow. The *Melody Maker* has gone as far as to call him 'the eternal star'.

In his early days, Marc was used by young female fans as a safe love-object, a good target for hormone practice. Just how safe he was as an object of fantasy female desire was hardly a secret even then. I remember a gossip column in a pop paper of the period, reporting that Marc Almond had been dancing 'with a hunk' in the gay club Heaven, which prompted a distraught letter from a besotted fan. 'How could you?' she asked the paper – not 'How could he?', interestingly enough, but 'How could you?' He laughs when I remind him of the incident, and is careful to point out that he still has teenage fans.

In concert these days he does everything from synthesiser pop to torch songs and ironic Jacques Brel numbers, accompanied sometimes by a solo piano and sometimes by a forty-piece orchestra. When he describes his recent Albert Hall concerts, though, it isn't in musical terms: 'I came on in a glittering dressing-gown. I threw it off to reveal a kind of black leather outfit. I then went and changed into a suit, a very smart suit and a shirt, dress shirt. Then I went off and came back in sequins. Different facets, that's what it's all about.'

His forthcoming album, *Twelve Years of Tears*, is a concert album. He has turned out, rather unexpectedly, to shine in a live setting. 'The days leading up to a concert I'm almost fainting with fear, but I'm still drawn to it. I come into my own. Once I get through the first song, when I'm terrified, it all starts to make sense.'

For once the obligatory question about a piece of current consumer product, the new single, is also the question I most want to ask. He dedicates the song to 'all those who dare to be different . . . all those who have the conviction to be different in the face of adversity . . . (there's a lot of it around, as well)'. After that, you expect some musical shout of affirmation, an 'I Will Survive' or an 'I Am What I Am'. What you get instead is Charles Aznavour's catchy but decidedly mawkish 'What Makes a Man a Man'. Doesn't that song betray the dedication he gives it?

For a moment he seems almost flustered, and goes into a disingenuous generalising mode. 'We're in a society that so often mocks people and laughs at people if they want to be themselves, to project their own individuality.' But then he takes a different tack. 'It's a song I've always felt in two minds about. I've always liked the song. It was the B-side of "She", the housewives' favourite. But if you flip over "She", it's "What Makes a Man a Man". I loved that idea. I thought that was fantastic of Charles Aznavour. He's always been one of my biggest influences. I thought it was amazing of him to sing it. As far as I know he's heterosexual.'

Might it have been brave for him, and not be brave for you? 'I don't think I see it in a self-pitying way. It's old-fashioned. For many years I've thought about doing it. I've seen it done by many drag artists who do it brilliantly – better than I probably do it – and I always thought there was a sort of strength I got from that song. I saw it as a song of defiance.'

Tearful defiance, though? 'Tearful defiance, yes, but I think there's a kind of strength to be gained from it. I suppose the verse that always bothers me is when he sings "When I go home alone and friendless". But there's something quite touching and old-fashioned about the song. I like its naivety. It's not untrue for a lot of people. What I love about it is that it paints a picture, it creates a character. I love songs that tell a story. I'm not saying, this is all gay men, this is all lonely people, this is all drag queens. I liked it because it's a song about a particular character, it's his story.

'I'm an unashamed sentimentalist. It's a moving song. It is appealing to the lowest common demoninators in a way, but I think sometimes in pop music you have to do that to reach an audience. Anyway, you can take the song's message as being anti-homophobia.'

But at a cost, surely? It's a song that might deter gay-bashing, but only on the basis that gay people are likely to drown in their own tears before you can lay a finger on them, so it's pretty poor sport.

Nervous laughter at this, and a further change of tack. 'I like to look at it as a strong song and a positive song, and I identify with it because there have been lonely times in my life, there have been times when I've gone home alone and friendless. I'm not saying, this is life and this is how it is. You have to listen to the last lines of the song. "Nobody has the right to be/ The judge of what is right for me." For me, that is the climax of the song. Those last two lines are what the song is about. We could argue about it all day.'

I take this last sentence to be a tactful indication from a polite man, who has allowed himself to be grilled fairly fiercely about his choice of what song to sing, that he would welcome a change of subject. I ask him, as a matter of interest, if he would ever be drawn to sing a more assertive song, like 'I Am What I Am'.

He thinks for a moment. 'It's too brassy for me. I like it, but it's not a Marc Almond song.' The formula, then, seems to be tremulous bravery, the eyes pouring out all their tears before the chin juts out at last. I mention that I can imagine him adding to his long list of successful cover versions, many years hence, with 'I'm Still Here' from Sondheim's *Follies*. He seems pleased. 'I actually jokingly referred to that in a way on the last album [*Tenement Symphony*], on "Vaudeville and Burlesque". "With some powder and some paint/ And the patience of a saint/ I'm still here." It was a humorous reference to that.'

I choose this moment to confess that there are two sorts of people in the world, those that think the song 'If You Go Away', one of Nina Simone's trademark songs and also a core item in Marc's live repertoire, is a profound statement about the human condition, and those who identify with the person who is supposed to be won over by this abject whingeing. I'm of the second party. For me, listening to 'If You Go Away' is like having a chihuahua strapped to your leg.

'It's a very cloying song,' he admits, before making the point that no one says 'If You Go Away' is about all heterosexual relationships. 'It's a much more self-pitying song, in a way, than "What Makes a Man a Man".'

He's a real fan of Nina Simone, it turns out, temperament and all. He admires her for forgetting lyrics and claims, rather endearingly, that he himself makes a special effort not to learn songs too well. 'The more I rehearse, the colder I get on a song. I like to know a song, but I don't like to oversterilise it, in a way.' He's shrewd enough to know that his fans don't mind it when he shows he's not a machine. 'I say, I'm sorry but I can't remember the song, and they love that and then *they* sing it.' As for 'If You Go Away', he's been singing it in concert for eleven years. 'It's a ritual. It becomes a song I sing to the audience, not to a lover.'

While Marc was brewing my tea, I spotted something that I've been longing to ask about ever since. Parrot owners in the arts have a special place for putting bad notices, and I couldn't help seeing that the *Daily Express* and the *Pink Paper* had pride of place – shame of place – at the bottom of the parrot cage. So what has the *Pink Paper* done to deserve this?

'The *Pink Paper* wrote a rather unpleasant review of my last concert, so it's found its way into the bird cage.'

Is it the actual issue with the review in it under the avian sphincters, or does he bear a more lasting grudge? 'Well, I've not been fond of the *Pink Paper* for a while.'

Does the gay press expect too much?

'They expect you to be very political-minded, always to be speaking out for the gay community. I actually feel that the gay community is a terrible myth. It doesn't really exist. There's so much bitching and backbiting and negativism. There's a lot of hypocrisy that annoys me terribly.'

This is dismaying guff, though all of a piece with someone who wouldn't dream of hiding his sexuality but doesn't see it as giving him common ground with anyone else. But then he says something that takes his point of view into the realms of high comedy. 'I went to the Gay Lifestyles thing the other day [an exhibition at Olympia, known informally as the Ideal Homo], and I said, Where is my lifestyle? I couldn't relate to it at all.'

This conjures up an irresistible image of a studiously unusual pop star surveying the glittering stalls and asking pertly, 'What, no pyjamas for my armadillo? Don't you even have the basics?' If there was a stall at the Ideal Homo selling wooden tigers, Peggy Lee records, joss-sticks, glitterballs, fake-fur cushions, parrots and tattoos, Marc Almond would be on the lifestyle-crisis phoneline by teatime.

I go mildly on the attack. 'But your family doesn't stop being your family just by behaving badly. Isn't community like that?'

'Well, my family are great, I love my family, but I don't feel a part of their lives.'

'But if there was a crisis you'd be there.'

'Oh yes I'd be there. I understand what you mean. I appreciate that. But I've never felt part of any group.'

The particular issue of the *Pink Paper* lying face down at the bottom of Marc Almond's parrot cage happens to have on its back page an announcement of a march, in support of those convicted for consensual sadomasochistic acts in the 'Spanner' trial. At the time of the interview their appeal was about to be heard by the House of Lords. The march took place on the same day as the Gay Lifestyles exhibition, as if gay London was being offered a stark choice between dreary activism and nice things.

Was this an issue he felt strongly about?

'It's everybody's issue. I mean, I'm a person who has a lot of tattoos on my body. Where does it stop? It's my right to hurt me. To do what I like with my body, if nothing else. It's all I have on this earth.'

But you didn't go on the march, and you haven't spoken out? 'I did an interview with *Rouge* magazine and spoke about it.' No disrespect to *Rouge* magazine, which may for all I know be the most radical journal around, but I'm not sure that counts as putting yourself on the line. He goes on: 'Where does it stop? Tattooing? It's like Fascism. It starts with a little thing.'

Yes, but what are you prepared to do about it? 'Doing an interview like I'm doing now and saying whether I support it is something. I have a platform for a media thing.'

I have to break it to Marc Almond that by the time this interview appears their Lordships will have decided the vexed issue of whether citizens own their bodies or lease them, under certain conditions, from a kindly state. It's almost maddening that he seems to identify with civil rights issues more urgently as a tattooed person than as a gay one.

He no longer does benefit concerts, partly because of bad experiences in the past. 'I'm very suspicious with pop stars that align themselves to causes. I feel I've become very – and it's a symptom of the country – I've become very what they call suffering from compassion fatigue. I see enough problems happening with friends of mine on my own doorstep that I'd rather help with. I'm talking about HIV here and things like that. I'd rather give support on a more personal level.'

If there has been a continuous thread to the interview, an underlying theme, it has been a refusal of groups. Marc Almond expresses this in terms of not needing to belong, but it can come across more as needing not to belong. It's as if he's morbidly afraid of his identity being swamped, if he doesn't keep himself apart. Even those tattoos say something of the sort, every indelible curlicue announcing I'M NOT ORDINARY, I'M *NOT*.

As the interview winds down, I set him a seasonal brain-teaser. I've bought my mum *Tenement Symphony* as a Christmas present, I tell him – no offence, the live album isn't out till the New Year – and I think she'll like it if she listens to it, but I'm afraid she won't play it unless I tell her what to expect. What am I allowed to tell her it's like? Can I say you're in the same area as the Pet Shop Boys?

'I'm a million miles from the Pet Shop Boys.'

Yes, I know that, but it's only to persuade my mum to give the record a listen.

'I'd rather be compared to people like – I don't know . . . I don't feel much in common with current pop . . .'

'But this won't define you, Marc. It's not going to go on your passport. How about if I say, Look Mum, remember you saw Erasure on television last week, and you thought they were fun?'

At this point the atmosphere becomes distinctly edgy. I think fast. '– Well, they learned a lot from Marc Almond. Would *that* be OK?'

A great burst of nervous laughter. Release of tension. Marc Almond's honour is satisfied, and we part on friendly terms.

Independent, 1992

III

Sharon Olds

Praise *The Father*. Praise Sharon Olds. Celebrate the autobiographical mode in American poetry, its risks and rewards. Praise directness cut with understatement, starkness with an obliquity that can still take the reader off guard. Salute, with unease, elegies that are also episodes of psychodrama, stages of a struggle that bereavement alters in key but hardly interrupts.

An elegy is a loss-lyric, the sifting and sealing of a life's leavings. What is startling about the poems in *The Father*, as they radiate outward from a death, is that their emotional depth does not correspond to a richness in the relationship being mourned – in fact, the depth of the poems is inversely proportionate to the richness of the relationship. The poet is so attentive to her father's dying because in his living he so comprehensively refused her. She is looking for their relationship to begin before it ends; his deathbed is her last chance and best hope.

Sharon Olds's language rises so readily to the biblical or mythical in its descriptions of her father precisely because he himself so rarely stooped to the human. As she puts it in 'To My Father',

> What have I worshipped?
> I ask you this so seriously,
> you who almost never spoke.
> I have idolised the mouth of the silent man.

The element in *The Father* that earns the definite article of its title is Olds's meticulous charting of physical changes – colour, texture, mass, smell – in the body close to death. She scrutinises these changes like a Roman augur over the entrails of a sacrifice, gravely frantic for significance. Her eyes are dry and very sharp; she finds a beauty in mortal process running parallel to all its ugliness. Her major theme-word is 'matter' (shadowed by 'earth'), its balancing, transcendent counterpart 'shining' (or 'glistening'). The actual phrase 'glistening matter' occurs halfway through the sequence, in the last lines of the poem 'The Exact Moment of His Death'.

The troubling distinction of *The Father* as a book of elegies lies in its exploring of what has been called in another context (by Richard Sennett in his book *Authority*) 'bonds of rejection': the way a person continues to be determined by forces or people that have consciously been thrown off. The structures underlying the emotions need not change just because the emotions now bear a minus sign before them: minus-love can be as profoundly shaping as love – more so, if it happens that what is denied persists, while what is acknowledged dies with its day.

We are impoverished by the deaths of those to whom we say yes, but in a strange way it can be the deaths of those to whom we say no that turn our worlds upside down. The millstone, at the very moment that it drops from our necks, is revealed also to have been a lodestone, all that long deluded time. Sharon Olds's father is not a new preoccupation: he features early and often, as a combined fetish and bogeyman, in *The Sign of Saturn*, a selection made from three previous volumes (published in 1980, 1984, and 1987). This, for instance, is from the second poem in the book:

> That love between us I called a stillborn
> hung by the feet – lately I have seen it
> move. Father.

There is something here of Sylvia Plath's accusatory masochism, even with 'Father' standing in for the more leeringly complicit 'Daddy'. In fact it is strange how little difference the advent of the women's movement, which has claimed Plath since her death, need make to a woman poet coming after. But then it's hardly reasonable to expect much in the way of gender solidarity from women who so hate their mothers.

The mother in *The Sign of Saturn* is granted the occasional cameo of functionality as in 'The Moment', when she gives her daughter's first period a welcome that might not have been predicted, but essentially she is turned away from, as the father, for all his destructiveness, is turned towards. There is no defiance of the father to match the triumph over the mother expressed in 'The Sisters of Sexual Treasure':

> As soon as my sister and I got out of our
> mother's house, all we wanted to
> do was fuck, obliterate
> her tiny sparrow body and narrow
> grasshopper legs. The men's bodies
> were like our father's body! The massive
> hocks, flanks, thighs, elegant
> knees, long tapered calves –
> we could have him there, the steep forbidden
> buttocks, backs of the knees, the cock
> in our mouth, ah the cock in our mouth.

The mother is the obstacle to pleasure, and the passage to the father that she bars is also the passage to a wider world.

Only one poem coincides with feminism, 'The Language of the Brag', and it has an instructive singularity. 'I have wanted excellence in the knife-throw,' says the poet, 'I have wanted some epic use for my excellent body.' Labour turns out to be just such an epic use, and the poem ends:

> I have done what you wanted to do, Walt Whitman,

> Allen Ginsberg, I have done this thing,
> I and the other women this exceptional
> act with the exceptional heroic body,
> this giving birth, this glistening verb,
> and I am putting my proud American boast
> right here with the others.

This works perfectly well as satire on American macho, but satire is not Olds's natural mode and it is clear that she has something particular to gain from it. This persona satisfies a need in her. She is enabled to shift motherhood out of the female realm and into the male, as she sees it, away from endurance and towards action.

Incest in Olds's poetry shades into exogamy without ever being rejected. In *The Father* incestuous emotion is still there, but it doesn't have the unembarrassed hedonism of the earlier volume, and is supplemented by a feeling for which there seems to be no name: the poet's desire to take her father back inside her – somehow *back*, though it is a place he has never been. In 'Nullipara', she will give him the safety he never represented for her:

> He knows he will live in me
> after he is dead, I will carry him like a mother.
> I do not know if I will ever deliver.

And in 'Close to Death':

> I always thought
> I had a salvation for him, hidden,
> even from myself, in my chest.

And 'The Pulling':

> drawn through my body like a napkin through a ring –
> as if my father could live and die

safely inside me.

This fantasy of providing salvation overlaps with a fantasy of power. It may be a benign revenge, but it is revenge for all that. The tension between the two roles shows up in a poem like 'His Terror', which concludes:

> Maybe his terror is not of dying,
> or even of death, but of some cry
> he has kept inside him all his life
> and there are weeks left.

That last line is in its understated way as intense as anything in the book, divided as it is between the father's need to keep that cry from being expressed and the daughter's need to hear it.

The fact of a power struggle is explicitly acknowledged in 'Beyond Harm', in which the father, mishearing the poet's routine 'How are you?' replies:

> 'I love you
> too.' From then on, I had
> that word to lose.

He could retract his inadvertent blessing at any moment:

> But then, a while after he died,
> I suddenly thought, with amazement, he will always
> love me now, and I laughed – he was dead, dead!

If there is a power struggle going on, it is one of which we necessarily have a partial account. The fact that the poet sees herself largely as her father's victim does not prevent her from being in her own way a predator, or a scavenger. In 'I Go Back to May 1937', from *The Sign of Saturn*, Olds imagines confronting her parents with their future so as to warn them off each other –

you are going to do bad things to children,
you are going to suffer in ways you never heard of

– before realising that she wants to live, and will pay a price for it.

I say
Do what you are going to do, and I will tell
about it.

That is her bargain: she will survive and testify. How well does she abide by it?

What the poet had to cope with as a child is hinted at in earlier poems from *The Sign of Saturn* and spelled out explicitly in 'Saturn' and 'What if God': cold, alcoholic father, sexually abusive mother. The father in 'Saturn' knowingly destroyed his son:

My brother's arm went in up to the shoulder
and he bit it off, and sucked at the wound
as one sucks at the sockets of lobster.

The mother in 'What if God', meanwhile, slipped the poet's soul

from between my
ribs like a tiny hotel soap

when she entered her bed. At least once the poet's sister urinated on her in bed ('The Takers'), knowing that their mother would assume the bed-wetting was the usual sort, any other story an attempt to shift blame.

This may be a house of dysfunction but damage is not a virtue. Though scars have become the guarantee of an autiobiographical poet, how you live with damage is also an issue. The father withheld love, the mother inflicted it in an intolerable form. The father never seems to have been human enough to explain why he wasn't being human, but the mother sought to make amends. We learn this from a poem in *The Sign of Saturn* called 'After 37 Years My Mother Apologises For My Childhood'.

There is no context offered, or indication given of how the conversation started, but the mother sheds tears that the poet recognises as showing 'true regret, the/regret of the body', and says: '*Where else could I turn? Who else did I have?*' The climax of the poem is the passage:

> I hardly knew what I
> said or who I would be now that I had forgiven
> you.

But there is another question unexpressed: who will *you* be, now that I have forgiven you? The answer to this second question would seem to be: no one. Forgiveness doesn't reinstate the mother, it abolishes her. Olds's tendency to think that she has only one parent, the male one, is not modified but exaggerated by the apparent breakthrough in family relations.

It may be a truth about emotional damage that it renders the traumatised party unable to conclude the relationship. By this account, the mother effects an abrupt release for the poet when she admits her responsibility, while the father continues to block her access to the end-game. There's something about this, though, that seems glib, psychobabblish. The mother gets it coming and going. Comparing 'Saturn' and 'What if God', the poems that directly address parental abuse, it is clear that when the mother is cruel she is threatened with a god ('reach down and/take that woman off that child's body'), but when the father is cruel he becomes one. Both parents are blamed, but only one is relentlessly eroticised and mythologised. Is it too insanely presumptuous to suggest, in the paradox zone that is autobiographical poetry, where dark material is obsessively rehearsed but its interpretation is tightly controlled, that the anti-maternal attitude predates and shapes the trauma that is used to prove it and justify it?

The mother is extraordinarily absent from *The Father*, not just as a person with some sort of stake in her ex-husband's death, but in other ways too. The poet condenses all her ideas of inheritance into the long legs she feels she derives from her father: those long legs are mentioned very often. The mother seems to have made no genetic contribution. Olds imagines, in 'Last Acts', her father carrying her in seminal form before conception, a seed that is also somehow a finished product, 'riding in his balls the day before he cast me'. Olds even contrives in 'The Swimmer' to feminise the sperm that became her while it is still within her father's body, making him the source of her femaleness too:

> the seed that made me raced
> ahead of the others, arms held to her sides.

There are other absentees from *The Father* besides the mother: until the last pages of the new book you could think, without the benefit of a recent reading of *The Sign of Saturn*, that the poet was an only child. The brother who was eaten, the sister who was also a victim, however complicit, in the hellish household, leave no mark. There might conceivably be an element of tact in these omissions, but nothing is more suspect than the tact of an autobiographical poet. All tact has been overthrown as a precondition of the mode, and any attempt to reinstate it seems surreptitious and sly. Also on the list of absentees is the poet's husband, who is physically present on occasion but not as the specific counterweight to the father he was in *The Sign of Saturn*. The most paradoxical absentee, however, is the one who is constantly there: the father's second wife.

That is always how she is referred to, as 'his wife' not 'my stepmother'. There is a possible courtesy in that – no word ending in those particular six letters could count as an honorific in Olds's vocabulary. There is no antagonism expressed for the father's wife, but there isn't any warmth either. The poems maintain an absolute neutrality, even where no such state can apply, and where the poem's structure demands an emotion of some sort. It's quite a feat to write a poem about a woman alone with the body of her husband ('After Death'), and so completely project your own preoccupations on to her:

> Did she lie on him, I think not, so
> breakable. Did she kneel by the bed,
> holding his hand, did she draw off the sheet
> and look at him, a last time,
> kiss his nipples, navel, dead
> warm penis. The man himself
> was safe, this was what he had sloughed.
> It lay between them like a child of their love.

The father's wife is a screen for one more round of incestuous fantasy, a stand-in not an actor. We know nothing about her. She only has a name (Francis, apparently) because the father's last spoken sentence included it: the name is preserved because of who spoke it, not who it referred to.

The same rule dictates the strange emotional blankness of a poem called 'The Want'. The poet confides:

> I had stopped
> longing for him to address me from his heart
> before he died.

The poem ends, though, with the father's wife spending time with him alone in hospital, settling him for the night:

> When she came out of his room she was shining –
> he had
> taken her hands and thanked her for all
> she had done for him for twenty years,

> and then he had said *I want to devote*
> *the rest of my life to you.*

That's where the poem ends, where most people's poems would just be building up steam. The poet must have feelings, somewhere on a continuum between rage and acceptance, about her father addressing someone other than her from his heart, before he died. What is the poem about, if not the conflict between wife and daughter over rights to the dying man? Yet the poem refuses this subject. It is important that the father's words are recorded, like any utterance of a god (dying does not make him any less a god) but the father's wife is allowed no role beyond witness of his words. She is nothing in her own right; the relationship between the women doesn't begin to develop any human texture.

That's just the point, to create a space where father and daughter can be alone in the world. Only then can every permutation of sexual and parental relationship be gone through without distraction. The poet is possessive of her father's body even after death, begrudging its dispersal. In 'The Dead Body' she writes:

> Don't take that
> tongue in transplant or that unwilling eye

– strange to single out the tongue, unless because it said *I love you too.* The insistent birth imagery has less to do with a religious perspective – a new beginning for him – than with a new beginning for her; signs of finally containing and controlling her father.

Sharon Olds's poetry is art and not therapy, but it is art with a high therapy quotient, and sometimes her diagnoses seem like symptoms in their own right. There are times when her assertions of her father's cold neglect don't match anecdotal memories cited in another context. One might ask how the father of 'Psalm' –

we had hardly
touched since the nights he had walked the floor at my arrival

– squares with the father of 'The Exam':

the way he used to do
the Itsy Bitsy Spider, slowly,
up my arm.

Sometimes the assertion and its undermining by evidence occupy the same sentence, as in 'The Pull':

only twice
did he urge me to live – when the loop of his seed
roped me and drew me over into matter;
and once when I had the flu and he brought me
ten tiny Pyrex bowls
with ten leftovers down in the bottoms.

This gesture is not just tender but dainty – self-conscious, flirtatious. There is nothing unpractised about it; it isn't plausible as a one-off. There may not have been other explicit *urgings to live*, but those are for special occasions, surely. There must have been a daily exercise of affection for the gesture with the bowls to be so eloquently playful, so imaginative.

This is not to accuse Olds of that darkest secret of the autobiographical poet, a happy childhood. One way of dealing with family hurts is to mythologise them. Easier to turn your father into the god who eats his children than to integrate the drunk slumped on the couch with the man who played Itsy Bitsy Spider, the cold spurner of affection with the preparer of delicacies in Pyrex.

There is a difference, though, in the way that the poets of these two volumes inhabit the mythology they have created.

The poet of *The Sign of Saturn* carries her scars outwards into the world. Her parents have given her rules for living after all, in spite of themselves. All she has to do is never imitate them in any respect. She feels a bodily affinity with her father, but she is able to move beyond him, to explore sex and found a family with a sort of defiant healthiness.

The poet of *The Father* has much less the psychology of a survivor. Longing for reconciliation but unable to delude herself, she relapses into an earlier set of emotions, ranging from a desire to be revenged to a desire to immolate herself. These desires combine in the fantasy of a place where she can keep him hers and intact for all time, a place that is both womb and tomb. Her book will provide such a place, but in perverse piety, like a woman in Greek tragedy, an Electra or an Antigone, she will join him there. *The Father* is a tomb for two.

The possibility that the poet is choosing to inhabit a structure of fantasy is confronted only once in the book, in the penultimate poem, 'Waste Sonata':

> I have learned
> to get pleasure from speaking of pain.
> But to die, like this. To grow old and die
> a child, lying to herself.

It is a tribute to the power of Sharon Olds's paternal obsession that this passage, which for once doesn't deal with the world primarily through the poet's relationship with the father, should seem so striking. Introspection is hardly a register alien to a book of elegiac poetry. It's fairly extraordinary for its appearance to be delayed till the 51st poem of 52.

The closing passage of the poem, though, shows that 'Waste Sonata' represents an air-hole for the poet rather than a way out just yet:

> My father was not a shit. He was a man
> failing at life. He had little shits

> travelling through him while he lay there unconscious –
> sometimes I don't let myself say
> I loved him, anymore, but I feel
> I almost love those shits that move through him,
> shapely, those waste foetuses,
> my mother, my sister, my brother, and me
> in that purgatory.

It must count as a breakthrough that the poet's mother and siblings return from oblivion but as a setback that she has chosen this particular setting for the family reunion. Sharon Olds may be seeking to free herself from the power of her father's myth, but she remains imprisoned in the web of imagery she has woven round him. The woman who wanted motherhood to be a male thing, as far removed as possible from anything her mother would do, who saw her father as a man who ate children, now shifts her fantasies to another register, where contradictions are not so much reconciled as excreted.

London Review of Books, 1993

Venus Envy

In these pages a spirit notorious for its mildness must summon up the necessary unfairness of polemic. Can I bloat my little grievance to impressive size? I must try. I must aim to be worthy of the price paid for paper and ink, by every squeezed octopus and melted tree.

Hobbyhorse, where are you? Come and be saddled. I see you there, lurking in the shadows of the stable block. The sunlight catches your long lashes, as they graze the slickness of your eyeball. Come from the shadows. Come and be saddled.

You are delicate, almost neurotic in your prancing. You sidle towards me, you push your muzzle of moist ultrasuede against my leg. Up close, your mane looks to be blow-dried – scrunch-permed, even. Worse, you are knee-high. Are you then *Eohippus*, the Dawn Horse, tiny ancestor of all the modern breeds, strumming a simpler planet with your foreshortened hoofs? No. You are plastic, you are pink and lilac. Are you in fact that bane of the tasteful parent, pastel nightmare that haunts Christmas lists – though any sensible Santa would hack you into rough steaks to feed the reindeer – My Little Pony? No matter. We must ride.

Feminism has changed the way men think but not in the way that feminists might have hoped. Although feminist criticism has made some male habits unfashionable in certain circles, masculinity has been quick to redefine itself, in terms not of nature or even of freedom, but in terms of responsibility. Lost ground has been recaptured, without any admission that ground was lost in the first place, or that any slow struggle is going on. A new style has arisen of faintly synthetic introspection, presented as a maturing process unprompted by contemporary debates, which nevertheless reads more convincingly as a rhetorical response to cultural pressure.

This is a subject of more than passing interest. A lot depends on how our culture comes to terms with the idea of its own destructiveness, an idea that can't be ignored indefinitely but is likely to appear in the form of bargains and wishful evasions. The longer these bargains are received uncritically, the less likely it is that we will make real changes in our behaviour.

This essay will examine how the redefinition has been accomplished, in two books of fiction published in the late eighties: *Einstein's Monsters* by Martin Amis and *The Child in Time* by Ian McEwan. Apologies to these two gentlemen for seizing on their work of that period as exemplary, apologies also to everyone else. If there's one thing more annoying than being singled out for analysis in a wide-ranging, witty, provocative essay on profound cultural change, it's being passed over by same.

I make no apology – is there a more defensive phrase in the language? – for analysing literature rather than softer material (newspaper articles, advertisements). A book of fiction is a very concentrated piece of mental behaviour. It is highly self-conscious, but it can also have the paradoxical property of shielding an author from his opinions, allowing them to develop independently. These books are also quite good enough to set up a sort of defensive force-field, a crackling barrier that throws off flimsy speculations, making them look as foolish as they are.

And if writers of this quality can't engage with the major issues of life without including a disabling amount of propaganda on behalf of their gender, how much can be expected of anyone else?

(Memo to self: praise in an essay like this sounds fishy,

hypocritical. No more of it. Sensible people would rather be slapped and have done, than be slapped and fawned on by turns.)

Einstein's Monsters is a book of stories preceded by an introduction, 'Thinkability', in which Martin Amis gives expression to his anti-nuclearism. I say *his* anti-nuclearism, because there is no standard form of opposition to nuclear weapons. You can for instance be against nuclear weapons and in favour of nuclear power, you can be against nuclear weapons and against unilateral disarmament. It is in the negotiation of those *ands* that things get ticklish.

Amis attributes the dawning of his interest in nuclear issues, in 1984, to two distinct stimuli: 'impending fatherhood' and a tardy reading of Jonathan Schell's *The Fate of the Earth*. He doesn't elaborate. But to contemplate, while waiting to become a father, the nature of the world into which a child will be born, though a common experience, is not exactly a logical procedure. The time to reach conclusions about the world, to decide whether it should be asked to bear the weight of another creature – or alternatively whether it can be trusted with a precious new person – was before conception, not before birth.

But there is in fact a deeper logic. Motherhood is a fact, while fatherhood is a fiction, perhaps the first fiction. There are women who have not suspected their pregnancy until some way into labour – even if in such cases it is a matter presumably of awareness blocked, rather than true ignorance – but no women who have become parents, as men can easily do, unawares. For the great majority of women, the physical and mental processes of prospective parenthood go hand in hand, while in men they are necessarily disjunct. Pregnancy has a huge prestige, but the corresponding period in the life of a father-to-be not only has no prestige, but no name.

But though conditional on the acknowledgement of a pregnancy, this period is a quite separate thing, of which women have no experience. In this period a man constructs the persona of the father, jettisoning some aspects of earlier selves and rehabilitating others long disclaimed. New material can be taken on, now that there is a place for it. The whole process may amount only to the displaying of a BABY ON BOARD bumper sticker on a car being driven with an unchanged recklessness – though a recklessness suddenly righteous – or it may be profound.

The essay 'Thinkability' is a rhetorical construction, its logic local rather than overarching. Amis states that we must 'find the logic of unanimity', but there is a striking lack of unanimity about the essay. Here for instance is a lovely lyric: '. . . we do not need the econauts of Greenpeace or *The Tao of Physics* to tell us that in our biosphere everything is to do with everything else. In that they are human, all human beings feel it – the balance, the delicacy. We have only one planet, and it is *round*.' And three pages later: 'If we could look at ourselves from anything approaching the vantage of cosmic time, if we had any sense of cosmic power, cosmic delicacy, then every indicator would point the same way: *down*.' The nearest to a syllogism that can be made of these elements is this: all human beings feel the cosmic delicacy. We have no sense of cosmic delicacy. Therefore we are not human beings – which has a strangely unhelpful feel to it.

More worrying than these contradictory flourishes is Amis's tendency to allow in a privileged context arguments that he would resist elsewhere. When he refers to 'the babies who will never be born' if nuclear weapons destroy the world, 'those that are queuing up in spectral relays until the end of time', he beefs up the rhetoric admirably, but he would hardly appreciate it if the notion of reproachful, non-existent babies hungering for life were to fall into the wrong hands, say the hands of a born-again Christian.

Above all, Martin Amis rejects his own suggestion that 'in our biosphere everything is to do with everything else'. He considers nuclear weapons as an issue in isolation, when in fact this question contains all others only in the limited sense that failure here destroys everything everywhere. As Martin Amis expounds it, the issue of nuclear weapons is an issue without edges, but it is still a single issue. Environmental considerations, for instance, get a look-in only with specific reference to the prospect of a nuclear winter ('the chemistry of ozone creation and destruction . . . is only partially understood'), as if apart from our gaffe of bringing nuclear weapons into being our relationship with the planet is going swimmingly, with bags of respect on both sides.

Amis hives off the issue of nuclear weapons intellectually from other subjects, but he also isolates the nuclear age historically from everything that came before. Nothing is as it was. This rhetorical construction of a Before and an After with nothing in common has the paradoxical effect of elevating the Bomb above history. The Bomb becomes something like the Uncaused Cause of theology. But it is only in its consequences that the Bomb is absolute: to imagine that the development of the Bomb corresponds to no long-standing ingredient of human nature is wishful thinking. The Bomb need never have been invented, but that doesn't make it a visitation.

Martin Amis announces early on in his essay that he doesn't know what to do about nuclear weapons, but he presumably doesn't intend the curious passivity that underlies the habitual agitation of his prose. It can sometimes seem as if equality under the Bomb is the first and last right of man in the nuclear age. The narrator of the story 'Bujak and the Strong Force' asks, in words that could have been transposed from 'Thinkability': 'Gratuitous or recreational crimes of violence, the ever-less-tacit totalitarianism of money . . . the pornographic proliferation, the nuclear collapse of the family . . . the sappings and distortions of a mediated reality, the sexual abuse of the very old and the very young (of the weak, the weak): what is the hidden denominator here, and what could explain it all?' If the Bomb underlies everything, and we can't do anything about the Bomb, then we can't do anything about anything. But seeking a single explanation for complex phenomena comes perilously close to being a confession of failure in any age.

In this context, as Amis acknowledges, 'questions of decorum present themselves with a force not found elsewhere'. But a certain amount of ingrained, reflexive indecorousness needs to be faced up to. We are always reluctant to admit that our most abstract speculations carry in suspension a silt of self-interest, and we have a particular taboo in this area. Surely, when we talk about Armageddon, we speak from our full humanity – not as men and women with axes to grind, but as people facing an axe as big as the world? We find it painful to admit that even here short-term thinking is our natural mode, so that we must force ourselves towards the sane perspectives.

But in fact this is an area where selfish distortion is more rather than less likely. Since someone who is authentically 'for' nuclear weapons is hard to find, the argument tends to be invisibly controlled, not by what we mutually oppose, but by what we individually seek to maintain.

These days the moral high ground can be claimed by just about anyone, and the ability to decode the real messages under the false has become one of the routine self-defensive skills of modern life. When a prime minister espouses environmental issues almost from one minute to the next, it isn't difficult to locate the disguised agenda – in this case a commitment to nuclear power – the ideology that lies unchanged at the heart of the turnaround. And when an acclaimed novelist, much admired for his cultivated scabrous cynicism, announces a concern for huge issues, or for one huge issue, the question should still be asked: what territory is being defended, consciously or unconsciously, by these manoeuvres?

With Martin Amis, the answer has to be the sexual status quo. His anti-nuclearism is conspicuously male: 'In this debate, we are all arguing with our fathers,' he writes, and the 'we' who are doing the arguing seem very much to be men. The essay 'Thinkability' makes no reference, for instance, to the most single-minded demonstration of nuclear protest, the Peace Camp at Greenham Common, or the larger movement of which it was part. The Peace Camp may have been only a symbolic gesture, but rather less symbolic than an essay, and the language of unanimity would be more eloquent if it registered the contribution of both genders.

At one point Martin Amis writes that nuclear weapons make him feel 'as if a child of mine has been out too long, much too long, and already it is getting dark'. The same sentiment, if it had appeared ten years ago in a book published by the Women's Press, or even been expressed late on at a party in the same period, would not have had a particularly easy reception from Amis as reviewer or fellow-guest.

But the persona of the father is a liberating construction, allowing for the safe expression of emotion in unprecedented quantities (the keyword here is *safe*) – provided it is bounced off children and not expressed direct. Men, moreover, have a freer hand in their rhetorical self-portraits than women, precisely because women are likely to be tied as a matter of day-by-day routine to the small people who are the basis and focus of the changed persona. (Those men who raise children tend to inhabit an aura of specialness, making ordinary things extraordinary by choosing to do them.) A man's children can be his property one minute, and his virtue the next.

As reported in 'Thinkability', the arguments between Kingsley and Martin Amis tail away as the two of them admire Martin's infant son, who will perhaps in time – Martin speculates – come up with a radical solution to the problem of nuclear weapons. Kingsley will have to die off, and so perhaps will Martin. But this imagined radicalism doesn't disturb the structure of patriarchy, which can more easily accommodate parricide than, say, the weakness of listening to your mother, sister, daughter, wife.

Clearly Martin Amis didn't choose to have sons instead of daughters; but if he were a father of daughters his rhetoric would be harder to sustain in its present form. He did, on the other hand, choose to marry, and it is also a matter of choice – literary choice this time – whether he presents himself in

'Thinkability' as husband and father, or just as father. Fatherhood in 'Thinkability' is a lonely responsibility, not an unobtrusive domestic fact, perhaps because on some primitive level children are an overflow of strength, while a wife is an admission of masculine insufficiency.

In fact the only reference to the author's having a wife as well as sons (and a father) is in his nightmare vision of having to travel through the firestorm from the flat where he works to his home, and then to kill her as well as them. Mrs Amis features in the essay only as one more mouth to stop.

The arguments of 'Thinkability' present nuclear weapons as an aberration, albeit the defining aberration of the modern world. There is no suggestion that anything about nuclear weapons corresponds to anything in the world before them, nor to anything profound in the world they hold to ransom.

But a century that saw Auschwitz and Dresden before Hiroshima can hardly claim to be taken aback by technological destruction on a vast scale. It isn't a parvenu principle of our culture that we do things, not because we should, but because we can.

This is not the logic that Martin Amis chooses to pursue, perhaps for fear of ending up on the wrong side of it. The feminist watchword that the personal is political is no longer in its first youth, and has kept some strange old company, but it still has a certain reproachful power, and any approximation to it in 'Thinkability' might crack open the vast latent ironies behind *Einstein's Monsters.*

The nearest that Amis comes to this is a paragraph about the regressive imagery of the Manhattan Project:

> the first bomb ... was winched up into position on a contraption known as 'the cradle'; during the countdown the Los Alamos radio station broadcast a lullaby ... scientists speculated whether the Gadget was going to be a 'girl' (i.e. a dud) or a 'boy' (i.e. a device that might obliterate New Mexico). The Hiroshima bomb was called

> Little Boy. 'It's a boy!' pronounced Edward Teller, the 'father' of the H-bomb, when 'Mike' ('my baby') was detonated over Bikini Atoll in 1952 . . . It is ironic, because *they* are the little boys; *we* are the little boys.

The emphasis that Amis places on the distinction adult/child draws attention away from the distinction male/female, where he isn't on such safe ground himself.

The notion that the entrenched destructiveness of our culture has something to do with the jealously defended imbalance between its sexes finds a place in *Einstein's Monsters* only in an inverted form. Bujak, in the story 'Bujak and the Strong Force', seeing gay punks in the street, interprets 'their plight, and their profusion, as an einsteinian matter also'. The idea seems to be that such violations of the sexual order stem inevitably from the Bomb's disturbing of cosmic balance. Presumably, then, in a world without the Bomb sexual roles would be properly harmonious. This, of course, is only a passing remark made by a fictional character, but there is an absence of characters who take any sort of opposing tack.

In the story 'The Little Puppy That Could', Amis imagines a post-Holocaustal future where the sexual status quo has been deformed and distorted along with everything else. Men have become interchangeable – Tim and Tam and Tom – subject to the rule of monstrous matriarchs who, horribly, demand to be pleasured. Now that fertility is a scarce commodity, the world is held to ransom by a womb and not a penis. The women are given names (Keithette, Clivonne, Kevinia) whose ludicrousness may be meant to derive from the supposed laughter-quotient of the male names on which they are based, but there is a definite edge of hysteria to the humour. What seems to bring out the rancour which the comedy disguises, at least from its author, is the very idea of women with male privileges.

At the end of the story the heroine, the intensely feminine Andromeda, has found herself a real man (a transformed puppy, innocent animal purified by fire): 'His arms were strong and warlike as he turned and led her into the cool night. They stood together on the hilltop and gazed down at their new world.' The logic here is arsy-versy, but consistent with the rest of the book's theorising. The Bomb has made men effeminate and women repellently assertive. Now a proper polarisation of the sexes will make possible some sort of renewal.

A feminist suggestion might rather be that it was a world in thrall to a distorted male identity that made the Bomb in the first place. It seems unlikely that Martin Amis is unaware of this line of thinking. What seems to be at work, here and elsewhere in *Einstein's Monsters*, is *disavowal*, that useful psychological word that means denying something without mentioning it.

The great irony of *Einstein's Monsters* is that a book dedicated to the unapproachable ideal of disarmament should be written by someone so opposed by temperament to disarmament outside the nuclear arena. Martin Amis's progress has been not so much a career as an escalation, the persona increasingly truculent, the style ever more bristling. His very method is overkill. There seems little doubt that in the silos of his notebooks there are stored enough explosive phrases to account for his readers many times over. Though Amis in 'Thinkability' may find the idea baffling, any reader of a page of his mature prose has a pretty good idea of what might be meant by *retaliating first*.

These analogies aren't flippant. Amis himself, despite his remarks about the need for 'decorum' in nuclear discussion, feels free to use the vocabulary of Holocaust figuratively. In 'Bujak and the Strong Force' alone, a man who is sensitive to potential violence is said to have a 'fallout detector', Bujak's fist is said to be 'neutronium', to kill a whole family is to 'nuke' them – perhaps to compensate for the nuclear preoccupations in the story seeming rather arbitrarily imposed on its plot. The story of a man whose family is murdered but who takes no revenge could be expressed in terms of the Old Testament giving way to the New, rather than deterrence unilaterally abandoned, but once you've used a nuclear vocabulary it's hard to go back to a conventional one. As the proliferation of nuclear images indicates, whether they are an integral part of the story or not, Amis concentrates on the way the big world infiltrates and corrodes private lives, rather than the other aspect of the traffic, the elusive way that individual behaviour subtends the status quo.

The aggressiveness of Martin Amis's style is of course artificial; it shapes its own highly contrived version of strength and weakness. The monstrous women in 'The Little Puppy That Could' are announced as all-powerful, but are relegated to the role of comic bit-players. The narrator of 'Bujak and the Strong Force', by contrast, is weak, but insistently, buttonholingly, Woody Allenishly weak, and – naturally enough, being the narrator – has control of the point of view, the true seat of power in a story. The hyperbolic phrases Amis gives him promote every flinch into a stylistic swagger, every whimper into a growl.

But if aggressiveness in a style does not correspond to aggressiveness in the world, it does correspond to the power of will. No other aspect of writing responds to pure willpower: sit down at a desk for four hours and you can't guarantee to come up with four satisfactory plot twists or nine convincing insights into character. But you can be pretty sure of coming up with twenty startling images or striking turns of phrase. Even when Martin Amis is treading water he breaks the surface so much it looks like a shark attack.

A style like Martin Amis's represents both a fear and a desire. It represents a radical doubt about the business of writing, an authorial identity crisis that can be postponed by having each sentence declare the presence of the author. Amis's narrators don't venture abroad without a suit, a shield, without a testudo of style to protect them. Here for instance are three of his narrators, the weak writer from 'Bujak', a disturbed pre-adolescent ('Insight at Flame Lake') and a citizen of the year 2020 ('The Time Disease'), all deploying one of Amis's favourite tropes, the cadenced triptych of synonyms:

'If the world disarmed tomorrow, he believed, the species would still need at least a century of recuperation, after its entanglement, its flirtation, after its thing with the strong force.'

'Meanwhile I stare into the brilliance and burnish, into the mauve of the MIRVed lake.'

'Up there in the blasted, the totalled, up there in the fucked sky.'

Fear of inauthenticity here leads to inauthenticity of a different sort, not an unsigned painting but a painting composed entirely of signatures. The reader who is reminded by each succeeding sentence of the looming designs of the author is denied much of the traditional pleasure of literature, the pleasure of surrendering to an imagined world rather than being bullied into finding it impressive. The supposed opposition between highly wrought and unambitious ways of writing on which Amis's style depends doesn't hold up in any case. There is writing which advertises its surprises and writing that simply springs them. Eudora Welty, for instance, when she writes a sly sentence like 'The librarian was the lady in town who wanted to be it', makes no obviously odd choices, but doesn't on that account go short of sleights and syncopations.

It is this absence of a neutral register from Martin Amis's work, oddly enough, that his father Kingsley complains of, the lack of workaday sentences not hell-bent on shock or charm. Here and there in *Einstein's Monsters* Amis hides his hand and aspires to such transparency, notably in the story 'Insight at Flame Lake', which alternates two diaries, of a disturbed pre-adolescent and his uncomprehending uncle. But all it takes is one electric adjective too many and the jig is up, the familiar antagonistic persona reaches criticality.

The other aspect of a style like Martin Amis's is the desire to make a mark at all costs – not the strongest basis from which to mount an attack on the moral blindnesses of the nuclear age. It is noticeable for instance that in 'Thinkability' he has a shot at rendering nuclear war in his particular tone of voice, in a sentence that ends with the distinctive juxtaposition 'the warped atoms, the grovelling dead'. Forget the ambition of finding the language of unanimity: this is a Holocaust with a monogram, almost a copyright logo.

The military analogies are irresistible, though the ugly sound you hear is only the dull clang of polemic against polemic. Martin Amis's anti-nuclear stance is in the nature of a pre-emptive strike, detonating an issue that might otherwise be used against him. A woman's hand on the button, after all, would do far more damage to his world-view. By striking first, he can cut the supply lines between the nuclear issue and other issues he doesn't want to engage with: feminism and environmentalism, half of humanity and the whole of its home.

In Amis's new novel, *London Fields*, there is a broadened concern with the whole degraded planet. But there is also an incongruous gleeful pessimism, a rush of satisfaction at making things as bad as they can possibly be. Amis is still in the business of making elegant terminal diagnoses, and has no interest in cures.

But there are other ways of engaging with the nuclear issue. To turn briefly to another writer who started his career as a bad boy and has metamorphosed into a good father: Ian McEwan's anti-nuclearism offers a useful contrast to Martin Amis's, in that he knows at least in general terms what to do about nuclear weapons. The crucial line of his anti-nuclear oratorio, after all, is 'Shall there be womanly times, or shall we die?' It isn't clear whether the phrase 'womanly times' invokes power for women or a less rigid identity for men – and the difference, believe it or not, is crucial. And of course the actual mechanism of change is unclear. The Maharishi Mahesh Yogi used to advertise classes in transcendental meditation with claims that the crime rate would plummet once 10 per cent of the population started to meditate regularly. It may be that in Ian McEwan's vision of things, a society where a true relation between the sexes exists cannot – in a similarly impalpable but effective way – sustain an impulse of destruction.

For McEwan, feminism and anti-nuclearism are inseparable:

but for Amis, anti-nuclearism is actually a substitute for feminism, performing the same rhetorical function of disengaging him from human destructiveness. But it is a rhetoric deeply suspect and divided. By saying a mighty No, in the voice that his sons lend him, to the nuclear negation, he aligns himself with life without actually saying Yes to anything, or committing himself to any sort of change below the superpower level.

But I don't at all mean that Martin Amis should break his pencil, and short the circuits of his word processor with the tears of his remorse. Quite the reverse. It is actually his need for absolution in the modern manner, surfacing most plainly in *Einstein's Monsters*, that threatens his stature as a writer.

Our culture is currently in the throes of a mania for self-exoneration. In every newspaper, polluting industries advertise themselves clean; the most compromised public figures somehow find their way to the high moral ground. If mere reality was as easily satisfied with gestures and good intentions as we are, there would be nothing much wrong with the world. But failing that, we have some dim obligation to treat things as they are, and not to join the stampede towards a fashionable innocence. Although writers may be on the side of the angels, they don't get to be that way by awarding themselves wings.

But already in Amis's *Money* there was the extraordinary move of including a character called Martin Amis, for fear that the reader might identify the author with his monstrous creation John Self. The resulting loss of tension would be disastrous for a less energetic book. It's not the case that a persona is a self-portrait unless the author testifies to the contrary, but nor are the ingredients for its making gathered on the Mountains of the Moon. There is a relationship, however shifting and elusive, between author and mask, and to announce their absolute separateness is to limit the power of each. The attraction for Martin Amis of the things he wants to dislike – a category that includes any number of impure appetites, sexual, social and even political – is actually the great subject of his work, a troubling burden he is the poorer for casting off.

*

Ian McEwan's *The Child in Time* may be the most sustained meditation on paternity in literature. It treats fatherhood, though, not as an experience – the hero's daughter is missing for the vast majority of the book – but as a condition. For the hero, Stephen Lewis, fatherhood is not a crude fact of biography but an irreversible existential state, not dependent on a current relationship with a present child.

The Child in Time is set in 1996, and flashes back two years to the abduction of Kate, then aged three. The novel doesn't spell out the year of its setting: I mention it here, perversely enough, to demonstrate that I can be true to a text when I want to, that I still have some residual power to read a text along the grain, rather than against it. The present tense of the book is set in a year of Olympic Games – which restricts the possibilities to the series 1992, 1996, 2000 . . . The year also contains what turns out to be 'the last decent summer of the twentieth century', a formula which disposes of the third of these candidates. As between 1992 and 1996 the evidence is softer, less definite. But if two years before, at the time of Kate's disappearance, Stephen is reassured rather than made uneasy by the 'oil and leather smell' of the gunbelts worn by policemen on routine duties, it seems reasonable to assume enough time from the date of writing not only for the necessary legislation, but for psychological adaptation on the part of the citizenry. The earlier date hardly leaves space for these legal and social changes.

1996, then. Two years earlier, Stephen takes Kate shopping, leaving his wife Julie to sleep. He returns alone; someone has abducted Kate in the supermarket, and her parents never see her again. But the actual circumstances of the disappearance are curiously unconvincing, as most readers of the book have acknowledged. (That is a flat lie – I know of no one who was even faintly troubled by the passage – but critics get lonely too.)

The difficulty is that Kate is taken while actually holding on to the supermarket trolley Stephen is unloading, in the tiny interval between his asking for a carrier bag and receiving it. Now, clearly you could draw a graph of abductions that plotted likelihood against culpability. In the case of a child, for instance, left in a trolley in the supermarket parking lot over a Bank Holiday weekend, the likelihood of her being taken would be high, the culpability of whoever had left her there also high. If on the other hand a master-criminal contrived to abduct Kate while Stephen was walking with her down the street, so that he noticed nothing until he glanced down and saw he was holding a small artificial hand, cunningly weighted, in a brightly coloured glove, why, that would have a very low culpability rating – what parent can guard against that sort of ruse? – but likewise a likelihood vanishingly small.

What McEwan has contrived in his book is very much towards the master-criminal end of the scale. It's highly improbable that a child could be snatched in this way unobserved; but if an experienced author chooses to present his material in this way, it must be because the compensations seem to him to be worth it. In other words, it is less important to him to be plausible than to defend a fictional father against accusations of negligence. The image and priorities of the father are paramount, and this sets a pattern for the book – both what it assumes and what it sets out to prove.

A moment that tends to confirm this follows almost immediately. As the alarm spreads through the supermarket, and the search moves to the street, male members of staff are suddenly 'no longer warehousemen or sub-managers or company representatives, but fathers, potential or real'. It's odd that fatherhood, potential or real, should be regarded as the precondition for human feeling, as if there was no other possible basis for emotion in a man. But at least *The Child in Time* is consistent in conflating fatherhood and humanity. It's ironic that McEwan, hardly a Thatcherite, should use the tactic, familiar from governmental rhetoric of recent years, of defining a universal experience in slyly narrow terms, though in this case the substitution is of 'father' for 'man' rather than, say, 'active citizen' for 'citizen'.

But why do men become fathers? How – psychologically –

do they become fathers? On these subjects, rather surprisingly, *The Child in Time* has nothing to say. Stephen's early life with Julie before they are parents, the pivotal period, is passed over. Fatherhood is assumed, without its even being mentioned, to be the male destiny, though Stephen is also privileged in the novel by not having any rivals, as if he was the only father in the world.

But in order to boost the option of fatherhood, still without mentioning it, other career possibilities for men are made to seem casual and contingent. Stephen becomes an author of children's books more or less by accident, and Charles Darke, first his publisher and then his friend, embarks on a high-flying political career after all but tossing a coin to decide his choice of party. When men's jobs are such arbitrary excursions into the world, paternity is bound to seem a thing of purposeful integrity, without needing to be addressed directly.

As for Stephen's partner in parenthood: Julie becomes estranged from him, when the paths of their mourning diverge. In due course she moves out, and settles in a cottage in the country. For the bulk of the book, Stephen deals with solitude or with his parents, either biological or symbolic (Charles Darke and his wife Thelma). But before Julie leaves comes a sentence with a faint jarring note: 'He suspected – and it turned out later he was correct – that she took his efforts to be a typically masculine evasion, an attempt to mask feelings behind displays of competence and organisation and physical effort.' The oddity is the clause between dashes. It isn't usual for McEwan to compromise his chosen point of view in this way, a formal puncturing even when the intention, as here, is to reinforce with corroboration. But it seems that even in a book that pays as careful a lip-service to women's perceptions as this one, male priorities must be defended. Men get points, not for changing, but for being right about women thinking they are wrong.

In his dealings with his biological parents Stephen is, not surprisingly given their relative times of life, tender and solicitous, protective of their reflex to protect him. At one moment he all but tucks them in for the night.

But Ian McEwan isn't content with the ordinary reversals that time visits on relationships. He contrives for his hero Stephen a paranormal experience, in which he is present, looking through a pub window, when his mother decides to defy Stephen's father and bring to term the pregnancy that will be Stephen. The experience is presented from Stephen's point of view as acutely distressing: 'His eyes grew large and round and lidless with desperate, protesting innocence, his knees rose under him and touched his chin, his fingers were scaly flippers, gills beat time, urgent, helpless strokes through the salty ocean . . .' But this is only an example of the book's strategy of taking one small step backwards and several big strides forward; the bolder the novel's advance, the more it is disguised with artificial shrinkings. Mrs Lewis when she corroborates Stephen's vision testifies to the power of the white and pleading face she sees through the window. It enables her to establish a relationship with her future child, and to defeat the forces ranged against this precarious but resourceful being. Stephen is not only present at this crucial moment, he intervenes in it. He creates himself. This is to extend the fantasy of paternity pretty far, with Stephen becoming in effect his own father, and overruling the wishes of his biological father to boot.

In the scenes of Stephen's vision, and its subsequent confirmation by his mother, the fantasy that underlies the whole book is uncomfortably naked. It becomes rather too evident that the desires of a man so taken up with the processes and privileges of reproduction actually move towards doing without women, or certainly minimising their part in the creation of life.

The nearest, by contrast, that the book comes to acknowledging that fathers can be manipulative, even destructive, is in its portrayal of Charles Darke, whose paternity is of course purely symbolic. Darke publishes Stephen's novel *Lemonade* and makes him famous, but exacts the price that it is marketed (not at all Stephen's intention) as a children's book. Darke promotes him in a way that is also a demotion, both making and unmaking him as a man. There is a similar pattern to Stephen's involvement in an Official Commission on Childcare – he is only appointed to it through Charles Darke's influence, but Darke also writes the unofficial document which pre-empts the Committee's work and makes its conclusions irrelevant. Darke gives, and Darke takes away.

But Darke is not a real father, and his sponsorship of Stephen is a manipulative perversion of the real thing. The conclusion of the novel's Darke-strand is that men who do not produce children are condemned to become them. Charles Darke produces a guide to childcare that is oppressively authoritarian, but himself longs to return to an infantile irresponsibility. In the novel, he gets to realise this fantasy, in a way that leads to his death. He becomes a failed and futureless child.

Each chapter of *The Child in Time* is headed by a passage from *The Authorised Childcare Handbook*, the volume written by Charles Darke. Darke functions in the book as a whole as a decoy, making Stephen's version of masculinity seem natural by the contrast with his highly unstable overcompensations, but the extracts from his book play an even more useful distracting role. They enable McEwan to conjure up a world in which the family is under threat from outside forces, so that the greater part of the book's energy can in fact be devoted to reshaping it from within.

However much the world has changed around Ian McEwan in the years since he started writing, it seems fair to say that he has changed more. In his early stories the only rule about sex seemed to be that it should *not* take place, with marital commitment and reproductive intent, within a fertile cleft – and the further removed it was from that situation the more it seemed to interest him. It would be hard to extrapolate this state of affairs backwards from *The Child in Time*, now that desire has been so completely mortgaged to the creation of new life. To read McEwan's novels in order, from the fixated adolescents of *The Cement Garden* through the drily passionate couple, childless and solipsistic, of *The Comfort of Strangers*, to the exemplary carers of *The Child in Time*, is to trace a drastic retraction of libido. (His new novel *The Innocent* seems to acknowledge that this progression has reached a dead end by starting again with virginity and romantic love.)

But it would be as much of a mistake to exaggerate the distance this author has travelled as to ignore it. Just as McEwan's early stories contained an element of artificial perversity, so *The Child in Time* conceals within it, for all its emphasis on universal experiences of love and loss, a fierce private agenda. There is a strong paradoxical thread leading from the apparent, but perhaps misleading, coldness of his early work to the apparent, but perhaps also misleading, warmth of the maturity announced by *The Child in Time*.

Charles Darke's wife delivers the verdict on her husband that his case ' "was just an extreme form of a general problem" ', men's inability to carry over the virtues of their immaturity into adulthood. Stephen agrees with this argument, and Thelma Darke then briefly turns it against him, saying that his indulgence of his emotions since Kate's disappearance has been a form of wilful blindness, and moreover a refusal of knowledge.

This fleeting indictment has a certain amount of authority, since by gender and profession Thelma unites the novel's two strongest images of a mutability profounder than the established order: femininity and the new physics. But it is the last of Stephen's ordeals before the novel gives him his reward. It will be everything he dreamed of.

The procedures of *The Child in Time* are intensely 'feminine', as men tend to use that word, indirect and dissembling, making each fresh inroad seem like a retreat. But now the book moves up a number of gears, from deferent advances to submissive annexation. McEwan mounts an extraordinarily daring raid on the very citadel of fertility. In the last, closely written scene of the book, Stephen attends the birth of a child he did not even know Julie was expecting. (The couple have hardly communicated since Stephen's visit to the country during which the child was conceived, the same visit that gave him his vision of his parents.)

The Child in Time is a narrative of pain and loss, but it is also a suppressed drama of symbolic ownership. The irony of its construction is that the disappearance of Kate makes the claims of her parents artificially equal. Only in the absence of the child does it become possible for the father's claims to be heard so favourably. The missing daughter becomes common property, and Stephen's feelings can dominate the novel.

Consequently, when Stephen finds Julie close to term, her pregnancy – suddenly looming, without preparation – seems more than anything an objective correlative to the development Stephen has undergone during the novel. But he receives more gifts from the fiction he inhabits than that. He and Julie make love, and their lovemaking flows into, if it doesn't actually trigger, the birth.

A little earlier, on his way to see Julie, Stephen has fulfilled his boyhood dream of riding in the cab of a railway engine. Now the older dream that haunts the book, of a man playing an immediate part not just in conception but in birth, has its fulfilment too, accompanied by a full-throated lyric: 'The silence resounded after all their promises, and merged with the stirring of a billion needles in the plantation. He moved inside her gently. Something was gathering up around them, growing louder, tasting sweeter, getting warmer, brighter, all senses were synthesising, condensing in the idea of increase.'

Stephen must forfeit this feeling of inclusion once Julie's labour gets fully under way. He falls back on the learned routines of the labour partner, though he feels that the basic purpose of such routines is 'to oppose the panic of paternal helplessness'. But on this occasion, unlike the last, his help will be all-important, since there is no one else around.

He casts his mind back to the time of Julie's first confinement. 'He had been brow mopper, telephonist, flower man, champagne pourer, midwife's dogsbody, and he had talked her through. Afterwards she had told him he had been useful. His impression was that his value had been more symbolic.' This could almost be the crux of the novel: the male exclusion, endlessly worried at and compensated for, from the reality of creation.

After all, no reason of any kind is given in the novel for the disappearance of Kate. There is no suspect and no motive, though on the naturalistic level many children would be easier to make off with than this particular one, loved and supervised, holding on to her father's supermarket trolley. Even on the symbolic level, there is nothing that her parents do, or fail to do, that would make them unworthy of her continued existence. The whole book resonates with Kate's absence, but into that resonating space is dropped only one infinitesimal suggestion of imperfection, which hangs in the mind only because it has no competitors: Stephen's role in her birth was only symbolic. Kate was fully mothered, but was only imperfectly fathered. There was an imbalance at the very moment of her coming into being.

If this was a flaw in the making of her, the Lewises' second child will not suffer from it. Stephen telephones the midwife, but until she arrives he must stand in for her. In fact the Lewises are parents again, and the action of the book is over, before she arrives.

Lifting the sheet clear on Julie's orders, Stephen sees, to his shock, 'a presence, a revelation': the baby's protruding head. It is silent and still. He can detect no pulse or breath. When he touches the head, he can feel a warmth of sorts, but it is too faint, and fading, a warmth borrowed from Julie's body. He is abruptly comforted by 'a memory, brief and clear like a firework, of a sunlit country road, of wreckage and a head'. This is another crucial elusive sentence, disguised by its brevity, its incongruity, and its being followed so closely by a sentence fuller of obvious significance, the trumpeted meaning of a novel's closing pages: 'This is really all we have got, this increase, this matter of life loving itself, everything we have has to come from this.'

The memory-firework flashes back to an incident when Stephen was driving down to the Darkes' country house. A lorry overturned in front of his car, and he escaped injury only by some inspired driving, aiming the vehicle into an impossibly narrow gap. Lightheaded in the aftermath of the crash, he tries to find the driver in the wreckage of the cab. He hears a voice, repeating a brief verbal formula, but can't locate the speaker. Then he hears that the words are in fact 'Look down.' He does.

There is a head at his feet, and an arm pressed into the face, obscuring the mouth. The man appears to be badly hurt, unable to feel anything below the neck, but eventually Stephen manages, with the help of a jack from his car, to deliver him from the wreckage. His injuries are in fact trifling.

Even on an innocent first reading, if you can imagine such a thing, there seems to be something slyly obstetrical about Stephen's handiwork with the jack. But the analogy becomes sharper and much more purposeful when the reader is referred back to it by the unemphatic sentence from the book's last scene. Although the compressed wreckage is compared to a tightly closed fist, or a toothless mouth held shut, a different anatomical suggestion is made when Stephen sees the driver's head protruding from 'a vertical gash in the steel'.

A writer as careful as Ian McEwan doesn't use a piece of taboo slang by accident, but the pun that depends on it is well disguised by its content. As that scurrilous, or mischievous, but certainly not neutral 'gash' indicates, this passage gives expression to a negative imagery of childbirth, to what Melanie Klein might have termed the Bad Womb rather than the Good. A man may think of childbirth as a mystery, as an apotheosis, or simply as an enviable power; or he may think of it as a piece of indifferent machinery, a bleeding trap, even an atrocity. This passage represents the second set of images, disavowed elsewhere in this determinedly feminism-friendly novel, tolerated here only in disguise and at some considerable distance from an appropriate context – as a gentle child might disfigure a doll and bury it far from the house.

Back to the nativity scene. In the light of the memory-firework, Stephen sees what he must do. He reaches into the wreckage and finds the umbilical cord, which is wound twice round the baby's neck and is already well on the way to strangling it. He works the cord clear, and as he does so Julie gives birth.

So it is that the hero of *The Child in Time* plays as decisive a role in the birth of his second child as he did, elsewhere in the book, in his own viability as a foetus. Twenty-five pages earlier, in a railway station, he has given his coat to a beggar, and this hint of Christliness has been admirably developed since then. Julie's baby was as cold and still as Lazarus, until he called it forth from the shadows.

In 1989 *The Child in Time* was a featured title in a festival of Green books, on the basis that it called for a more nurturing relationship with the environment. That may be true, but it is also true that a few green sprigs can be used to brighten up almost any ideology. Ian McEwan may be one of the few successful literary examples of the New Man (there it is, the dreaded phrase at last), but in his vision of the relationship between the sexes there is much that is atavistic, patriarchal, even patristic. It was an idea of the Early Fathers of the Church, after all, following Aristotle, that woman was responsible only for the body of a child, man for the soul. Woman the factory of flesh, man the author of breath, as Stephen is so literally. On this reading of fatherhood, maternity is brute and gross, paternity spiritual, and the men have nothing to envy.

Only in the last sentence of *The Child in Time* do the new parents think to discover the sex of their infant. They are described, as Julie reaches under the covers to find out, as being about to rejoin the world – the world by implication of definition, of fixity. But the reader has learned to be just a little suspicious by now of the contrived preceding flux: not a true indifference to gender, let alone a transcendence of it, but a temporary artificial blurring of identities, under cover of which the male, all the while loudly extolling the sanctity of her privileges, usurps the female.

Clearly the two writers considered in this essay adopt utterly different attitudes to the problems of the world, and to their places in it. Martin Amis declares a separate war against the Bomb, a private treaty of antagonism, while Ian McEwan tries to smuggle himself across the border of gender. But their situation is similar. Each is seeking to align himself with qualities traditionally associated with women, with a certain tender-mindedness. Each in his own way bears witness to the tidal pull of feminist thinking, and to a nagging doubt about the authenticity of male experience (the Venus Envy of my title).

Anthropologists use the word *couvade* to denote patterns of male behaviour that seek to upstage or to appropriate potent moments in the lives of women. The women go into labour, but the men – it varies from culture to culture – either cry out in stylised agony, or else persuade themselves they actually feel the pangs.

There is certainly something poignant about a man seeking to make fatherhood a binding contract, the linchpin of his identity, at roughly the same time that Angela Carter, newly and maturely a mother, was saying in interview – with splendid defiance of biology – that no one should think of having children until their forties, because at that time of life you don't so much mind giving up your evenings. Angela Carter was trying to find a style of motherhood that was casual, breezy, matter-of-fact – just as fatherhood has traditionally been – while Ian McEwan, and to a lesser extent Martin Amis, was trying to turn fatherhood into an experience as immediate and binding as motherhood has been, on the traditional model.

Presumably these writers will ease up on the paternity motif as their actual children grow up to be more obstreperous, less completely contained by their parents' world, not such handy screens for the projection of masculine emotion. Fathers of teenagers lose the habit of wearing paternity as a medal. Till then, it would be refreshing if writers were a little more even-handed in their treatment of such material.

If two people decide to have a child, they are doing one thing, not two. It can't be the case that one of them is capitulating to her biology, while the other is making a commitment to the future. Children have no absolute value, and nor do parents, unless people do, full stop. A BABY ON BOARD bumper sticker ignores the fact that the children it seeks to defend, if spared an early death on the road, are no less likely than any others to go joyriding in a borrowed car with a snootful of cider the weekend they turn fourteen. You may want to preserve your children, your genetic possessions, but that isn't enough by itself to turn you into a conservationist.

If, above all, a man finds that becoming a father changes his opinions on all manner of related and unrelated subjects, then he shouldn't simply entrench himself in his new status, and the authority it seems to confer. He should also think about *change*, and how it has happened that his view of the world has shifted through 180 degrees, without any admitted inconsistency. One of the bases of sexism has traditionally been an imagery of women as changeable, unreliable, fickle and so on, with a corresponding exaggerated ideology of male fixedness and stability of purpose. This ideology could usefully be renounced, or at least revised, by those who no longer hold it as they did. But in practice, fathers hold tight to their new fixity, and rapidly forget the old one.

The result is a streamlined account of masculinity that leaves out everything disreputable, in a display of presentational skills that might make you wonder if British Man plc isn't being rejigged in the run-up to privatisation. But disreputability has its own story to tell. Alasdair Gray is a writer of an older generation than Martin Amis and Ian McEwan, with less sophisticated reflexes on issues of sexual politics, and in his 1984 novel *1982, Janine* he concentrates almost exclusively on the disreputable, telling the story of a Scottish supervisor of security installations fantasising in a hotel bedroom. The fantasies are intricate, and constantly threaten to be unforgivable, though Gray knows just how to rehabilitate the fantasist with humour, at the very moment when the reader is poised to reject him. The fantasies all concern having sexual and physical power over women. And then, after nearly 200 pages, Gray makes his move, in one of the most audacious passages in modern British literature:

> . . . I had started to tell myself stories about a very free attractive greedy woman who, confident in her powers, begins an exciting adventure and finds she is not free at all but completely at the disposal of others. As I aged that story became very elaborate. The woman is corrupted into enjoying her bondage and trapping others into it. I did not notice that this was the story of my own life. I avoided doing so by insisting on the *femaleness* of the main character. The parts of the story which came to excite me most were not the physical humiliations but the moment when the trap starts closing and the victim feels the torture of being in two minds: wanting to believe, struggling to believe, that what is happening cannot be happening, can only happen to someone else. And I was right to be excited by that moment because it is the moment when, with courage, we change things. Why *should* Janine feel helpless when she realises Max has lied to her and is abducting her? He is driving a fast car along a motorway, his hands are occupied, if she removes one of her ridiculous shoes and threatens his eye with the heel he will certainly stop or change direction if he sees she is serious. But she is not used to acting boldly, she finds it easier to pretend Max is honest and decent, hoping her act will make him more so, and thus he drives her into the mire. My fancies keep reliving that moment of torture for Janine because I have never fully faced it in my own life and I am travelling in a circle again.

This passage finds a new emotion and a new truth in the feminist criticism that when men talk about women they are usually not talking about women at all. Alasdair Gray chooses as his subject the part of the male psyche that is almost by definition the most distorted and destructive, and finds in it, safely encoded, a simple message that has been scrambled everywhere else by the high-minded censors of consciousness. A profound truth has survived by allying itself with the strong unexamined current of sex, and has only been recovered by a willingness to start from the most unprepossessing materials. The more fashionable tendency in British literature is to present masculinity in its more reputable aspects, but it is a tendency, as this essay exists to show, with its own inbuilt drive towards distortion.

But there is a further irony lurking. These late accommodations of feminist ideas are affected by the blowing of quite another wind. Our understanding of the stranglehold we have on our planet has changed, and must change a lot more. The phrase 'doomsday device', once applied specifically to the nuclear arsenals, now seems to cover a much wider range of apparatus: aerosols, fridges, cars. As our fear of national leaders with their fingers on the Button recedes, we must acknowledge that our own hands have been busy, with nozzles and switches and ignition keys. If as Martin Amis suggests it has taken us all this time to learn to write about what uranium can do, how quick will we be to address the issue of carbon dioxide?

In this altered climate, we must learn to accept that our culture suffers from more than a bout of bad breath which some gargle of the future will rid us of. Every time we oust a species or vaporise a habitat we add another clause to the long eviction order we are serving on ourselves. Somehow we must bring together our experience of our lives as meaningful – since without that we will have no motive to improve matters – and our abstract knowledge of their unsustainability.

It will take more than the 'womanly times' prayed for by Ian McEwan to bring this about. In fact it may be that the special and restricted female prestige of recent decades, based on a recognition of women's submerged social and political identity, will suffer in the years to come, rather than sweep the field. It was a powerful piece of rhetoric, after all, on the part of women's peace groups, to characterise the Bomb as inherently masculine, a piece of diabolical machinery that no woman would invent or think of using (tit for tat, this, for the dreary question Why no great female composers?). But if our idea of our destructiveness stops being vested so absolutely in nuclear weapons, and comes to be seen as diffused through all our lives, then female innocence is likely to show up as an illusion. When hairspray and nappy bleach are added to the list of doomsday devices, women may find that the personal is political in a way that no one had quite bargained for.

For a while yet, men of good will and imperfect conscience will try to find an existential niche in the traditional realm of female values. But the phantom of human virtue is set to become still more elusive. The womb cannot survive for ever as an innocent organ in a body otherwise discredited. The island of exemption offered by caring for children can only be eaten away, as time passes and the waters rise.

And you, my hobbyhorse, how is it with you? Once or twice I heard the finger-drumming of your gallop, once or twice I thought you would lift me off my feet, while I urged you onwards with my rubber spurs. Let me loosen your girth-straps. Surely that is sweat, darkening the nap of your cheekbone? Your mane lies in lank strands, rinsed by passion of all its chemical bounce. And this foam that trails from your mouth, isn't that the authentic foam of unreason, positively proof that rancorous emotion has achieved its orgasm?

(Bring the camera in close, close as you can. Focus. *Focus!*)

I can only apologise. It appears in fact to be toothpaste.

Cinematically Challenged

The film is a well-known one from the early nineties, a touted return to form by a famous director. The hero's lawyer, representing him in connection with a murder, is in a wheelchair. There is no particular symbolism to his condition – he isn't for instance an Ironside, paradoxically powerless champion of the truth, a person possessing moral force exclusively. Nor is he presented, like so many wheelchair-users in films, as having a special affinity with technology, whether by supposed virtue of being a disembodied brain or as a person who is already in part mechanical.

The character is in a wheelchair, essentially, because some people are. The chair says no more about its owner than, say, a bicycle or a skateboard – except that its user doesn't ride a bicycle or a skateboard. The actor playing the character may or may not use a wheelchair when the camera isn't turning. The hero's lawyer occupies only a brief time on screen, measured in a high number of seconds or a low number of minutes. If there is a more than casual point to his disabled status, it must be that by this stage of the hero's experiences, his life is so out of control, so free of an unfolding logic, that nothing can surprise him.

This is that rare thing, a neutral portrayal of a disabled character in a Hollywood film – a film about Hollywood, at that – and perhaps that's why, perversely, it's so easy to forget. It makes the point that it's not making a point, and then it vanishes from the memory. This is the double-bind governing representations of minorities in cinema: distortion resonates, while matter-of-factness leaves no trace.

It isn't a new observation that being cast in a physically disabled role does no harm to an actor's Oscar chances (actresses have rather fewer opportunities to experience this beneficial effect, but remember Patty Duke in *The Miracle Worker* and Marlee Matlin in *Children of a Lesser God*). A feigned impairment can be a real boost. But does anyone imagine that there is anything particularly difficult about sitting in a wheelchair for short periods, about pretending to be blind or deaf? Part of the hysterical applause is of course self-congratulatory, saluting the presence of an 'issue' that has been properly distanced from raw experience. But perhaps there's more to this great need to emphasise the gap between the actor and the part.

Why single out these performances for praise? Actors act. The performer is not continuous with the role. Isn't that the point? Not always, apparently.

One other set of portrayals is given a somewhat frantic endorsement: impersonations of homosexuals by actors certified straight. Sometimes the most inert caricature receives frothing acclaim (case in point William Hurt's turn in *Kiss of the Spider Woman*). Here the thinking behind the brouhaha is more transparent: having defined homosexuality as a set of stylised gestures, Hollywood thereby creates the fear that anyone reproducing the gestures, for the best of reasons, will become homosexual. What follows is hyperbolic insistence on how hard it was technically (but really how risky, morally) to loll the wrist and simper. Somehow contamination was avoided.

So what is it about the able-bodied stars in their wheelchairs, beyond the fluffy feeling that Hollywood Cares? Perhaps it's something to do with the particular characteristics of the minority (the substantial minority, if we accept the figure of 10 per cent) made up by the disabled.

The majority values crispness of contour in a minority, clarity of definition. Disability does not oblige. There is considerable fuzziness of boundary involved, even when there aren't institutions with different agendas doing the assessing. This moreover is a minority that grows by osmosis across a membrane, as the hard-of-hearing become definitively deaf (the partially-sighted blind, the residually-mobile wheelchair bound), but also appears to recruit by catastrophe. The minority also loses members across its membrane, as people are successfully treated or rehabilitated, but miracle cures aside, the journey between motorcycle and wheelchair is made in one direction only. This is a minority for which all non-members are on a waiting list, with a real prospect of jumping the queue.

Anyone can speak for the rights of the disabled, but disability is not a unitary experience, and nor is fear of disability. It condenses many fears – of age, of dependence, of mutilation. What the Academy voices from time to time on Oscar night is perhaps a willed exoticising of disability, making it something that exists at a vast distance from real life, a remote territory that can only be reached by the most intrepid of cinematic explorers.

Hence the particular *frisson* behind the press coverage of Christopher Reeve's riding accident and consequent paralysis. An actor professionally identified with invulnerability lets the able-bodied side down, and allows repressed fears to return. Everyone out of a wheelchair needs to believe in Superman, in vigour that is self-sustaining and endless.

A book called *The Cinema of Isolation* by Martin F. Norden, published by Rutgers University Press in 1994, sets out to trace the history of disability in film. By its own admission the book goes for breadth over depth in its survey. In fact like many a cultural archaeologist coming upon a rich site, Martin Norden does what Schliemann did at Troy and sinks his shafts in haste, turning up many treasures but profoundly disturbing the strata in the process.

Norden lists a vast number of early silent films featuring people with disabilities – slapstick offerings like *The Invalid's Adventure* (1907) or *Near-Sighted Mary* (1909) – which would have to come into the category of mocking the afflicted. He is sometimes moved to sarcasm in his descriptions: 'Gaumont also found it necessary to share with the world its enlightened views on the subject of disabled people and marriage.' He goes so far as to label such films 'assaults' on physically disabled people in the name of humour.

His introduction to the book has the feeling of a historico-theoretical framework run up after the event, but in it he has at least touched on an explanation. He quotes from Freud's 1919 essay on 'The Uncanny': 'anxiety about one's eyes, the fear of going blind, is often enough a substitute for the dread of being castrated' – fear of castration being 'what gives the idea of losing other organs its intense colouring'. If disability raises in the able-bodied viewer the spectre of castration, then the so-called humour of those early films becomes not more attractive, but at least more intelligible, as a form of compulsive dis-identification. This refusal of empathy is perhaps symmetrical with the attitude prevailing later, of sympathy offered as if from an invulnerable height, sympathy that denies any claim of kinship. Those who murmur 'There but for the Grace of God go I', after all, disclaim their entitlement to an able body on a humble level, while reasserting it on a more elevated one. God wants them as they are – and God wants the others other.

If Norden has an overall message, it is that the representation of the disabled in films confirms their status as inherently different: 'most movies have tended to isolate disabled characters from their able-bodied peers as well as from each other'. The social ideal would be for the two not so very different groups to mix on a regular basis: studies such as Nancy Weinberg's 'Modifying Social Stereotypes of the Physically Disabled' (1978) have shown that 'as contact between able-bodied and disabled is intensified, the stereotype of the disabled as different diminishes . . . There is a positive relationship between contact and perceived similarity: as contact increases, perceived similarity increases.' It isn't clear how this attempt on the social level to reverse the mutual impoverishment of minority and majority could be realised or abetted by films.

His unrealistic expectations have the consequence of making some of Norden's judgements seem faintly absurd. No doubt *The Invalid's Adventure* and *Near-Sighted Mary* are lamentable pieces of entertainment, but how many other films of the period 1907–9 are congenial to modern taste? It seems a little quixotic to expect higher standards of artistic achievement from films that happen to have disabled characters in them.

There is the occasional whiff of good intentions even in early films, but the results seldom tickle Norden's nostril. *Deaf Mute Girl Reciting 'Star Spangled Banner'*, a single-shot film of about 75 seconds made in 1902 (perhaps at Gallaudet, the famous institute for the deaf), can make some faint claim to progressiveness, with its Old Glory backdrop and patriotic performer of American Sign Language. What is it saying, if not that the deaf are also citizens? Yet Norden sees only the 'desire for freakish entertainment', and a pandering to that desire. The deaf girl had novelty value, to be sure, but is that really the same as 'freakishness'? Norden is at risk here of presupposing the attitudes he seeks to rebuke.

A leitmotif that Norden discovers in early cinema is of the disabled person as fraudulent. Silent films swarm with beggars feigning. Again, he becomes incensed that the able-bodied world should libel a disadvantaged minority in this way (though it is the fate of minorities to be libelled). It might be rewarding to characterise this motif in another way: the desire to represent the disabled in movies is constantly shadowed by the desire not to represent them, somehow to separate the person and the disability. To expose a disabled person as a sham is the antagonistic version of this desire, while an insistence on curability (never entirely absent from films, but having as Norden shows definite seasons of prevalence) expresses the same drive in an apparently more sympathetic version.

Norden looks for a social-realist depiction of disability in films, with particular reference to economic conditions, which again seems a little naive. Hollywood cinema has only ever had spasms of realism in these matters – why would it make an exception in favour of the disabled? The workings of money are fairly thoroughly suppressed in mainstream cinema.

He also seeks to assess 'audience positioning' – whether viewers are encouraged to identify with disabled characters or with the able-bodied ones who look at them. With reference to blindness, he doesn't explain how a visual medium could appropriately accommodate the priorities of the sightless. In general, his judgements have an insensitivity to tone that can sometimes verge on the deranged: 'Though commendable for its explicit recognition of able-bodied exploitation and relatively balanced in its representation of character gazes, Heidi otherwise deals with issues of physical disability in a simplistic and facile way.' *Heidi* deals with *the Alps* in a simplistic and facile way. It's a simplistic and facile film. Who ever thought any different? We're not talking about *Persona* here, we're talking about *Heidi*!

With other films, by contrast, Norden's rudimentary analyses, particularly of camerawork, don't do justice to sophisticated strategies. A case in point would be *The Elephant Man* (1980), a still from which appears on the cover of the book. David Lynch's film may indeed demonstrate 'time-worn points of view' in some ways, and its central figure may indeed combine the stereotypes of the Sweet Innocent and the Saintly Sage (Norden is inordinately fond of categories like these and the 'Elderly Dupe', 'Noble Warrior', 'Civilian Superstar' and so on). But his camera plays an ambiguous game, in two stages.

First of all it withholds the full sight of John Merrick (John Hurt), tantalising the audience with reaction shots, glimpses, a silhouette against a screen. The viewer's appetite for freakishness is played with, worked up, and then strangely shamed. After Lynch has shown Merrick at last, the camera dwells on his appearance until it acquires its own integrity, if not actual beauty. Lynch questions in turn both the rights that make up our position of privilege: first the right to look, and then the right to look away.

In his watchfulness about 'ableism', able-bodied bias, Norden sometimes overstates his case, precisely where one might expect him to ackowledge distinctive efforts. This, for instance, would be a fair comment about a great many films: 'the fulfilment of actions ordinarily associated with mainstream members is an acceptable substitute' for miraculous recoveries temporarily out of fashion. 'In other words, the characters should start acting like majority members if they cannot be cured outright.' It's just that this verdict is passed on *The Miracle Worker* (1962), of all films. When Helen Keller made her first communication with another human being, it wasn't a lot like selling out a considered political position. What it was like was a painful birth, and Arthur Penn's film doesn't play down the pain of her entering into language.

The distinctive element in *The Miracle Worker*, which makes it still so eminently watchable, is the acknowledgement that in her isolation Helen Keller's resistance to communication was all that she had. Before she could express No explicitly, she was entirely clenched round a No that she had to give up. The film does what it can to honour that.

Martin Norden isn't the first cultural commentator to discover that Freudianism works wonders in small doses, but small doses aren't available. The Freudian scaffolding rigged up to buttress the introduction ends by threatening to pull down the whole building. Norden spoils a valuable point about the way disabled characters are arbitrarily inserted into screen adaptations of literary originals (he singles out the deformed lab assistant in Rex Ingram's *The Magician* [1926], drawn from a Maugham novel, mysteriously incorporated into the James Whale *Frankenstein* and subsequently acquiring the generic name of Igor) by his grudging response to one of the few occasions when a disability materialises as an aspect of the hero. Howard Breslin's short story 'Bad Day at Honda' has an explicitly able-bodied protagonist, while Spencer Tracy in *Bad Day at Black Rock* is famously one-armed.

All Norden can think of to say is that Tracy's character is

' "remasculinised" through his heroic deeds'. Since when was he *de*masculinised? He looks pretty tough from the word go (even Norden describes him as 'a self-assured, goal-orientated fellow'). The dismal equation of disability with an internal defectiveness is so widespread that it seems to have bewitched him into overlooking a rare exception, where the character who is physically impaired is the one to embody integrity.

Norden seems not to notice that the film's theme is that difference need not be the same as Otherness: you can be one of Them and still be one of Us. The self-consciously liberal message of the film is that xenophobia cannot plausibly be the philosophy of the melting pot, cannot be an American value. The town's secret is that during the war some of its inhabitants murdered a farmer of Japanese descent. The guilty parties assume that John Macreedy has come to investigate the crime, when his mission is much simpler: to deliver a bravery medal to the father of the man who saved his life in combat. The two quests, though, the feared and the real, necessarily converge since the father in question is the murder victim.

Bad Day at Black Rock also includes an early appearance of oriental self-defence techniques: Macreedy fights off his attackers with some basic judo and karate. This is a more plausible resource for a one-armed man than Hollywood fisticuffs, and has the advantage of showing the hero's willingness to absorb non-Western skills without compromising his Americanness. Perhaps it even signals to the viewer the possibility that minorities in general might be able to use the majority's strength against itself. But all Norden sees is the disability platitude he projects on to it, and a highly unlikely Freudian reading of geography to bring about that redundant recovery of virility: if film-makers 'did not provide female figures to accomplish this remasculinisation, they at the very least offered female-like environments that allow the males to engage in heroic acts (e.g., the hostile landscape that John Macreedy penetrates in *Bad Day at Black Rock* . . .)'. Since when is a hostile landscape a female-like environment? Are women deserts? Since when, come to that, is Spencer Tracy a phallus? Someone who has taken on the task of exploring our complicated investments in the bodies we see on screen should be able to provide a less preposterous gloss.

It's never explicitly stated in *The Cinema of Isolation* that commercial films can be made exclusively, or even primarily, for a disabled audience, but the assumption lurks in many passages. In his discussion of *The Heart Is a Lonely Hunter* (1968) the author remarks: 'anyone who knows the language can readily tell when the hearing actors who play deaf characters are basically fumbling their way through it . . . A scene in which Singer interacts with a black deaf person played by Horace Oats, who truly was deaf and knew the language well, only accentuated [Alan] Arkin's lack of facility with the language and underscored the impropriety of casting a hearing actor in such a role.'

Yet Norden has just finished telling us about the five-year struggle to get Carson McCullers's novel filmed at all (the industry reaction was 'It's absolutely beautiful and I wouldn't touch it with a barge pole'), and the decisive contribution made by Alan Arkin, who had long coveted the role of John Singer, and told the screenwriter: 'You gotta give me the part now . . . I've gone to all the trouble of becoming a star just so I could play it.' Arkin is clearly more fluent in Hollywood hyperbole than in American Sign Language, but he deserves more than a ticking-off for his 'impropriety'. No doubt his signing was substandard. But there's little point in comparing the film that exists with one that could never have been made – the same project with a deaf actor. Disparaging comparisons with the impossible don't make for effective criticism.

Perhaps the makers of *The Heart Is a Lonely Hunter* deserve praise for the fact that Arkin's faulty articulation of ASL is the only barrier to a deaf audience's understanding. Consider these strictures on *Children of a Lesser God* (1986): 'many signings [were] cut off by the edges of the frame, executed in bad lighting, or obscured when the performer ([William] Hurt, usually) turned away from the camera, and hearing characters would sometimes talk without signing'. Norden doesn't spell out what is implied here: that for signing to be properly intelligible it must take precedence over lighting, composition and editing. It isn't insulting to suggest that many deaf viewers (whose exclusion from movies, after all, began only with *The Jazz Singer*) might consider this a bad bargain.

As Norden points out, the defective signing in the film could be made good only by a subtitled showing – and less than 5 per cent of American cinemas showing the film in its first run offered captioned versions. (Captioning for television is one area where technology may usefully be prevailed upon to cater to minority needs, and it's worth mentioning that ASL travels a lot less well than written English.) But if you're going to caption a film anyway, why bother to try even as hard as *Children of a Lesser God* does to represent sign language?

Though this isn't an argument made by Norden, any film that gives importance to sign language is by that very fact less likely to treat deaf people as sensitive outsiders who should be allowed by the big-hearted majority to partake more fully in a wider world. The point here is not what sign language communicates to the deaf, but what it communicates to the hearing.

Norden's thesis is not wrong: that many Hollywood films encourage audiences to consider disabled people's experiences as being remote to the point of unimaginability. *If I went blind I'd kill myself. I don't know what I'd do* – that is the basic premiss magnified and distorted by the movies. But there is also the assumption that the majority's experience contains and excludes the minority's. Nothing is more provocative, and sometimes more politically useful, than the claim to an unshareable life.

Coriolanus's response to banishment – 'I banish *you*.' Long-ago weather reports on the Home Service – 'The Continent is cut off by fog.' T-shirts in the high street: *It's a black thing. You wouldn't understand.* When deaf people sign, they make no such rhetorical statements, but discomfit the hearing no less. It's not simply that a group is inherently a more resisting object than an individual, when it comes to certain fixed responses. It's more that the majority is always eager to strike an emotional attitude – that feels good – but intellectual effort is something else again. The idea that *you* might have to go to some trouble to make yourself understood isn't half so welcome. When deaf people sign, they pass the message to a wider audience: *Evening class first, sympathy second. Listen, and then talk.*

Yet Norden, in his analysis of *The Heart Is a Lonely Hunter*, speaks up for the majority in this particular matter: 'Singer seems forever isolated not only because of the other characters' lack of responsiveness to his needs but also because the filmmakers refused to make his signed conversations accessible to audiences unacquainted with American Sign Language.' *Refused* is a strong word, implying something more wilful than merely *deciding against*, as one of their many choices. Doesn't there come a time when isolation plus resources equals something like resistance to being annexed? Something like autonomy? Or can disabled people only hope to be accorded their rights by flattering the majority's illusions? By making some conversations in the film opaque, the film-makers place a trifling obstacle in the path of facile identification.

Deaf critics of *Children of a Lesser God* seem to have been less hard-line than Norden, and to have taken it for granted that this was a mildly progressive film aimed squarely at hearing audiences. Clearly there's nothing more tedious for a minority than to be offered overwhelmingly grotesque or sentimentalised images of its existence, but it might also be mentioned that minorities are under no obligation to bond with the positive images they are offered.

It may be, for instance, that a deaf viewer watching a properly captioned print of, say, *Edward Scissorhands*, will identify with difference as expressed in a strongly poetic register. Something similar might even apply to the sequences in *Planet of the Apes* where Charlton Heston is abused by monkeys who refuse to understand what he's saying, regarding him as by definition stupid.

It is also possible to prefer negative images over positive ones, provided they offer some bonus of power. The fatal woman in *film noir* magnetises female viewers as well as male. Gay audiences of *No Way To Treat a Lady* (1968) could be under no illusions that Rod Steiger's campy vaudeville turn was any sort of sympathetic portrayal of a homosexual, but they took to their hearts the taunting catchphrase he used: 'Doesn't make me a *bad* person.'

So too with the stereotype that Norden calls the Obsessive Avenger. Clearly it is not the case that disabled people seek revenge on the able-bodied, but there might be times for finding that fantasy delicious. Norden can't bring himself to appreciate Tod Browning's *Freaks* (1932) because of the notorious finale, in which an entire community of circus performers undertake to punish a pair of sinners (they kill the man and mutilate the woman). They're not by any stretch of the political imagination 'role-models', that desirable thing, but it certainly makes a difference that the disabled on screen at this point are in the majority, that wrongdoing was associated with able-bodiedness first, and that there is no come-uppance for these particular Obsessive Avengers. The subversions of *Freaks* are more thoroughgoing than Norden is prepared to admit.

Norden points out in his survey of recent films with a disability theme that it is particularly dramas with disabled people at their centre that are 'problematic' ('they have registered mostly regressive qualities with many of the old stereotypes still in force'). Less direct approaches are likely to be more rewarding, as in the case of the irrelevantly disabled lawyer in Altman's *The Player* (1992).

An old episode of *Hill Street Blues*, for instance, dealt with disability issues in a glancing way. While a police car was parked while on urgent duty so as to block one of the cutaway sections which since the 1970s have been required in American pavements, an activist in a wheelchair sprayed angry graffiti on to its bodywork. He was arrested. Later in the episode he was found guilty of the vandalism, but his punishment – with soap-opera glibness of closure – was to give the police classes in disability awareness. Nevertheless, between the arrest and the cutely didactic resolution was an extraordinarily painful sequence, in which the man in the wheelchair needed to use the lavatory. The facilities in the police station were not accessible to wheelchairs, so a policeman had grudgingly to escort him. Trying to hold the disabled man upright at the urinal, the policeman lost his grip. The two men's encounter with shame, loss of control and urine was powerful precisely because it wasn't part of some standard parable, some partronisingly smooth learning curve. The issue wasn't neatly aligned with the dramatic structure: there was a welcome element of syncopation.

On the big screen, it is in cameos and bit parts that ragged little bits of reality are more likely to show through the Hollywood gloss. In Viggo Mortensen's brief appearance in *Carlito's Way* (1993) – he plays a wheelchair-bound criminal – two points are made with surprising force. Referring to his wheelchair, the character says that when they really want to punish you, they don't put you in a grave, they put you in one of these. The idea that life in a wheelchair is worse than death, actually a form of torture, is unusually stark for a thriller that is routine in most respects. And when the character is found to be wired for sound, and to have been hired to entrap Carlito, his defence of his actions is also striking: What else can I do to earn a little money, except sell out my friends? The economic powerlessness of the disabled, with the corollary that certain moral choices can become unaffordable luxuries, is rarely addressed by a cinema predicated on the power of individuals to transcend fate.

There's one film which receives no mention in *The Cinema of Isolation*, but nevertheless uses disability themes in a uniquely disorientating way; Michael Mann's *Manhunter* (1986), best known as a sort of 'prequel' to *The Silence of the Lambs*, with Brian Cox doing a turn as Hannibal Lecter. The serial killer in the film is an Obsessive Avenger with a vengeance, murdering entire families of strangers carefully selected on the basis of the perfection of their normality. His psychology is obliquely explored in the film – the murders are transformational rituals – but the source of his (to put it mildly) alienation isn't explicitly stated.

In the middle of the film, after following the police investigation exclusively, *Manhunter* switches abruptly to the murderer's world – his professional world, not his handiwork. He is tall and odd-looking. He works in a large-scale film-processing plant. We see him talking to a female colleague, offering her a lift home after work. That part of us that is already unsettled by the film shrieks silently: *Noooooo! Don't accept a lift home from the monster!* She says thanks, but she doesn't need a lift. He explains that his offer was selfish, since it would give him pleasure to drive her home. She accepts.

The viewer has been deprived of a piece of information known by both parties: the woman is blind. And yes, in her way she is a grown-up (and sexually competent) version of the Sweet Innocent. But in her discussion of her blindness and her job she shows a wry political awareness, of the sort that Norden searches for in vain in so many films: corporations in America must hire a quota of the disabled if they are to be considered for government contracts, and employing a blind woman in a darkroom doesn't require much in the way of modifications to the premises. No expensive wheelchair ramps, for instance.

It's too much to expect the film to allow this character to wield the power of the gaze, but she does something remarkably similar. She wields the power of knowledge at a distance, which the sighted equate with sight. She congratulates her colleague on the clarity of his articulation, and on the excellence of the corrective surgery to his harelip. She remarks that he has trouble only with a few consonants – no one who hadn't worked as a speech therapist, as she has, would even notice. This is one of the most forceful pieces of self-presentation by a disabled person in all cinema. She goes on to make a request: may she touch his face? He refuses, and she doesn't insist.

He mentions that if she has time, he has a surprise that he would like to show her, on her way home. Again we bite our tattered tongues so as not to shout, in a crowded cinema, *Noooooo! Don't let the monster show you a surprise!* She says yes. She likes surprises.

When the killer shows his colleague the surprise, *Manhunter* enters a territory of perverse and extraordinary richness. The surprise is a tiger, anaesthetised for the removal of a wisdom tooth, flanks stirring faintly as it comes round after the operation, its threat for now suspended. The blind woman touches the beast with wonder and then something like greed, an *amour fou* of the fingers and the sensing skin.

This is an astounding sequence quite apart from its almost surrealist strangeness. We are being shown that evil can be imaginative, can identify with other people's lacks and desires. We are being reminded that blind people are particularly cut off from nature, our access to wild things being so largely ocular. And the murderer is conveying to her without using words that he too is dangerous, but not to her.

It should come as no surprise that the romance on which these two people embark does not turn out well – if this is Beauty and the Beast, then the Beast can't rise above his bestiality. But what is salutary about the film's approach is that the murderer chooses to draw the dividing lines differently, not as we do between her and him, representatives of good and evil, but between both of Them and Us – they with their difference, we with our defective normality.

Martin Norden has praise for a handful of films in Hollywood history, but there are two pieces of work that bring out something like actual acclaim: *The Best Years of Our Lives* (1946), directed by William Wyler, and *Coming Home* (1978), directed by Hal Ashby. Both films represent responses to a recent war, and are perhaps part of a social surge of awareness in different decades about a class of newly disabled men, wounded soldiers: men with an interrupted sense of entitlement, recently dispossessed of privilege, and also men with a feeling of having kept to their side of a bargain with their country. In a sense, then, these are films about the honouring of – or reneging on – a social contract that may or may not extend to all disabled people, including those who cannot present their condition as a manifestation of sacrifice, negative trophy of patriotism.

Both films seek to address the intimate aspects of disablement, with a comparable mix of forthrightness and equivocation. Wyler's film, highly unusually, uses a disabled person, Harold Russell, in a major role. For once, disablement in the movies is a matter of visible absence rather than disguised presence (Lon Chaney's strapped-up legs visible in profile in *The Penalty* [1920], Spencer Tracy's theoretically missing arm bizarrely present in publicity stills for *Bad Day at Black Rock*). *The Best Years of Our Lives* goes as far as a bedroom scene, in which Russell's character is helped by his girlfriend to prepare for the night.

This sequence is in its way highly daring, in what it invites an audience to contemplate. Yet it is striking that there is one area where the film-makers made the character of Homer Parrish less functional than the actor who played him. Russell could put on his prostheses by himself, and wasn't helpless without them. Could anything signal more clearly the reassuring (in this context) fact of impotence?

The character's girlfriend reacts with true love rather than pity, but this need not mean more than that in a 1940s film caring for men was still felt to be the female destiny – with *nurse* as only a special case of *woman*, and a nurse who married her disabled patient making a satisfactory contract between two people exempted from desire.

In *Coming Home*, by contrast, the wheelchair-bound veteran played by Jon Voight is able to give Jane Fonda's character sexual pleasure in a way her macho husband cannot. Here the equivocation is in the casting rather than the screenplay. The other inhabitants of the Veterans Administration hospital in the film were disabled in real life, while Voight is a familiar face (best known from *Midnight Cowboy*) attached to an able body. *Coming Home* contains sequences that are almost documentary, but it is the familiar actor in the standard triangle with whom audiences are expected to identify.

In films like *Coming Home* (or Brando's early film *The Men*, 1950) the paraplegic supporting cast guarantee the seriousness of the lead actor in the wheelchair, which is only to say: the disabled people in the background certify the excellence of the star's performance. We never forget that performance is what it is. When Jon Voight pleasures Jane Fonda on the screen in front of us, we know we're not really being invited to imagine the sexual experiences of the wheelchair-bound.

The logical next step from the actor-surrounded-by-real-sufferers strategy of *Coming Home* is represented by the Gary Sinise character in *Forrest Gump* (1994). Here the actor and the 'real' disability have been fused by special effects. Sinise's legs aren't there, because some expensive digitised manipulation of the image has seen to it that they're not. There is no strapping-up to see in a profile shot. This is one of the most visible absences on screen since *The Best Years of Our Lives*, but its significance is the opposite of the earlier one's. It becomes less and less likely that actual disabled people will appear in films, now that anyone can be a temporary amputee. The authoritative visual shock of seeing the body Harold Russell inhabits is lost, when kids seeing the film that earned him his Oscar (a statuette that he was forced in time to sell off) may only be impressed that they could do that back then. After virtual disability realised to such high specifications, who will have (screen) time for the real thing?

It takes only common sense to understand that the sex lives of the disabled are a taboo subject because this private area is one where the majority sensitively prefer not to trespass.

So much for common sense. In reality the able-bodied imagination intervenes with great intensity in this area. The disabled are insistently sexualised – it's just that they are sexualised in a highly particular way. What is sexualised is not the life but the loss. For the majority, the disabled are by symbolic definition unable to function sexually. If on the level of individual fantasy we equate disability with impotence, as if the wheelchair or the white stick were only outward and visible signs of an inner castration, we can hardly expect more realism from our films.

It should tip us off to the way our thoughts are being shaped that the limbs of the disabled in movies – Lon Chaney's legs, Spencer Tracy's arm, Gary Sinise's reverse prosthesis – are body parts that both cannot and must be there; a formulation classically applied in psychoanalytic theory to that necessary phantom, the mother's penis.

Yet Freudian theory is problematic in its own way. The Oedipus complex may contribute to an explanation of our compulsive dis-identification with the disabled, but its root-myth itself both begins and ends with disabilities viewed symbolically. Oedipus is 'orthopedically impaired' (to borrow a recurring phrase of Norden's) as a result of being exposed on the mountainside as a baby. As an adult he blinds himself in a highly expressive piece of self-mutilation: he has seen too much, and at the same time up to the day of his blinding he has seen nothing at all.

The Oedipus complex is not an optional experience. Freud proposes it as universal and unchanging. But if disability is symbolically viewed by the able-bodied as castration, how is it viewed by the disabled themselves – by the estimated 15 per cent who are born disabled, but also by the remaining 85 per cent? Do they negotiate the complex in its female version, irrespective of gender, viewing themselves as already castrated? (And does this also mean that Freudian theory in effect constructs femininity as a disability?)

The theory of the Oedipus complex depends fairly heavily on *seeing*, on the glimpse of the mother naked that reveals her genital anomaly. (In Freud's essay 'Medusa's Head' it is stated that the terror of castration is always linked to the sight of something.) Freud presented his theories as contributions to science, but if he had really wanted to test them scientifically, he might have taken an interest in the sexual development of those born blind.

Freud features only intermittently in *The Cinema of Isolation*, in the introduction and then in the concluding pages, but he's present quite enough to destabilise the whole enterprise. Freud is invoked in the first place to explain hostility towards the disabled, as if this was a minor thing that could easily be disposed of, but then Freudian analysis itself seems to endorse able-bodied fantasies about what disabled bodies represent, and even to be composed of them.

The final paragraph of the book tries to put the genie from Vienna back in his bottle. It starts with a tone of modest confidence: 'Though the Oedipal crisis cannot entirely account for the construction of movie images of physical disability, there is little question that the Cinema of Isolation [Norden clearly has hopes of his title becoming the technical term for his chosen subject genre] – good films, bad, and everything in between – is heavily indebted to it.'

The confidence reaches a peak a few lines later: 'Though the Cinema of Isolation has hinged so strongly on this retrograde male fantasy, it need not continue to do so. The Oedipal framework remains a formidable challenge to movie makers wishing to represent the physically disabled experience with some measure of equity, but it is not insurmountable.' At this point on page 323, we are four lines from the end of a long book, and it begins to look as if the author has left it rather late to show us how the future can be made to differ from the past.

Here is his attempt at it: 'If movie-makers, disabled and able-bodied alike, can break away from this narrative structure that has served as the foundation for the whole of mainstream narrative media (and indeed the whole of patriarchal society) and pursue alternative strategies for telling their stories, we may at long last see some real progress.'

In the course of a single paragraph the Oedipus complex has gone from being one factor among others in the shaping of cinematic images of disability, to being the strong hinge of the genre, and finally to being the foundation of the entire society that makes and consumes the films. The Freudian tail has wagged the critical dog throughout *The Cinema of Isolation*, but with this particular convulsion even a sympathetic reader may wonder whether the doggedness which is the book's chief virtue is merit enough.

What is needed is a study that takes disability less for granted as a category. Something of the sort is attempted by Lennard J. Davis in his ambitious and intermittently thrilling book *Enforcing Normalcy*, published in 1995 by Verso. His title gives fair warning of polemical intent, the subtitle being rather more neutral: *Disability, Deafness and the Body*. As he puts it, 'disability as a subject is under-theorized – a remarkable fact for this day, when smoking, eating a peach, or using a bodily orifice are hyper-theorized . . . The general population does not understand the connection between disability and the status quo in the way many people now understand the connection between race and/or gender and contemporary structures of power.'

Davis starts as he means to go on, with an epigraph from Aristotle (*The Poetics*) that defines those born disabled as outside the scope of rights: 'As for the exposure and rearing of children, let there be a law that no deformed child shall live.' This is hostility *a priori*, a pre-emptive holocaust.

Davis practises what might slightingly be called a politics of punctuation. He seeks to insert inverted commas round the word 'normal' in whatever context it is employed, and to confer an initial capital on Disabled, on the analogy of *Black* as against merely *black*. The upper case of absorbed identity as against the lower case of untheorised experience.

Even Davis's euphemisms, with few exceptions – 'mentally delayed' hardly seems an improvement on *retarded* – show less embarrassment than a sly instinct for destabilisation. He accepts the term *disabled* as being older than 'handicapped', closer to neutrality, and then gets to work on the less examined term: able-bodied. He prefers a term which emphasises the precariousness of what it is more comfortable (for those with an interest at stake) to imagine as stable. He uses 'temporarily abled' – that is, occupying a privileged and correspondingly ignorant interval between the uncontrol that follows birth and the uncontrol that precedes death.

Davis plays a game of epistemological striptease when it comes to declaring what *his* interest is: 'Here we come to a point I am sure many readers are asking themselves: is Lennard J. Davis a person with disabilities? And what is his disability?' Is he disabled himself, and vulnerable to a charge of special pleading, not to mention the fractionating, factionalising questions about whether the deaf can speak for the blind, the blind for the wheelchair-bound? Or is he himself *temporarily abled*, gaining in authority but losing authenticity? As he puts it, 'Can someone without disabilities ever understand what it is to be disabled? Is there a subject position that one can occupy without being subjugated?'

Temporary mystification is rhetorically justified, as a way of illustrating a double-bind, showing that either answer to the question entails a loss. But there is something disingenuous about the next step in the argument: 'The question demands an answer. I must tell you the status of at least some portion of my body. Unlike other kinds of interventions around the issues of race, class, or gender, there is a powerful policing mechanism that demands I answer your question.'

In fact deployment of the authenticity detector is all but universal in identity politics. To be a Queer scholar married to a member of the opposite sex, for instance, is a circumstance that calls for some fancy justificatory footwork. (In the case of Eve Kosofsky Sedgwick, she explains that she is in effect a gay man trapped in a woman's body, whose apparently conventional domestic arrangements are mined with transgressive double-bluffs.) Davis's desire to establish a politics of disability that is *not* merely an identity politics is unusual and admirable, but he must be aware that the kind of critical writing he practises insists on the unmasking of discourses that pose as disinterested.

Davis prolongs the suspense, knowing that the answer, when he consents to have it squeezed out of him at last, will in any case confound the categories: 'I was born into a family with Deaf parents. My first "word" was uttered in sign language. The word was "milk", a sign I made through the slats of my crib. I grew up in a Deaf world, in a Deaf culture, and with a Deaf sensibility. So in this sense, I am not deaf (hearing-impaired) but I am Deaf (culturally Deaf).' He now has an acronym to describe his condition – he is a CODA (a Child of Deaf Adults) – and a sense that his liminal position, straddling the categories or falling between them, gives him a place from which to write.

He makes the valuable point that even disabled people have to make the leap of identifying with their category – just as men who have sex with men are in a sense not 'gay' unless and until they realise they are. A number of respondents in the 'Cleveland Cripple Survey' of 1918, for instance (a source not quoted by Davis), were 'amazed that they should be considered cripples, even though they were without an arm or a leg, or perhaps seriously crippled as a result of infantile paralysis. They had never considered themselves handicapped in any sense.'

Like many CODAs, Davis wanted to join the hearing world as soon as possible. This was also what his parents wanted for him, yet there is a sense in Davis that he betrayed them by assimilating – though that word seems too drastic in this context. It was only in his forties that Davis 'began to make a return', as he phrases it, to his childhood culture.

Enforcing Normalcy makes some sort of retrospective amends to Davis's parents for struggles he was necessarily unaware of at the time. In a footnote he mentions that he is also working on a memoir about his background 'which may or may not see the light of day' – a book to be looked forward to, if it materialises, but also incidentally an unfortunate formulation for someone with such sensitivity to prejudicial phrasing to use.

To see the light is one of the most ancient ways of saying *to be alive*, but it equates blindness with death no less for that.

The central claim of *Enforcing Normalcy* is that disability is a political category. Davis argues that it was only with the mechanisation of labour that workers needed to be physically interchangeable, and disability became a stigma. It would be useful to know, in this context, how many of the respondents to the 'Cleveland Cripple Survey' – the ones who didn't recognise themselves in the mirror of Handicap – were from rural areas or from milieux where mechanisation was not as yet a factor. As Davis expresses it, the demands of the factory system require 'another version of the body' as well as another version of time.

When disabilities are elided from accounts of historical figures, it isn't always clear whether this is because disability was not perceived as affecting a person's essence and ability to function at the time, or because of a conspiracy of tactful silence. Davis's list (which inevitably recalls gay culture's lists of the great ones claimed or outed) includes King James I – unable to stand at the age of seven, constantly leaning on the shoulders of others by reason of weakness – and Stephen Hopkins, who when he took the pen to sign the Declaration of Independence referred to his cerebral palsy by saying, 'My hand trembles but my heart does not.'

Davis asks whether those university administrators who resist the legitimacy of the disabled as a minority 'realize that when they encountered the work of Rosa Luxemburg (who limped), Antonio Gramsci (a crippled, dwarfed hunchback), John Milton (blind), Alexander Pope (dwarfed hunchback), George Gordon Byron (club foot), José [*sic*] Luis Borges, James Joyce, and James Thurber (all blind), Harriet Martineau (deaf), Toulouse-Lautrec (spinal deformity), Frida Kahlo (osteomyelitis), Virginia Woolf (lupus), they were meeting people with disabilities? . . . Why it is that when one looks up these figures in dictionaries of biography or encyclopedias their physical disabilities are usually not mentioned – unless the disability is seen as related to creativity, as in the case of the blind bard

Milton or the deaf Beethoven? There is an ableist notion at work here that anyone who creates a canonical work must be physically able. Likewise, why do we not know that Helen Keller was a socialist, a member of the Wobblies, the International Workers of the World, and an advocate of free love? We assume that our "official" mascots of disability are nothing else but their disability.'

Franklin Roosevelt's polio is not exactly absent from the historical record, though it was treated at the time (with a degree of press collusion now unimaginable) as something he had overcome. Yet in 1995 a memorial to FDR could be approved despite the fact that none of its three sculptures and bas-reliefs showed Roosevelt with wheelchair, crutch, brace or cane – the mechanical aids he in fact needed to approximate mobility. Davis quotes extensively from contemporary accounts to show how large the gap was between reality and the required image – a gap that had to be closed by FDR himself with careful planning and great pain.

As Davis puts it: 'In the perverse logic that marks the political imagination of the United States, only an aristocratic WASP could embody the aspirations of the working classes; only a physically intact man could represent those who were crippled by the ravages of an economic disaster.' This is perhaps suitably dry and cynical, but it's disturbing that the word 'cripple', hardly acceptable in a physical description, is permitted to return as metaphor. If the author of this book, of all books, doesn't see that all bodies are made to bear the burden of metaphor, but disabled bodies receive a second dose of disadvantage in that area, then there's not a lot of hope for the rest of us.

Politics is very much the business of deploying symbols in public life, and FDR couldn't opt out of that business and remain in politics. But having the body he had, how could he offer it as material for metaphor? By saying, 'My fellow Americans, your lives have been ravaged by the Depression as my body has been ravaged by poliomyelitis. Vote for me and together we will . . . ?' Together we will what?

To symbolise wholeness comes closer to escaping from the system of symbols than to symbolise imperfection. Is it really so surprising that another president with a debilitating condition, Kennedy, had his Addison's Disease cunningly masked by the way he was presented to the world, the pain of it referred back to the war? – a war wound, if short of disfigurement or amputation, being the only element of disability that can make a public man wholer than his whole opponents. The rocking chair which Kennedy used to lull his pain was turned into an eloquent prop signifying New England approachability.

An American president is an individual functioning as the embodiment of a country, but one particular physique must continuously underwrite the symbolic function. However adroitly the spin-doctors spin, a latent anxiety becomes patent every time a Ford stumbles, a Bush vomits, or a Reagan just plain forgets to duck. The individual lies of the press corps nevertheless map out a collective truth: that the body fights a losing battle. Yet in practice this does the disabled prospective candidate no good, since even a losing battle has the advantage over an apparently foreordained defeat.

One of the assumptions that Lennard Davis is most concerned to refute is that able-bodiedness somehow precedes disability, making disability a falling-off. His most striking suggestion in this area is that sign language might be the master category of speech, rather than the other way round, as is always assumed. People have ingrained in their minds a scenario that has all the plausibility of a dinosaur-and-fur-bikini exploitation movie, in which grunts and pointing gave way to rudimentary speech. But modern sign language is a true language, able to express any concept however abstract, fully equipped with a grammar traced in space, and processed in native speakers by Broca's region of the brain, which deals with language as opposed to gesture. The brain had an expressive potential that predated the larynx (relatively recent, at a mere quarter-million years old), so why should signing not have provided the armature for spoken language, which would at first have had only the advantages of being effective over distances and at night? The question isn't likely to be resolved, as between the claims of sign and speech. Davis's point is that the issue is never phrased so as to consider the argument of the minority. The majority grants itself a superiority that is indefinitely backdated.

In his preface Davis acknowledges that disability – he calls it 'the bodily state that dare not speak its name' – is anything but a hot topic in professional circles: 'When I talk about culturally engaged topics like the novel or the body [his previous books include *Factual Fictions* and *Resisting Novels*] I can count on a full house of spectators, but if I include the term "disability" in the title of my talk or of a session the numbers drop radically.' *Radically* is perhaps precisely the wrong word here, since what is involved is fear of examining the status quo by which one benefits.

It exasperates Lennard Davis that people who are self-consciously politically aware resist adding disability to their list of the modalities of discrimination. The example he gives is of people of colour who perceive disability as a side current likely to muddy the waters around the central issue of racism. To this position he offers a profoundly paradoxical rebuttal: disability needs to be added to race, class and gender because it is already there. The relationship between class and disability, for instance, is profound. Poverty causes disability, 'since poor people are most likely to get infectious diseases, more likely to lack genetic counselling, more likely to be injured in factory-related jobs and in wars . . . The chief cause of traumatic pareplegia and quadriplegia in American cities now is injuries sustained from gunshot wounds – and most of the people so injured are drawn from the lower classes, particularly from people of color.'

But if political exclusiveness frustrates Davis, a corresponding cultural exclusiveness among his intellectual colleagues in the academy positively outrages him. He denounces them in a passage of extraordinary and in some ways bewildering intensity: 'The body of the left is an unruly body: a bad child thumbing its nose at the parent's bourgeois decorum; a rebellious daughter transgressing against the phallocentric patriarch. The nightmare of that body is one that is deformed, maimed, mutilated, broken, diseased. Observations of chimpanzees reveal that they fly in terror from a decapitated chimp; dogs, by contrast, will just sniff at the remains of a fellow dog. That image of the screaming chimpanzee facing the mutilated corpse is the image of the critic of *jouissance* contemplating the disfigured, the mutilated, the deaf, the blind. Rather than face this ragged image, the critic turns to the fluids of sexuality, the gloss of lubrication, the glossary of the body as text, the heteroglossia of the intertext, the glossolalia of the schizophrenic. But almost never the body of the differently abled.'

What is being rehearsed in this violent projection of a scream on to the silence of the academy? Perhaps the fear that disability in our culture represents to the temporarily abled the thing that Freud posited as unavailable to the unconscious: death, death not as an idea but as a presence, death present in the body.

Davis's intellectual model is clearly Foucault, but he wishes, as so many other critics have wished, to derive a political agenda from analyses that warn against such a thing. He wants to say that disabled lives contain the buried truths of able-bodied lives, though Foucault seems never to have endorsed sentences with the word 'truth' in them. Having shown how the category of the disabled is historically constructed, he then wishes to empower disabled people, just as gay critics who pay lip-service to Foucault's archaeology of homosexuality rather resent his warnings not to take the created category as a new essence.

If gay identity seems pretty real to someone who suffers from its negative definitions, someone who is excluded from sexual expression, or the right to marry or to inherit from a lover, without a will being challenged by more orthodox kin, so disabled identity looks pretty secure to someone in a wheelchair facing a flight of steps. And no doubt it would be naive to expect the respondents to the 'Cleveland Cripple Survey' who did not see themselves as handicapped to remain indefinitely in the innocence of citizenship.

In theorising the origin of hostility to the disabled, Davis recruits Lacan rather than Foucault: 'The disabled body, far from being the body of some small group of "victims", is an entity from the earliest of childhood instincts, a body that is common to all humans, as Lacan would have it. The "normal" body is actually the body we develop later . . . One might even add that the element of repulsion and fear associated with fragmentation and disability may in fact come from this very act of repressing the primal fragmentariness of the body . . . The homeyness of the body, its familiarity as whole, complete, contained, is based on a dynamic act of repression.'

This is intriguing, but a long way from a politics of Disability. Lennard Davis has moments of something like naivety himself, when he attempts a definition and then passes on an anecdote: 'The person with a disability is just that – a person with some kind of limitation or difference. One student told me that her mother had no fingers on one hand. As a child she had never considered this particularly strange, and she was always surprised when strangers stared at her mother's hand. To her it was a loving, caressing hand that she might joke about, kiss, or hold. The point is not that she was habituated to what others might consider a horror, but that she had not received the instruction to cast the hand away.' It could also be said of Davis himself that as a child he didn't consider his parents' deafness an oddity – their deafness preceded his existence and he didn't question it until later. But then he did receive in some attenuated version the instruction to cast them away: 'In my growing up I identified with the Deaf, and yet, to be completely honest, I never wanted to be deaf. I wanted to be hearing, to do what the hearing did, and in many ways I sought to leave deafness behind me. But I discovered that what I was fleeing was not deafness *per se*, but the deafness constructed by the hearing world. My parents themselves, born in 1898 and 1911, lacked coherent political explanations about the Deaf world, growing up as they did before this era's activism. Their defense was to say "We are as good as anyone else" – the subaltern's defensive response.' By this account, just as Lennard Davis is Deaf without being deaf, his parents were deaf without being Deaf. This doesn't seem a satisfactory conclusion, if only because the son's Deafness was only two pages earlier attributed to growing up in what is now being unsaid, 'a Deaf world . . . a Deaf culture'. The sentence which distinguishes between deafness *per se* and deafness constructed by a hearing world is especially enigmatic.

Those born hearing-impaired in an era of activism presumably have more prospect of achieving Deaf identity, but it remains unclear in Davis's book how the Disabled can ever earn that elusive capital. In his preface Davis refers to his theoretical focus on deafness, describing deafness as 'the best-case scenario' for analysing general attitudes to people with disabilities. Yet this turns out to be true only if we define a 'best case' as an exception. Where the Deaf lead, the disabled by definition cannot follow as a group, because the political strategy of Deafness is to repudiate the category of disability.

According to this ideology Deaf people make up a *linguistic* minority: 'They feel that their culture, language and community constitute them as a totally adequate, self-enclosed and self-defining subnationality within the larger structure of the audist state.' Inability to hear and return speech is by this logic no more a defining characteristic than an inability to speak Spanish or Dutch.

The Deaf, as Davis explains it, having been reared in specialised institutions, tend to see themselves as different from people with disabilities who have no supporting network or shared culture. The Deaf have no desire to link their subnationality with other conditions where communication is problematic, such as autism or schizophrenia. Davis seeks to honour these arguments but is understandably troubled by them, since they represent less a trail being blazed that others might follow than a wall being erected in a new place, with a new agenda of exclusion. Not for the first time, a minority claims prestige at the expense not of the majority but of another minority.

Davis's arguments are distinctly queasy at this point: 'I would never say that a Deaf person and a paraplegic were the same. They are not. But to the ableist majority, they may be . . . It is not my aim to insult the Deaf by saying they are people with disabilities; rather, I wish to explore how people with disabilities, at the risk of insulting everyone perhaps, can be Disabled.' Even his book's subtitle (*Disability, Deafness and the Body*) keeps the categories tactfully apart.

It's certainly true that deaf people have a political presence that other disabled groups may envy. The last episode of student unrest in America was the successful campaign at Gallaudet in 1988 against the appointment of a hearing president, who did not seem to regard the learning of sign language as any priority. That campaign was in many ways the high point in the short history of disability activism, but Davis, recognising perhaps that even a subnationality constitutes itself by who it excludes, ends on a note of bleakness. He tells a few case histories of deaf people without sign language and with a limited ability to communicate, who have become stranded in the American penal system.

Junius Wilson was discovered in Cherry Valley mental hospital in North Carolina in 1993. He was ninety-three, and had been 'lost' in the system since 1925. In that year he had been arrested for attempted rape, and deemed to be mentally incompetent, though his incompetence was merely linguistic. He was never tried, but was later castrated as a sex offender.

Davis takes care to dispel the comforting illusion that such things could not happen nowadays. They still happen, because no state has a penal code including the concept of linguistic competence – mental competence is the only determinant, a criterion that someone who is unable to communicate can hardly meet. José Flores, for instance, has been in jail in Passaic County, New Jersey since June 1992, awaiting trial on various charges including kidnapping and burglary. Raised in a rural area of Puerto Rico, he had no access to appropriate education or a Deaf community. In his incarceration, he has not attracted the advocacy of the Deaf people who might seem to be his brothers and sisters, since to them he represents what they are trying to get away from: deafness as raw disability.

Davis's peroration deserves to be quoted extensively: Flores 'was never taught to sign, a skill that would have turned his disability into merely an impairment. His lack of normality makes it impossible for him to be processed through the judicial system. Had he just been poor and Latino, he would have fit the known categories and been tried and, given prevailing attitudes, convicted. But José Flores's impairment means that he is disabled, so profoundly disabled that he can never be released from jail, never be tried. Like part of a jigsaw puzzle that has been lost, he fits into no system. He is guilty of disability, and under a system that demands normality he will remain in limbo. In a recent discussion with his attorney, I found out that he will probably be committed to prison under a civil action as a danger to himself and others and placed in jail until such time as he is no longer a danger. Given the fact that he will never be taught sign language, that means he will be in jail for the rest of his life.' At the time of Davis's writing, Flores was twenty-nine.

In an ideal history of culture, *Enforcing Normalcy* would have appeared before *The Cinema of Isolation*, so that the dogged researcher of disability themes in the movies could have the benefit of the passionate academic's theoretical illuminations. (Instead Davis politely credits Norden's book as having alerted him to the extraordinary prominence of those themes.) Cultural interest in disability is so faint that the market can be saturated and even supersaturated by a single book. *The Cinema of Isolation* is likely to remain the standard work, without reaching any very elevated standard.

If Martin Norden had been exposed to the sophistication of Lennard Davis's thought, and to the fieriness of his paradoxical engagement with disability, he might have adopted a more rigorous approach. He might, for instance, have asked himself the apparently stupid but actually necessary question: What are films about disability about?

On the first page of his preface, even before his acknowledgements, Norden refers to the mainstream movie industry's 'fascination' with 'the physically disabled experience'. This last formulation bears tell-tale traces of euphemistic embarrassment – the physically disabled experience as against the Jimi Hendrix Experience? – but if it is sincere then it is already crucially wrong (no mean feat for a point in the book so early that the pagination is still in Roman numerals).

As all the evidence adduced in the book goes to show, if Hollywood has attempted to represent the disabled experience it has made an astoundingly bad job of it. So why not take another approach, and suggest that what is being represented is not disability? – or certainly not disability as an experience.

Martin Norden may teach film as a professor of communication at the University of Massachusetts at Amherst, but in his book he doesn't address the governing paradox of cinema. The movie camera shows us the outside of things, and the outside of people. In this sense film is a literal medium, and a literal medium has a crying need for metaphors. So when cinema wants to show a state of mind, it tends to show a state of body instead.

Films with a blindness theme tend to be about trust, films with a deafness theme tend to be about isolation. Both genres express the simultaneous fear of and need for other people. Films with a theme of wheelchair-boundness tend to be about a metaphorical powerlessness.

Disabilities on screen stand in for negative mental states, and clearly it's a good thing to turn a negative mental state into a positive one. But where does that leave real-life people for whom the conditions are not allegorical? When disability is metaphorical, there is no such thing as incurability. Cure becomes a moral obligation.

Gender intervenes in the metaphors, not as it does as a factor in real-life disability (as part of a triad with race and class) but in accordance with well-established fantasies. There can be something especially appealing about a blind woman on screen, someone who can't meet the gaze that appropriates her, while a deaf woman is practically advertising her need for a male intermediary between her and the world. Powerlessness is felt to be more threatening for a man than a woman, since power is inherently his domain, and so wheelchair-users in the movies are with rare exceptions male.

If this is exploitation by metaphor, then it doesn't have to be signally pernicious. To object to the various blind-woman-in-jeopardy thrillers would be to object to the thriller itself. If we have devised a genre that arouses and then dispels fears, we have to accept a vulnerable central figure (the bodybuilder-in-peril genre has never got off the ground). In the case of *Wait Until Dark* (1967) or *Blind Terror* (1971) the supposed blindness of Audrey Hepburn or Mia Farrow is more of a gimmick than a metaphor.

We know where we stand: the appeal for a director is that the heroine's unawareness of her danger, which must normally be conveyed by cutting from her danger to her unawareness of it, can be compressed into a single shot, with great consequent intensification of *frisson*. (It takes a different class of director to attempt a similar trick with deafness, but Hitchcock manages it in *Marnie* [1964], when he shows the heroine robbing a safe while an office cleaner gets on with her work in the same shot on the other side of a partition. The scene builds a mighty suspense as it moves towards Marnie's 'inevitable' detection, which is inevitable only if the office cleaner can hear.)

If Martin Norden wasn't so addicted to the form of words that gives his book its title, though, he might have noticed a different trend, one that in recent years has more or less driven out the old cinematic ideology of disability. Far from saying that disabled people are creatures of a different order, this new trend sees no barrier to the consumption of any lives whatsoever. The catch, of course, is that *we* can be like *them*, but the proposition is not reversible. They're not allowed to be like us.

Call it not the Cinema of Isolation but the Cinema of Specious Sharing.

There are traces of specious sharing even in fine and much-loved films. At some point in *My Left Foot* (1989), for instance, Christy Brown's psychological survival becomes a triumph of the human spirit. Obscurely it accrues to us, just as (in this context perhaps an appropriate comparison) an Irishman who wins an international prize immediately becomes British. Many people have walked out of screenings of the film inspired and energised, to the point of not noticing that the cinema where it was shown was about as wheelchair-accessible as a lighthouse.

The classic example of the Cinema of Specious Sharing, though, would have to be Penny Marshall's *Awakenings* from 1990. There are very many bad films, but *Awakenings* is significant in its badness. Its badness is its only significance. It isn't inertly bad but positively teeming with bad things, repugnant in its strategies and the manipulative meanings it imposes on real-life disabilities.

Between 1916 and 1927 there was a world-wide epidemic of encephalitis. A third of those affected died. The majority of those who survived developed forms of Parkinsonism which made them progressively contorted and paralysed. It was a peculiar paralysis, resulting from a deficit of dopamine in the brain, which could sometimes be outwitted in certain circumstances by those who suffered it. Over time, nevertheless, most of the sufferers were placed in institutions.

Then in 1969 a young doctor, aware of the paradoxical nature of the paralysis, had the idea of prescribing L-DOPA, a new drug which promised to restore dopamine levels and therefore physical function. The results were spectacular in the short term but not sustainable in the long.

Penny Marshall's film tells the story of the Parkinsonism patients, particularly of one played by Robert de Niro, but also of the doctor, played by Robin Williams. The doctor is shown to be almost as self-enclosed as the paralysed people he tends, pathologically shy sexually and easily flustered by the most routine social approach from the charge nurse played by Julie Kavner. Over that eventful summer doctor and patients come out of their different trance states. They share a learning curve, except that at the end of the film the patients sink back into their previous condition, while the doctor has attained a minimal but secure ability to function socially. He can go out for coffee with a woman.

To link the two 'awakenings' is of course a wholly grotesque narrative device: to suffer from a dopamine deficit in your brain is not a form of shyness. But the film has more crassness to offer. Much, much more. When the charge nurse is convinced that the post-encephalitic patients, though seeming little more than the living dead, might be worth some treatment, she rallies her forces. But the nurses are absorbed in watching soap operas on TV: she has to clap her hands to break into their absorption.

Here in effect the director adds the helpful gloss that we're all in a trance. We could all be more fully alive. Which makes this viewer want to growl: Sure, Penny, we're all of us in wheelchairs. But some of us can walk.

What makes *Awakenings* more than simply a schlocky piece of Hollywood tear-jerking is that it was based on a very powerful book of the same name, written by the doctor, Oliver Sacks. *Awakenings* the book was even a sort of landmark. Without being the product of a hippie sensibility, it offered an interpretation of illness that was in some sense holistic. At first Sacks could give his patients back their animation with L-DOPA, but over time their reaction to the drug became unstable. It was impossible to find a maintenance dose.

Sacks's conclusion was as much philosophical and psychological as narrowly medical: that an illness endured over decades, especially one that straitens sufferers' lives to the point of vegetation, becomes effectively part of the person. His patients couldn't resume their lives at the point where they had been left off, as much as half a century before. They could discharge energy and emotion, they could make a brief return to a changed world, but they had made an accommodation to their illness, and were dispossessed when it was taken away.

To coincide with the film, a new edition of *Awakenings* was published, with a cover chiming with the film poster and a new and rather star-struck appendix in which Sacks wrote about being on the set with the lead actors (whom he called 'Robin' and 'Bob'). But if the film people had made an impact on the book, there was no sign of a reciprocal invasion in the movie. What went missing from the film version were the people the book had been about.

In the book there were twenty or so patient case histories – after all, Sacks wanted 'something of their lives, their presence, to be preserved and live for others, as exemplars of human predicament and survival'. In Steve Zaillian's screenplay twenty-odd had effectively become one, the character played by Robert de Niro, Leonard. This wouldn't be so bad if this character was left unprocessed by the screenwriters. The real Leonard L. was a highly articulate man – when finally he could speak – a Harvard graduate who had been closing in on a PhD, aged twenty-seven, before post-encephalitic disease closed in on him. He also had a backlog of libido. In May 1969 he was masturbating for hours every day, not concealing what he was doing. In June he wrote his memoirs – 50,000 words' worth.

Of this complex human being virtually nothing survives into the film, certainly not those twin enemies of sentimentalism, the intellect and the libido. The twenty-odd have been boiled down to one, and then the one has been diluted with many times his original volume of syrup. If you ask someone to buy you two dozen free-range eggs, and he comes back with a can of Coke, you're likely to point out this wasn't what you asked for. In Hollywood, you say instead, 'Thank you for the sensitive screenplay, Steve. It taught me a lot about myself.'

There was a time when awkward inmates of institutions would be lobotomised or castrated by their keepers. Dr Sacks would never dream of such a thing – so why does he give his blessing to a film which makes the same subtractions on the symbolic level? Leonard L. in his book had an unruly body, which subjected the nurses at Mount Carmel hospital to insistent sexual harassment, and a sophisticated mind which had done little for decades but reflect on its own experiences. 'Leonard' in the film is all heart. The original has been mutilated in the interest of greater wholeness.

'Leonard' is an ordinary-Joe-regular-guy, whose sudden quoting of a Rilke poem, of all things, comes across as a bizarre aberration. And of course he doesn't, you know, touch himself *that way*. He has a chaste romance, mainly in the cafeteria of the hospital, with the daughter of a patient who has had a stroke. She thinks he works there, that he's maybe a doctor. Doesn't that just make your heart *break*?

When Leonard starts to be able to move and communicate, the nursing staff line up to be introduced to him. They use his name now, now that he's a person and not a dreary zombie. Now it's a privilege to meet him, where before he was just a sack of unresponsiveness. But the 'Leonard' to whom they are introduced has been turned by the screenplay into a child.

Before he published *Awakenings* in 1973, Oliver Sacks had written a single book, a technical book of less than universal appeal, on the subject of migraine. *Awakenings* put him on the map culturally. He did a lot for his patients, but in that sense they did a lot for him too. Their lives were the material which gave him his reputation. They were unexplored, hardly knowable territory, and he was the explorer of that territory.

When he sold his book to Hollywood, all that changed. If Sacks didn't mind being represented on screen as a virtually autistic virgin, every bit as removed from life as the people he sought to help, that was an eccentric choice but it was certainly his privilege. He did not however have the right to feed his patients' lives into Hollywood's blender of kitsch.

What Sacks did when he let the rights to the book be bought was a betrayal and also a fraud of a rarefied kind. He sold on that which he did not own. The lives of his patients, who trusted him not just to medicate their bodies but to tell their stories. He continues to refer to them in the current edition of *Awakenings* as 'not only patients but teachers and friends', which is charming, unless you feel that you shouldn't take any of these three categories of person to market.

The post-encephalitics tended to be elderly at the time the book was published, and only one was around by the time the film was made. Sacks and the stars visited her, and so did the director. 'Bob, Robin, Penny and I,' he remarks in his 1990 appendix, 'all marvelled at her toughness, her humor, her lack of self-pity, her realness.' Ah yes. Her realness.

It isn't even the case that Oliver Sacks sold the rights to the book and then kept his distance from the trivialisation of his work. He was employed by the production (hence his access to 'Bobby' and 'Robin') to teach de Niro and other actors how to behave physically as his patients had. How to 'do' post-encephalitic Parkinsonism.

The great strength of the book had been that it insisted on patients being more than the sum of their symptoms. Now Sacks was defining them as symptoms all over again, and showing actors how to impersonate their restricted movements, with no interest in their individual lives. He gave classes. 'I showed the actors how Parkinsonian patients stood, or tried to stand; how they walked, often bent over, sometimes accelerating and festinating; how they might come to a halt, freeze, and be unable to go on. I showed them different sorts of Parkinsonian voices, and noises: Parkinsonian handwriting; Parkinsonian *everything*.' Well, not *everything*. Just a crash course in the gimmicks.

The more photogenic gimmicks, at that. Sacks's patients tended to drool, but he gave the actors no drooling lessons. The film-makers wanted authenticity, sure, but not drool. Drool would be icky. They wanted, like, the broader picture. The nicer picture.

Perhaps Sacks wasn't aware of the use to which the director would put the tricks he showed the cast; perhaps he doesn't even notice when the movie is screened. But for instance there's a moment when de Niro is using a flight of steps in one direction, carefully, tentatively, and we are shown a toddler going in the other direction with a similarly touching gait. The disabled are really children, you see. Children at best.

Sacks even went on the publicity tour for the film. When asked, he did not seem to understand that he might be thought to be endorsing the film in any way, though he would be delivered to television studios for interview in cars sent by the film company, and ushered on set by the company's publicity people. Cuddly adorable bear-like man as by all accounts he is, Oliver Sacks seemed to be entirely insensitive to the rights of the people he had once, so long ago, been employed to look after. Yet that same season he was promoting his excellent book on deafness, *Seeing Voices*, which includes an account of the Gallaudet disturbances of 1988, when the Deaf students had decided that enough was enough.

The film of *Awakenings* is an extreme case, because the same person who wrote a classic account of illness, and tried to imagine some very inaccessible interiorities, also benignly watched over the turning of his work into an obscenely sentimental confection, and did what he could to help.

The appendix about the various adaptations of the book survives in the current paperback edition. The Acknowledgements thank the actors, the producers, the director and the screenwriter, though the movie tie-in cover has been replaced by something rather more classical. It no longer shows the doctor indulgently watching from the prudence of the jetty while 'Leonard', the patient who is also his friend and teacher, stands triumphantly on a rock in the ocean, trouser legs rolled up, reaching out to the sky with the sheer joy of being alive. The big kid!

Published in part by the *London Review of Books*, 1996. Thanks to Howard Schuman for his suggestion of a title.

Blind Bitter Happiness

My mother was born on 20 August, 1923, and christened Sheila Mary Felicity Cobon. At some stage she was told the supposed meaning of these names, or looked them up in a book. Her forenames meant by derivation Blind Bitter Happiness. As an adult Sheila found this augury ruefully amusing or faintly annoying, in its mixture of the appropriate and the hopelessly wrong.

Sheila was both a wanted and an unwanted child. Charles and Gladys Cobon already had a daughter, three-year-old Margaret ('Peggy'). What they wanted was not Sheila the eventual alto but a boy, who would in time sing treble in the same choir as his father. There was a name prepared for the invited guest: Derek. Sheila was a failed Derek, a fact which was not entirely kept from her.

Sheila was keenly aware of the difference in status, as far as her father was concerned, between herself and her sister. The family lived in Wembley, while Charles worked for a firm of marine engineers in Rotherhithe. As a matter of routine, Peggy would meet Charles's train after work on a Saturday. When Sheila was old enough to deputise for her sister in this coveted duty, Charles's first question would always be: 'Is Peggy ill?' This was before parenting skills. He didn't have the sense to wrap it up. To say: Lovely to see you, Sheila. Kind of you to come and meet your old man. How's your mother? Good, good. And Peggy?

As children, Peggy and Sheila competed over such important

matters as who could eat slowest. Peggy was particularly skilled at hiding, say, a straggling line of peas in the shadow of a folded knife and fork, so as to thwart Sheila's triumph and eat the stragglers with a relish out of all proportion to their deliciousness.

As a girl, Sheila's candidates for the title of Naughtiest Words in the World were *bosom* and *spasm*. She would say them in her head continuously, until the laughter burst out of her. Bosom spasm bosom spasm. A litany of taboos. A wicked prayer.

Sheila was ten when Gladys died, after a stroke, and it was Sheila who found her stricken, incapable, labouring for breath.

Ever after, Sheila was hysterically distressed by physical impairment, by paralysis and mutilation, even the malformation of a London pigeon's feet. A pigeon with fused feet was still a wounded symbol to her, and a flyspecked mirror held up to her of bedraggled suffering, loss of self. Her reaction was complex, being made up of both identification and disgust, the desire for things to be whole and for them to be dead. If anyone asked about this phobic affinity, she would refer to the conspicuous presence in her childhood of veterans injured in the war, but not everyone of her generation was so deeply affected.

In the months after her mother died, a new routine established itself. Sheila would come home from school first and let herself in, but was not trusted to make a fire on her own or for her own benefit. She would have to wait for Peggy's return before she could think of getting warm.

When Charles himself came home, he would cook supper, which would be chops or else steak, and boiled potatoes. Sheila was in a phase of revulsion against meat, and ate only the potatoes. At weekends the girls' Aunt Mimi, who lived in Rotherhithe, would cook Sunday lunch and prepare sandwiches for them to eat at school the next day, using the meat left over. On the way home Sheila would be revulsed all over again, seeing the wrapped sandwiches in the glove compartment of the car. She was prone to carsickness anyway, but the closeness of the meat made things worse. At school she would throw the meat away, convinced it smelled of petrol, and eat only the bread.

Those around her did not for some time connect the fact of her developing boils with her near-exclusive diet of bread and potatoes.

Charles was not a worldly man. His father had been an organist and had published a *Te Deum*: Charles himself not only sang in the choir but was a lay preacher. If he had a passion besides God and marine engineering it was trains. He didn't share his bereavement with his daughters, but then bereavement is not for sharing. If it can be shared, it is something other than bereavement. Still, Charles can't be accused of anticipating his children's needs with overmuch imagination. He did know, though, that girls need a mother. He found one for them.

Lilian, his second wife, was a schoolteacher in her forties. Her motives for the union are more obscure than her new husband's. Perhaps there was sly triumph in the casting off of a maiden name, at a time of life when the label Old Maid was firmly attached to her. Perhaps too, as a teacher who had met the Cobon girls in their mother's lifetime, she responded to Charles's appeal on their behalf, and to the challenge of shaping a child's character more directly than she could in the classroom.

It was 'a child' she had ambitions to shape, rather than children, and her first choice was Peggy. She would have had more of a chance if she had played her cards better. It was a mistake to insist that the girls both wear ankle socks and frilled red velvet dresses at the wedding. Peggy at fourteen thought herself too grown-up to be dressed as a child, almost a doll, and never forgave the ankle socks.

It was also a mistake to expect to be called Mummie, or at least to make an issue of it. Peggy would never call Lilian Mummie. Sheila would.

Now at least there was someone who noticed whether she ate properly or not. Boils stood no chance against Lilian. Lilian was also determined that Sheila should have a proper education, and in due course be financially independent.

This was in part a recognition that Sheila was bright, but also reflected a colder agenda. It was Lilian's feeling that women should always be financially independent, because women should have as little as possible to do with men anyway.

By the time she was fourteen, Sheila had been told by Lilian that she had never let Charles come near her in 'that way'. No carnal congress for Lilian, thank you very much. No bosom spasm.

What did Lilian think she was doing by passing on so grotesquely inappropriate a confidence? There are a number of possibilities. To establish as a general principle that Men Are Beasts. Or to offer reassurance that she was playing by the rules of the marriage: the girls' new mother, not Charles's new wife. Perhaps, too, it was a way of striking a bargain. Showing that she had no secrets from Sheila – a rare sort of trust. And trust must be returned.

By being mother of a sort to at least one of his children, without being functionally Charles's wife, Lilian effectively split the family in two. At one point she had a maid who performed some duties also for Sheila, but had instructions not to attend on Charles or Peggy. From there it was only a small step to separate the two half-households.

In her early teens Sheila was not expected to choose what clothes to wear – she would put on what was laid out for her, schoolday or holiday. So there could be no question of her being allowed to choose which person to live with. Lilian always said that when she was sixteen, Sheila would be able to exercise a choice, but it was clear that Lilian had fixed expectations of the choice.

Looking back as an adult (and a legally trained adult to boot), Sheila realised that Lilian was careful all this time to avoid making herself vulnerable to a charge of deserting Charles. What she wanted was to negotiate her demands from within the married state, not risk a departure from it. So Sheila would spend the time after school at Lilian's mother's house, 92 Upward Road, and then be brought back to sleep in the family home, the house with the grandly pretty name of Foxes Dale.

The prospect of being allowed to choose somehow suggested to Sheila that she was considered relatively unimportant. Charles hardly seemed anxious to claim her. Sheila didn't even particularly look like a Cobon, unlike Peggy, with her bony face and prominent eyes.

Sheila had masses of dark curly hair, cause for pride, and a nose she felt was beaky, cause for shame. There were other things about which she felt self-conscious. Her feet were so narrow that she would leave school-issue shoes behind, even tightly laced, if she ran upstairs. The man who operated the X-ray pedoscope in the shoe shop said gravely that she would be in a wheelchair by fifty. Did he think that she had been born with wide fat feet, and that the narrowing was progressive?

There wasn't actually a moment for Sheila of decision between guardians. Before she was ever sixteen, rights over her had imperceptibly been transferred to Lilian. She had been kidnapped piecemeal.

Sheila was too young to wonder whether the bisection of the family was a legally sanctioned or an informal arrangement. In later life she assumed it was informal, and therefore that Lilian took her because Charles didn't want to. It was not in Lilian's interest to tell her that Charles contributed to her maintenance, and that both parties had put their signatures to an Agreement assigning custody.

Lilian's care, which had from the start contained an element of overidentification, of vicarious living, shaded bit by bit into abuse. Sheila never used that word about her experience of subjection, even when it became ubiquitous so in the culture that people could be routinely described as abusing alcohol, or a racquet during a tennis match. It was 'only' emotional abuse, moreover: but abuse it was. Lilian pumped the breathable air out of the house, and replaced it with oxides of rancour, her grudge against the world.

Lilian would give her stepdaughter the silent treatment for three uninterrupted days, until Sheila begged to be told what her crime had been. It would turn out to be misbehaviour on the level of failing, at a school concert, to let the applause die down fully before coming on stage to announce the next item. Just *bouncing* on to the stage, full of herself in a common way.

By this method Sheila's mild extroversion was obliterated. Yet she never thought of Lilian's behaviour as normal. She had memories enough of the time before her mother's death to know that it was Lilian's coldly boiling rage which was disordered. She developed a hatred of confrontations and of 'atmospheres' which would last all her life.

Lilian had no real prospect of imposing a hatred of men on this adolescent girl. The part of Sheila's sensibility which had been so tickled by *bosom spasm bosom spasm* would later take joy in a school joke that Lilian would certainly have found smutty:

> *Girl's Father*: I should inform you, young man, that the lights go out in this house at 9.30 sharp.
> *Young Man*: I say, sir, that's awfully sporting!

If this was smut, it was more wholesome than what Lilian dished up daily.

Though Sheila wasn't temperamentally able to assert herself against Lilian, she wasn't altogether biddable either. On one occasion she ran away, and fulfilled her ambition, fuelled by teenage reading, of sleeping in a haystack. She loved to read. Once she'd been so wrapped up, perched half-way up a tree reading *Lorna Doone*, that she missed lunch, and didn't even mind.

From Lilian's reign onwards, although Sheila was widely regarded as bright, anyone who wanted to make her feel stupid could do so, and there were those who produced the same effect without intending or noticing, purely in passing.

One day, staying with a schoolfriend, she picked up a book

which her hostess's older brother was studying as part of his university course. She had been given his bedroom to sleep in, and law books were everywhere. This particular volume was called *Winfield on Tort*. She opened the book at random, and her eyes fell on a bracketed phrase: '(Married Women and Tortfeasors)'. There was something irresistibly comic about this combination – a tortfeasor sounded as if it should mean a small spherical sweet, honeycomb with a coating of chocolate. *I'll have a box of tortfeasors, please – they're the torts with the less fattening centres.* It happened that Maltesers were her favourite sweet. It seemed plain to her that somewhere lurking in the legal system was a great dry sense of humour. She read on, and found herself, if not exactly rocking with laughter, then certainly intrigued by the system that the book spelt out.

Sheila was a good student, and Lilian could hardly object, in view of her stated ambitions for her stepdaughter, to the plan of reading law in due time at London University, relocated in wartime to Cambridge. Sheila and her lodgings-mate smoked five cigarettes a week each, on principle. They were sending smoke signals. This was their way of signalling that they were approachable, not nuns or prudes but Modern Women.

In the evenings Sheila helped at a canteen set up for forces personnel doing courses: the bolder men called her the Girl with the Gypsy Eyes.

The war brought both enlargements of horizon and setbacks to Sheila. She had especially been looking forward to the appearance of American troops in the global conflict, but in the event she was disappointed. Their buttocks were large and slack; they looked nothing like the men in the movies. Could that be why they were called Doughboys?

In June 1943, when Sheila was nineteen, Lilian made some sort of appeal to Charles, desiring him to reinforce her authority with his. It was odd that she should make such an approach, when she had hitherto been so steadfast in separating father and daughter.

Charles had come to regret the Agreement that gave Lilian

her power, and seems to have made the suggestion that Sheila should return to his care, if she was proving troublesome. Lilian's response to Charles's solicitors was sharp. She would of course continue to respect the Agreement, and to offer Sheila parental affection as and when she proved worthy of it. It was not possible however to offer care to a headstrong young woman who was abetted in her opposition by outsiders.

She was disgusted by the motive of Mr Cobon's interference. If she had known he would seek to exploit the situation she would never have thought of involving him.

Charles asked his solicitors if there was any prospect of having the Agreement set aside. They told him this would only be possible by mutual consent, while in this matter the parties hardly seemed to be *ad idem*. By professional reflex they translated the idea of being in agreement into the dignified extinction of Latin. They did however object to Mrs Cobon's withholding information about Sheila's whereabouts, information to which he was certainly entitled.

After that, Charles adopted a more conciliatory, even a wheedling approach. He started his letters 'Dear Lily', and wrote a rough draft so that he could add a little more soap to the final version. He was grateful that she was doing so much for Sheila. He would send any gifts or pocket money to Lily rather than Sheila, for her to pass on as she saw fit. He would be grateful for an opportunity of seeing Sheila, in London if that was more agreeable to Lily. Perhaps he could take her to a show. He would of course meet all expenses.

Between the ages of fifteen and twenty-five, Sheila saw her father twice, and her sister not at all. The estrangement extended even to birthday and Christmas cards. The second meeting, when she was nineteen or so, was perhaps the rendezvous requested in the letter to Lilian. Charles surprised his daughter by treating her as a grown-up. This recognition was conveyed by the offer of a glass of light ale.

Charles kept the correspondence that had been conducted through his solicitors, and also the drafts of his letters of entreaty. After his death in 1980, aged ninety-four, they passed to Peggy, who rather oddly, since there was no bad blood between the sisters, didn't show them to the person they chiefly concerned.

There was no testamentary reference to the letters, so no direct duty was owed. Peggy had lived with and looked after her father all her life, though even in old age he had an independent streak. He would usually cook the dinner (steak or chops), took short holidays on his own even in his nineties, and wasn't above directing the occasional perfunctory kick at the current embodiment of Peggy's love for emotionally inadequate dogs. Quite properly she inherited the bulk of his modest estate.

So why hang on to those letters? It was as if she was back with the ingrained competitiveness of the nursery, hiding peas on her dinner plate from Sheila one last time. Only after Peggy's own death, in November 1995, did the letters, with their fragmentary story of an attempt to reverse an abandonment, find their way to Sheila. Even then she was shy of them, not in a hurry to learn what they implied.

After Part One of her degree, Sheila joined the Wrens, and was duly posted to a Wrennery in London. The premises were very grand, a town house in Cheyne Walk, and she slept in the ballroom, but she shared it with thirty-one other Wrens. Sixteen of them would want the windows open at night, and sixteen wanted them shut, so half of them were always simmeringly resentful. They were a mixed group: one girl never changed her clothes, until eventually they had to be taken from her by a little deputation of hygienic Wrens. A kangaroo court, come to lynch a dirty shirt.

There was drudgery, admittedly, in the effort to keep smart. You had to wash your white shirt every night, and iron it in the morning, either getting up at crack of dawn or queuing for the iron. Then after breakfast Sheila would walk across the bridge to Battersea and learn how to assemble radios. Luckily her hair was short: girls with long hair were always having it brush against the soldering iron. The smell of burnt hair became familiar, almost consoling. In the evenings she would do her Bates exercises, for perfect sight without glasses, before washing her shirt again. If the exercises had worked for Aldous Huxley, who had been as good as blind, why not for her?

Lilian's plan to make Sheila a career woman, independent of men, had the inherent drawback that the world of work was full of them. After the war and the completion of her degree, she was called to Gray's Inn as a barrister. By the time she met Bill Mars-Jones in 1946, it was no novelty to be romanced by a stranger.

He projected on to her a strongly romantic account of their future together. But he also – and this *was* a novelty – seemed bothered by his lost virginity, and introduced the subject with a jarring urgency into their early conversations. Why in the world does he think I care one way or the other? she thought. She also found it odd, if virginity was so important to him, that he seemed to entertain no doubts whatever about her own. This was almost unflattering enough to pique an interest. Did he think she'd had no offers?

Still, he had merits. One of them was that although he had served and even earned a rather smart little gong, he didn't go on and on about the war, the way so many men did. Maybe that was an advantage of the Navy, that either everyone went down together or they were all more or less OK. You could see action without seeing casualties directly, without being scarred or turned into some dreary hero. Bill had had his share of dangerous duty, on Russian convoys, but his closest brush with death proper came when he was posted to HMS *Hood*, sunk before he could take up the post.

It was almost a shock when Bill turned out to be Welsh. He'd lost the accent in pretty short order. His voice was musical, but he sounded more like someone on the Home Service than a country boy who was going to say 'look you' at the drop of a hat. Perhaps she had met the only Welshman in London at that time who didn't dream of being mistaken for Dylan Thomas.

Bill was still thrilled to be living in London, which made Sheila feel almost old, but in a nice way. Bill was still, deep down, the teenager who had hidden his face in fear at a screening of *King Kong* on his first visit to London, grateful to have his father sitting next to him – not because the old man made him feel strong by example, rather the opposite. His dad gave little suppressed yelps during the great ape's appearances, and prayed under his breath in Welsh.

Bill was smartly dressed, even a bit of a dandy, what with his tie always in a tubby Windsor knot, but it was pretty clear he wasn't a wolf. From the way he told her about his past philandering it was clear that a philanderer was what he was not.

It was only much later, on her first visit to Bill's family in North Wales, that she understood some of the fuss about his fallen sexual state. He came from a different world. She had been briefed to do without make-up and cigarettes, at least until Bill's widowed father got to know her. It was bad enough her being English rather than Welsh, without being *painted* and English, and the smoke signals that spelled out Modern Womanhood in Cambridge would convey the same all too inflammatory message here.

In Bill's world, the woman you married would be as pure as your mother had been – and he had mourned his mother intensely. Most men of twenty-one (his age at the time of bereavement) have passed the stage of thinking that their mother is a truly perfect being, but Bill had not. He had been unable to sleep at home when his loss was raw, and families in the village had taken him in for a few nights at a time, on a rota basis, until he could bear to return. The dead woman had been popular, but still there was an element of bafflement at Bill's behaviour, at his taking on so.

Bill would have it that his intended recapitulated his mother's virtues. She was entitled to expect a virgin, and he broke the bad news to her as soon as possible, before he lost his nerve. Never mind that his seduction technique with local girls had been not only rather successful but rather calculating: day trips by rail to

Manchester with their parents' permission, without chaperonage since no night away was involved. A brisk poke in an unshared compartment, with no fear – on a train without a corridor – of being seen. Getting into trouble precluded by a protective from Denbigh's leading dealer in rubber goods, a tradesman known to all as Lord Dunlop.

Impossible to go into these coarse details with someone of Sheila's refinement (whose railway-related adventures, by contrast, had tended to involve artificially missing the last train).

Nor did Sheila learn until much later that there had been a particular urgency in Bill's desire to get married. Looking at his hairbrush one day, he found it matted with shed fibres, and convinced himself he was going rapidly bald. He was already thirty, after all, and his younger brother David had gone bald in his twenties (admittedly David had made matters worse by forever wearing a cap).

Their mother had been all but bald, at least until the day of her Transformation. One day Father had said, Your mother has had a Transformation, and when Mam had come downstairs, radiantly smiling, the top of her head had a quite different aspect. No one in Llansannan used the word *wig*. Perhaps no one even thought it. It was always: 'Your mam's Transformation is so smart', 'Doesn't your mam look magnificent in her Transformation?' The sudden change in Mrs Jones's appearance was received in that Chapel community like a biblical miracle. It was not to be questioned. Lazarus was dead and just now came stumbling from the tomb. Mrs Jones was all but bald and has a fine head of hair.

Still, Bill thought he'd better get married, just to be on the safe side, rather than rely on a miracle. Better get a girl down the aisle while there was still some thatch remaining. So Bill looked through his address book, in search of women who were potentially marriageable, women in other words who had turned him down sexually. It wasn't much of a list.

If in fact Bill's hair had given him cause for concern, it must have been that he was going through some sort of seasonal moult. He continued to produce scalp fur in large quantities. Or perhaps it was that being married acted as a hair restorative . In later life Sheila, watching him brush it with daily devotedness, would experience a rueful pang. Hospitalised for an intestinal abscess in 1995, Bill would sweetly ignore requests to do physiotherapy, but would brush his hair for hours.

As a young man, Bill was known for his charm. He played the guitar, and would improvise comical calypsos at parties. At university (Aberystwyth and then Cambridge) he had done as much acting as studying: his advocacy was a professionally promising mixture of careful preparation and theatrical flair.

He seemed so very sure that he had found the right woman, and who was Sheila to say he was wrong? Her extroversion was a shadow of its former self after the Lilian years, and she would never find it easy to make the first move. With Bill, she might never have to. Very early on in their relationship, Bill started relying on her to prompt his patchy memory, to remember the names and histories of his friends – including those she hadn't met. She experienced a twinge of irritation flooded out by the joy of being needed, a combination of emotions she recognised as promisingly marital.

If Bill's father had taken to Sheila, despite Bill's fears, no such rapport could be expected between Bill and Lilian. Learning that Bill's father was a lifelong teetotaller, she wrote to him warning him that his son had a serious drinking problem. She did however agree, when this revelation seemed to have no effect on the proposed union, to take on the traditional duties of the bride's mother.

Her motive, though, was to sabotage them. She consented to Sheila's father attending, but Peggy received no invitation. The list of Bill's guests was firmly restricted.

Sheila was given away not by her father but by her Uncle Harry. Uncle Harry, a civil servant, could not quite grasp the concept of the bride's tactical lateness on her defining day. All Sheila's procrastination could not succeed in making her more than a little late, and she had the symbolic humiliation of arriving earlier than her groom. Bill and the best man, his brother David, had stopped off for a quick one – a sharpener – on the way to the church.

Sheila trembled so badly during the ceremony that she thought everyone must notice. She was sure her wedding dress was shaking right down to its train. When the ceremony was safely over and she arrived at the reception, a waiter offered her a mixed drink. Accepting, she asked what it was. The drink was so potent and so timely that it took away all her tension, but as it did so it took away also the name of this utterly necessary, utterly restoring drink. She was never able to remember what it was.

At the reception Bill's father, a teetotaller but not a fool, fixed Lilian in the eye while he drank a glass of champagne, without visible distress. But perhaps the sparkling wine in his glass was changed, as he drank it, into untroubling water: a reversed miracle-at-Cana, reworked with abstainers in mind.

Sheila hated the photographs of herself at the wedding and destroyed them. She did however permit the pictures of the couple in going-away clothes after the reception to continue to exist.

The newlyweds honeymooned in Ireland. For the first time Sheila ate potatoes that had been boiled in their jackets, a simple pleasure. They went to the Abbey Theatre, a sophisticated one.

Bill had been in charge of the arrangements and had got the dates wrong, so the marriage got under way not in the intended suite but in the only room their Dublin hotel had free for the first night: an attic room whose bed had comically squeaky springs. A bed like a prop in a bad farce, not the sort of theatrical fare for people who bought tickets for the Abbey.

On the way back from Ireland the two of them spent two nights with Bill's father and (fair's fair) two nights with Lilian. Lilian however had moved from attempted sabotage to a sort of flailing revenge, and claimed back from Sheila every present she had given her over the previous decade and a half. There was a particularly undignified squabble over a pair of ice-skates that were too small for Sheila anyway, but had not become quite worthless to either party.

Lilian unleashed revenge on a new front by sending the invoices for the wedding and reception expenses to the groom. Bill got the bill. This was a particular imposition since the newlyweds' assets at the time of their marriage amounted to (this is the statutory phrasing) two briefcases, two umbrellas and a £1,000 overdraft. As an index of the ominousness of that figure: the rent at Clare Court, their first home, off the Euston Road, was £3 a week.

Bill had stayed with a friend for a few days before his wedding, learning how to cook. What he learned how to cook was bacon and eggs, which he prepared for Sheila on Sunday mornings in the first year of their marriage.

Despite everything, Sheila didn't cleanly break with Lilian. Perhaps she felt free enough of that influence to be magnanimous. Perhaps she was beginning, even, to feel pity. Lilian came to call while Bill was away on circuit, and warned her fiercely of the danger she was in from poisoning. She must avoid eating anything that Bill had prepared or even touched.

Luckily one weekend Bill was so tired that Sheila cooked breakfast for him, and he never offered again. The danger of poisoning at his hands, never great, dwindled to nothing.

In the summer of 1949 Bill and Sheila took a holiday in Spain. Sheila was the linguist of the couple, but had only basic Italian to make stretch, so as to fit this rather different country. She had brought with her a new bathing suit which was smart by British standards, but as she saw on her first visit to the swimming beach, was potentially a scandal in Franco's Spain. It wasn't remotely a bikini, but it *was* a two-piece, and Fascist beachwear had not yet taken that path. The señoras chose to veil their midsections, while Sheila felt much more self-conscious about her (as she thought) knobbly knees than about her firm young midriff.

She felt less conspicuous when she was actually in the water, and undertook to teach Bill the long-overdue lesson of floating. Bill swam short distances with vigour, especially if women were watching, but had not yet learned to suppress the panic reflex that prevents relaxed floating, particularly when he was out of his depth. She tried to persuade him to put his trust in the basic unsinkability of the body.

Rather than run into town and buy a less challenging costume, Sheila and Bill decided the next day to find another beach. Sheila thought she had seen a party of nuns take to the water in the next bay. They would swim there. With them went a hotel acquaintance who had been a champion swimmer not so long ago.

The sea was rough, and thanks to the unfamiliar pleasure of being knocked off balance by big brusque waves they didn't immediately realise that they were being swept out and were out of their depth almost at once. As it turned out, the beach was notorious locally for its appetite, and the nuns glimpsed the day before were optical illusions, or else only paddling.

The hotel acquaintance resolved to swim back to shore and raise the alarm. Bill and Sheila needed only to stay afloat. They were soon separated in the water, however, and Sheila, knowing that floating was a very shallowly rooted skill in Bill's repertoire, gave him up for dead. Mentally she was widowed as she trod water in the heavy swell, waiting for death or rescue. She had time to absorb the full meaning of the phrase *lost at sea*.

The third member of the party managed with difficulty to reach the shore. He tried to explain the situation to the few people on the beach. One of them was a young man called Xavier Cremades, who as soon as he had understood, seized a child's inflatable boat – a tiny thing, only a toy – and charged into the water. He let himself be swept out in his turn, reasoning that this would bring him to the approximate position of the floundering English.

If Sheila had been visualising rescue, it was not in the form of what looked like a teenager holding on to an inflated toy boat rather smaller than an airbed. She had left her glasses with her towel and her book on the beach, but she had no difficulty seeing him approach. Her first thought was, What a clot! What a clot to be out in this sea with that cockleshell.

Then he swam up to her, and she realised that if this was a clot she should be thankful for it. He was nodding and smiling, having no English and prevented from gesticulating by the need to hold on to the infant lifeboat. Sheila gestured wildly in all directions at the heaving sea, shouting hoarsely *Il marito!* This was Italian, and she conscientiously repeated her distress signal in what she hoped was the corresponding Spanish idiom: *El marido!* Xavier Cremades had understood the first time, and the two of them started to search together.

Of course he wasn't Xavier Cremades to her then, simply a figure as unlikely and as inherently sunlit as a boy on a dolphin.

Each of them now held on to the little boat, and when a swell lifted them briefly up they tried to stare at different sectors of what was revealed to them. Sheila's eyes were less sharp than Xavier's, but she had the advantage of having a clearer mental image of what they were looking for: his dear hair matted with seaweed, the view of his pale back under the water that would mean he had forgotten yesterday's lesson in floating.

Bill was actually only a little distance away, unconscious and blue in the face but undeniably floating. Without being able to communicate verbally, Sheila and Xavier nevertheless managed a very tricky piece of manoeuvring. At this point the boat expands from its previously stated dimensions, and becomes big enough for a woman and a boy to heave an unconscious man on to it. So be it. Or compromise by saying that what they were doing, despite the emphasis on *teamwork* and *heaving*, was closer to slipping the boat underneath Bill, with the same happy result of flotation.

Sheila didn't dare to hope that Bill would be all right, even now. She had no way of knowing how much water he had swallowed, but at least he was breathing. On he breathed. She wanted him to cough, to clear his lungs of what they had taken in, and she managed with Xavier's help to turn him face down so he could safely vomit. For any more ambitious rendering of first aid, the little boat would have had to go through another, more drastic expansion, to the size of the vessel that eventually rescued them, a ship of the Spanish Navy.

Bill, Sheila and Xavier Cremades were briefly local celebrities. Some of the speculation was romantic – the English couple mistakenly thought to be honeymooners – and some of it mildly prurient. What sort of bathing suit would make even a foreigner have second thoughts?

The parents of Xavier Cremades gave a little reception in honour of the rescued visitors, once Bill had recovered. It might have been expected that any entertaining should be the other way about, which only made the gesture more charming. Pride too has a right to a party.

The event was announced as a tea and took place at the appropriate hour, but Bill in particular was pleasantly surprised by the Spanish interpretation of the meal, in which sherry of many different styles was served in tiny glasses. Tea the liquid featured only by special request. In that period of intense currency restrictions, this was a bash that few British tourists who hadn't been lucky enough to near-drown could hope for.

Bill was the one who had been despaired of, but Sheila took much longer to recover. Bill after all had known nothing of being despaired of, while Sheila's despair as she trod water out of sight of land, her sense of being rescued from Lilian and then abandoned all over again, had been an overwhelming mental event.

Back in London, with Bill away on circuit, Sheila started to show the early symptoms of some sort of breakdown. She was prey to obsessional thoughts. Sitting on a bus, she would be aware of people looking at her oddly, and only then realise that she had been silently weeping for some considerable time.

Medical advice was sought on her behalf: her state of anxiety was diagnosed, perhaps unsurprisingly, as an anxiety state. Being given a description and a name for what she was experiencing did her some small good in itself. The suggestion was made that she was reliving, in an oblique way, the marine despair she had experienced before Xavier Cremades paddled into view, of which she had no direct memory. Time would bring a cure, time that steals all wounds.

It became increasingly difficult for Sheila to let Bill out of her sight, and for a while she stayed with him on circuit. Bill's professional life, though, with its institutionalised male camaraderie of circuit mess and circuit dinners, its heavy smoking and drinking and sessions of frantic preparation through the night, was essentially a bachelor zone in a married life, and Sheila couldn't indefinitely share it.

Her symptoms gradually abated, though she would always think of a time 'before Spain' and a time afterwards, almost as if she had seen action with the International Brigade. The simmering of her brain as it cooled percolated through to her skin, and a few months after Spain she started to suffer from psoriasis. Stress is recognised to play a part in this condition. From then on, her quest for clear skin took over from any direct quest for emotional peace. Over the years, she tried a number of remedies, from acupuncture and PUVA-plus-sunlamp to (in the 1970s) methotrexate, which proved the most effective treatment for a condition which was never as obvious to others as it was to her. But why is that always offered as a consolation? To say the same thing with a different emphasis: it was a condition that impinged on her sense of herself as much as it affected her dermis.

Sheila had never wanted children, partly because every baby whose pram she had ever leaned over lost no time in bursting into tears. Bill, however, had always made it clear that he had a paternal destiny, and wanted four sons. Eventually, after a few years of marriage, Sheila leaned over a friend's pram and was greeted with a gurgle rather than a howl. It seemed to her that a jinx had been lifted. Perhaps children of her own would gurgle too.

Though she had never wanted children, it hadn't occurred to Sheila that they wouldn't come when they were called. They tried. They monitored cycles and ringed dates in the calendar.

On one occasion Bill was away on circuit, appearing in an important case, for almost the entirety of Sheila's time of ripeness. He would be cutting it fine. Never short of bravado or a lawyer's access to official favours, he arranged for a police car to meet his train at Paddington. The fretful sperm travelled under police escort as it went to meet the shivering egg.

Nothing worked. Every time they had 'tried' early in the day, Bill and Sheila would catch a show, hoping to cheer themselves up. But that year in the theatre the controlling metaphor of every play seemed to be infertility. Every time they sat down in the stalls, the curtain rose to show them a childless couple symbolising the emptiness at the heart of modern life.

Bill took tests, and so did Sheila. She knew she had only one fallopian tube, since the other had become gangrenous during her time as a Wren, and been removed. Now it turned out that the other one was blocked. She had an operation, in which the tube was blown through. Having your tube blown through conjures up a mental image of something from an Old Master painting, a bright Botticelli angel in a surgical smock setting sexless lips to the reproductive trumpet, sounding the high true note of fertility. It sounds like an Annunciation under anaesthetic. The reality of the operation was presumably a little different, but she fell pregnant in 1952.

Bill had wanted four sons, for no better reason than that in his Denbighshire childhood he had known a farming family with four sons, which had seemed ideally happy. It didn't occur to him that this family's happiness might have had other sources than brute number and gender of offspring, or indeed that happiness for a farming family may require sons rather than daughters, as it need not for a metropolitan lawyer. He wanted four sons; and so did Sheila.

Babies carry a magnetic charge which can act unpredictably on their carers, and it seems unlikely that Bill and Sheila would have treated daughters with coldness. They maintained a slush pile of tolerable female names, in case: Victoria, Hilary, Zoe. But in the event Sheila bore a son in February 1953, another in

October 1954, and a third in November 1957. After that her vindicated ovary rested on its laurels.

The 1950s was not a period in which men attended labour. Bill developed a rather abstract ritual in which he would mark Sheila's confinements by eating out in his favourite restaurant, Leoni's Quo Vadis, extravagantly, and donating a celebratory case of wine to the staff. He could never fully explain why he chose this gesture as against, say, giving something to the nurses in the hospital. But then it was his ritual, not anyone else's, and he didn't really see that there was anything to explain.

Sheila was morbidly afraid that she would drop her first-born, surprised that the nursing home allowed her to take him with her when she left. Shouldn't they have held on to him? They knew what to do. This must be a common fear in first-time mothers, but with Sheila the fear returned only slightly diminished with her second child, and full force with her first grandchild. It seemed that she needed to convince herself every time from scratch that she was not going to drop or break this leaking treasure.

Bill too was uneasy holding his children, until they were old enough to play with the boisterousness he enjoyed. His father Henry died before the third son was born, but relished bathing the first two, going so far as to tease Bill for his reluctance. But then as a farmer he was used to handling livestock; possibly he was reminded of dipping sheep.

Henry's hands were steady, while Bill's had tremors, tremors both gross and fine, which after he gave up the habit in the 1970s he attributed to his heavy smoking. Sensibly he magnified his vices once they were past, and concluded that his lifestyle was now fine-tuned for longevity. Drink he gave up only for short sprints of abstinence, at health farms in the 1980s.

Early motherhood was the happiest time of Sheila's life, expressed by her in the formula *I knew what I was supposed to be doing*. From parenthood she had expected no enhancement of self, but that was what she experienced, or at the very least a lifting of conflict.

Her thirties and early forties were lived by Sheila as her prime. She had children and some help with them, au pairs at first foreign and later Welsh: Jutta, Gisela and Ceri – remembered in no particular order as the one who danced on tables. The one who had a pregnancy scare. The one who married a policeman, and turned out to have been methodically sweeping her cigarette butts under the carpet of her room. Sheila had a successful and devoted husband, who spent much time away but who could be relied upon for a ritually caressive phone call at least once a day.

Soon before the birth of their first child she and Bill moved into No. 12 Gray's Inn Square: soon before the birth of their second they moved to a much larger flat opposite, at No. 3. Both rents were cushioned by Gray's Inn, which had yet to feel the vulgar necessity of getting the most out of its assets.

Gray's Inn had suffered considerable damage during the war. They were the first tenants of the new No. 3 Gray's Inn Square, rebuilt in a paraphrase of the original's Georgian style, and could even modify some of its specifications. So the windowless room at the end of the hall, designated a wine cellar, was instead added on to the sitting room, making it L-shaped. A cupboard inside the front door was adapted to contain a spiral staircase: the extensive attics thereby made accessible were turned in due course into a children's bedroom, a playroom, a little gym complete with horsehair mats, rings and trapeze, and a further room to accommodate a growing model railway layout.

This garret, lit only by skylights, was occupied by sons long after Bill and Sheila might have hoped to be free of them, despite the low lintels and the childish beds, two foot six wide, that were the largest that could be carried up the staircase.

Above the attics was the roof, which Sheila could reach up a ladder on sunny days so as to assuage her psoriasis with a tan. On one side the flat overlooked Gray's Inn Walks: Sheila lay in the bath when big with her second child, soon after moving in, and watched sunlight through mature, even overgrown, London planes. On the other side was Gray's Inn Square, also well planted with trees, where babies could be left in their prams with no closer watch kept on them than a mother's casual eye from three floors up.

In those days the ozone layer was as plump as a fresh pillow, though the aerosols that would dent and crease it were already proudly displayed in select bathrooms and kitchens, and sunlight was still considered good for babies. Ten minutes' walk away was Coram's Fields, with playground equipment and a marginally earthier social mix.

Ten minutes' walk in the other direction were Bill's chambers in the Temple, where Sheila's maiden name (under which she had practised) was also on the door. It was possible for her to think of herself as being in the informal sense 'out of practice'. Not that she missed the Bar, and her inglorious career largely devoted to uncontested divorces.

Sheila hadn't practised for long. When novice lawyers stand up in court and speak, they either experience a swelling of chest and voice and brain, an ability to fill the high-ceilinged space with compelling audible logic, or they remain exactly as they were before. She was the second type of lawyer, and realised that she would never know the barrister's joy of being given a red bag to replace her blue one.

This is a ritual recognition by a silk of a junior's outstanding contribution to a significant case, but she knew it was something more: the blue bag changing colour as it leaves the alkaline environment of mediocrity.

She was better suited to law reporting, despite the mad rush to get copy to *The Times* at Printing House Square before five o'clock. She went back to law reporting for a term after the birth of her first son, until she was offered work she could do from home, sub-editing the *Weekly Law Report*. Her workload could be within reason contracted and expanded. She had passable shorthand, and made her sons' eyes widen, when they were only a little beyond The Cat Sat on the Mat, by demonstrating her favourite Pitman hieroglyph, the expert arbitrary squiggle that meant *necessary*.

Still, a door-tenant always has a foot in the door, and the door with her name on it was only a short walk away from Gray's Inn. Not that Bill often attempted the walk home from chambers: growing professional success allowed him to indulge the innocent vice of a taxi addiction.

Her lull of fulfilment as a mother allowed Sheila a discreet expansion of personality. After driving the children to school, she would make herself a cup of coffee and sometimes even feel that she deserved it. She was always tense in her pleasures, as if at any moment she might be told she hadn't earned them.

It took her many more years to throw off the conviction, instilled by Lilian, that reading for pleasure by daylight was immoral, and it required some steeling of nerve on her part to take up so much as a newspaper before sunset. But she signed up for dance lessons with Bill, who took with surprising agility to that not very Welsh dance, the tango. Only the bossa nova, when that became fashionable, flummoxed them with syncopation.

Sheila had no instinct for housework, but learned to run a household by a sustained act of will. In the end she was even able to derive a penitential satisfaction from a campaign of spring cleaning waged with the proper fierceness. One legacy of the war years was that she found it psychologically very difficult to throw food away, and would hang on to an egg, for instance, if it had the slightest whiff of viability about it. The memory of scarcity carried over into something subtly different: a disbelief in abundance. Far from hoarding supplies, as might be expected from someone who had experienced years of rationing, she never acquired the habit of buying in bulk, preferring to shop every day long after supermarket habits had made inroads into the lives of the middle classes.

Sheila's neighbour and best friend Cynthia, one of those 'best friends' whose differences are savoured as much as their similarities, loved running her home and expressed her personality in intensely feminine touches like the collection of little cats on her mantelpiece. Sheila so relaxed in these years that she felt it was legitimate for her too, career woman or no, to collect something ornamental. She decided on bulls rather than cats, not realising that cows outnumber bulls, on the market stalls of the world, by thousands to one. Finding a bull she liked became a challenge in the short term, and a minor annoyance in the long. Finally she changed the rules of her hobby so that anything quadruped and of bovine aspect was admitted.

In her continuing education, which she pursued strongly in these years, Sheila showed both an appetite for knowledge and a strain of masochism. The City Lit (City Literary Institute) was ten minutes' walk away from Gray's Inn, and offered tuition in a huge variety of subjects. Yet over the years Sheila tended to choose classes that would make her feel slightly inadequate – not French conversation but French grammar, not a continuation of long-ago piano lessons but a grounding in Harmony and Counterpoint. Why brush up on a Chopin prelude when you can be notating a juicy retrograde inversion? She seemed to be seeking a sort of mortification of the intellect by this recurring impulse to take a course too far.

It was as if she needed to prove to her own satisfaction that she wasn't really all that brainy, and consequently that she wasn't wasting herself in the life she had. When she started studying Welsh, she not only set herself to running the gauntlet of that language's notoriously difficult consonantal mutations, but found an area of study where she would always by definition perform less well than the native speaker she had married.

Bill and Sheila and their sons spent the famously idyllic summer of 1959 in Rhosneigr, a village on the west coast of Anglesey. Rhosneigr with its beaches and sunshine seemed to offer an even more propitious setting for the happiness of children than Gray's Inn with its square and its gardens, and the next year Bill used his inheritance from his father, who had died some little time before, to buy a house a little outside the village. The white house he chose (always called The White House, with no presidential irony and no recourse to Welsh) had the great advantage of being separated from the main road by an extensive common, so there was a strict limit on development in the immediate area. Fourteen steps led down to the beach. In September gales, spray would blow from the breakers to strike the kitchen windows with considerable force.

The sea. One day in the early 1960s Sheila was swimming with her two older sons, while Bill rolled up the trouser legs of his Prince of Wales check suit to paddle. Suddenly Sheila saw that her boys were swimming out of their depth. As she reached them, she realised that she was barely in her own, and where she put her feet down they met not sand but rock.

She then managed the difficult task of grabbing her children and half-swimming, half-wading with them to safety. She wanted to alert Bill to a crisis without letting the boys know this was anything but a game. And in fact they had no sense of danger in the water, although they were marked with different memories of the event. One son, looking down, was mesmerised by the sight of mother's blood swirling thinly from a gash on Sheila's leg. The other, looking to shore, was awed by the sight of his father rushing fully clothed into the water. It was only Bill's willingness to endanger his Prince of Wales check suit, and the sodden banknotes from his wallet, which dried out slowly on a radiator for the rest of the day, that made the swim seem to contain anything momentous.

If Bill and Sheila collaborated on rescue, that day, they were not always so secure in their teamwork. Every generation should have at least one complaint, properly filed and docketed, against the one that went before. That's good form. It prevents bad feeling. The complaint of her sons would have to be that Sheila's hatred of confrontation led her to accept a discrepancy in disciplinary styles.

She didn't punish physically, and Bill did. Bill's punishment normally had the spontaneity that is its excuse or mitigation, but he sometimes fell back into a lawyer's habits. He might cross-examine, looking for inconsistencies, and in the face of denial he would gather evidence. By the time punishment came to be delivered, there was a coldness to it, made worse by his saying, 'This is for hurting your mother', when the sons knew that if she was there she would extend her mercy.

Between them Bill and Sheila wrote a script by which the male parent acquired a certain vengefulness. Indirectly therefore they also shaped their sons' particular versions of the sentence starting 'If I have children I will never ever . . .', and often running to many thousands of clauses, which constitutes the mental life of a teenager. A sentence like the tie-breaking slogan in a newspaper competition.

Sheila's hatred of atmospheres could sometimes prevent her from intervening. Otherwise her life offers no support for a trickle-down theory of trauma. In general the damage done her trickled down only into herself, and wasn't allowed to spill out over others. Is it a characteristic of women as opposed to men, or of the abused as against the respected, that they absorb injuries rather than pass them on as they should? Great abuse, of course, breaks the pattern by exceeding any power to absorb.

In 1969 Bill, after an escalating series of recorderships (Birkenhead, Swansea, Cardiff), was made a High Court judge. Such an appointment carries with it a knighthood. Bill glowed with prestige, and talked sweetly to Sheila about having made a Lady of her at long last.

Sheila was wary about having a title, often too shy to include it when asked her name. She was moving now in a world of compliments and stylised attention for which nothing in her background had prepared her. Lilian had not used compliments; she preferred the other weapon. Sheila came to assume that most of the attention she was receiving was either mildly or intensely false, and greeted it with a smile of blankness. One of the things she enjoyed about the winter sports holidays in Austria which the family took at this period was that social life *après-ski* for once had no connection with legal London and its tortuous skirmishings.

In her forties Sheila undertook two small pieces of editing on herself: she deleted her glasses and she rephrased her nose. She had already tried contact lenses, rather earlier in their technical development, when they covered the entire eyeball and gave those who could tolerate them a permanently startled expression. Sheila had not been one of those who could tolerate them for more than a few minutes at a time, but now that lenses had shrunk to a corneal discreetness she was more successful.

The decision to have an operation on her long-hated nose was mildly unusual in her social circle at that time. But then her motives too were unusual. She wasn't trying to make herself attractive to a new audience, or even an old one. The decision hardly involved other people at all, but it wasn't slackly narcissistic. Sheila was engaged on a rather effective exercise in what would now be called something like self-esteem management. She rid herself of neurosis about her body the way squirrels rid themselves of ticks.

Squirrels, supposedly, pull out a tuft of fur and hold it above their heads while they wade hoppily into a river. It may help to imagine them holding their noses with the other little hand, as the water rises round their heads. Understandably the ticks swarm upwards on to the decoy tuft. The submerged squirrel then simply flings away the tuft, and regains the safety of the bank. The infestation is over.

Sheila focused her self-hatred on her nose and then flung it away. Her new nose wasn't even quite what she had specified, which had been something jauntily snubby (*tip-tilted* was the word she used), but she had no regrets. The new nose was *not* her nose. That was its virtue and justification. Passing a mirror, she could meet her eyes without rancour.

In May of 1973, leaving Moorfields Eye Hospital at the foot of Shaftesbury Avenue, where she had been doing voluntary work, Sheila made a small dent in a Ford Transit van. The van made a much larger dent in her.

It was a rainy day, with a wind, and Sheila may have held her umbrella in such a way that she could not see the approach of the van, released from the traffic lights nearby and bounding towards her. She was certainly much preoccupied at that time with the fate of her best friend Cynthia, who was suffering from a bone disease. These contributory factors have to be reconstituted artificially, since she had no memory of being struck. Like her despair at sea, these were some of the many moments that go missing from a life: missing but immense, the amnesias of ecstasy and accident.

An ambulance was called, to take her to the Middlesex Hospital not far off. Sheila was alert enough to give a name when asked for one, but not quite alert enough to give the right one. The name she gave seems to have belonged to the last person she had talked to, during her morning stint of wheeling round the trolley of cassette players and books on tape.

At the hospital, she was booked in under the name she had given, and was X-rayed. No one, however, looked with any attention at the resulting plates, so it was not noticed that she had suffered a comminuted fracture at the base of the skull. *Comminuted* is posh for *like a little jigsaw*. There was only one superficial injury, to the scalp, so they sewed that shut. In the process they sewed hair into the wound, which subsequently became infected.

Of all the professionals through whose hands she passed that afternoon, it is only the ambulance men who emerge with any credit as diagnosticians. They at least realised that this was a woman who wouldn't be in good shape any time soon, and wouldn't be asking any awkward questions about the disappearance of her earrings.

Sheila's medical problems didn't end with the little jigsaw of skull fractures. There was also the question of the contrecoup injury. The brain suffers when a sharp blow causes it to strike the side of the skull away from the impact. The brain suffers.

Sheila's first bit of good luck that day was that an acquaintance, who had also done some voluntary work at Moorfields, was told by the staff there that her friend had been knocked down and was now in the Middlesex. Someone therefore turned up at the hospital who was able to clear up the question of the name, and also to sit with Sheila long enough to realise that she wasn't merely shocked and confused but seriously ill. The pressure of blood in the brain was building up to a dangerous extent. She was beginning to have small stroke-like seizures on one side of her body.

From this point on, her luck changed abruptly. At last the X-rays were looked at properly, and John Firth, a brain surgeon with an experimental technique, was alerted for duty. Messages could finally be sent to Bill in court in Cardiff, and relayed by him to the sons, at their various educational establishments.

John Firth operated for five hours. He was a good surgeon, so good in fact that he dreamed of something better. Subsequently he stood as Parlimentary candidate for the constituency of Orkney.

He had already started operating by the time any family member was able to attend. The technique he used involved removing an area of bone and refrigerating it for later reinsertion. In the meantime the brain would be able to expand after its trauma, and if there was a complication there would be no need to cut healing bone all over again. From the point of view of an era of keyhole surgery, this seems more like barn-door surgery, but it was the state of the art in its day. One of the first things that Bill was told by John Firth, when he arrived, was that this was a good time to have a neglected comminuted fracture of the skull and consequent subdural haemorrhage. A few years ago there would have been no hope, and he had used a new ventilation technique which allowed him to operate for longer, and so be more thorough.

Even so, he wasn't exactly optimistic – to the extent that anyone wearing rubber gloves stained with the blood of a man's wife can communicate optimism to him. Sheila might recover physical mobility and mental power; she might lose either, or both.

In fact her recovery was good. Sheila's first gesture on regaining consciousness, even before she had taken in what exactly had happened to her, was to reach a hand up to her nose. It was safe, it was still there: the new improved nose, the nose she could live with. Only then did her hand go further up, to explore the alien head-dress of the plaster cast that now protected her head.

The trapdoor of bone from her head was kept in a fridge for six weeks. She was told about it in terms of a tennis ball. Bill told her that a piece of bone the size of a tennis ball had been removed. A tennis ball, a rough sphere. Had they taken some brain as well? It was confusing, it wasn't reassuring, this domesticating description of what was gone from her head.

But then we make clumsy assessments of the size of delinquent body parts. If it isn't sport it's fruit – it's always either sport or fruit. Of swollen testicles or sinister growths, we say that they're the size of a tennis ball, or the size of a football. The size of an orange, the size of a grapefruit. Pathologists perhaps sometimes see things they compare to watermelons or medicine balls.

What Bill meant was that the piece of skull that went missing from Sheila's head, and was then reunited with it, was the size of a flattish section of a tennis ball, or the *slice* of an orange. In a separate operation, the little area of bone that had gone septic after hair was sewn in her wound was cut out. The size of a marble, the size of a cherry.

In a way, when she reached her hand up that first waking day in hospital and met the firm reassuring prow of her chosen nose, what she felt was a mirage. In a manner of speaking, her nose was missing, and didn't come back. Sometimes it seemed that doctors could do anything these days, that they could open an inspection hatch in the brain and knot the dangling wires together, but they couldn't bring her nose back. They couldn't do that. Her nose was dead, or at best in a coma.

Whether because the sensing fibres had been flattened by the van's impact, or because the area of the brain that interpreted their signals had been closed down while the blood pressure built up unnoticed, Sheila never smelled anything again, not fresh bread nor burning hair. The technical term for this is anosmia. Strange: loss of sight or hearing are privileged with an

Anglo-Saxon term, while loss of smell remains in Greek, as if this is a rather fancy deprivation. Never mind that smell is the most basic sense, the one that crouches lowest in the brain.

Her sense of smell was the only absolute loss from the accident, and a good bargain by any standards, compared with how her prospects were announced on the night of the operation. She had sustained damage to the trigeminal nerve that runs down the side of the face, and it was a long time before the neural frazzling settled down, giving her relief from adjacent areas of numbness and a tingly distorted sensitivity.

Her hair grew back from its pre-operative shearing, though less curly than before and perhaps less full – but then few women of fifty (an age she reached a few months after the accident) are natural casting for Rapunzel. She had kept the shape of her chosen nose, losing only its function. Yet loss of nasal function is not nothing.

The structural logic of perception dictates that if you are nose-blind, nose-deaf, then you are palate-impaired, 'hard of tasting' as people are said to be hard of hearing. You may sense only the basic categories of taste as they are exemplified by what is actually in your mouth. What happens on your palate is no longer vivid dinner, but your taste-buds attempting a slightly muzzy after-dinner game, a round of charades. Spice or condiment, two syllables, let's see, must be garlic. Ginger?

You may have a sort of speckled insensitivity, able to detect some subtle flavours, defeated by ones which your fellow-diners pronounce strong. Texture in food tends to become more important in this domain of straitened sensation, celery's crunch being less elusive than its tang. If you have weight to spare, you will tend to lose it: having your jaws wired is a clumsy procedure compared to having the wiring of your nose disconnected. Without the flaring alarms of the nostrils sending any signals, you will have to remind yourself to eat, and if you are slim, like Sheila, you must guard against unhealthy weight loss.

This was a period in which brain surgeons were just

beginning, while talking to relatives of those on whom they had operated, tentatively to invoke comparisons with computers. In 1973, when even a major hospital such as the Middlesex had no great investment in hardware, and private individuals were even less familiar with the subject, to say that a brain was like a computer was to make a rather abstract statement, but at least it might convey the information that an injured brain heals differently from a broken leg. Bill was told that with luck Sheila, though technically brain-damaged, would retain her skills and her memories. Important 'files' of memory in damaged tissue would somehow be transcribed, in the weeks to come, on to fresh pages of the mind. The word 'file' sounded old-fashioned, even bureaucratic; it had yet to take on a modern overtone. It suggested tall cabinets of olive-green metal.

It was likely that Sheila's short-term memory would be impaired – the idea seemed to be that it would get squeezed out by the demands of all that transcription – though the prognosis overall was remarkably good.

Sheila gingerly took the morning sunlight in the little hidden garden of the hospital. During those early days and early nights, dozing or solidly asleep, Sheila was visited by marvellously humdrum dreams. She dreamed entire days of inconsequence, from morning tea to evening toothbrush, while her brain absorbed the fact of damage.

The transcription was certainly accomplished, but there were perhaps hidden costs. Sheila was bound to feel more anxious about her mental quickness. No one to whom the label of *brain damage* has been attached will venture into conversation without subliminal hesitation: am I talking sense, am I even using language? Perhaps I'm talking in numbers, and people are only pretending to understand out of politeness, or for their own reasons.

After 1973, Sheila would become unduly anxious about the pronunciation of disputed words, words like *controversy*, *decade* or indeed *dispute*. At moments of trivial stress she would run out of words altogether and resort to a small handful of coinages, so that *I've spilled a bit of wine on the carpet* came out *I've spoobed a bit on the doo-dah-day.*

She had never had much taste for the sort of film or play that keeps you guessing, for suspense of any ambitious kind, but after 1973 indifference turned to positive aversion. All it took was one plot twist or unexplained development and she would defensively withdraw her attention, convinced that in her stupidity she had missed something vital which would make the entire plot clear to everyone else in the world.

She found it harder to make decisions, particularly about trivial questions. She would spend what felt like absurd amounts of time deadlocked about stupid things, like what to prepare for dinner, as if a marble in her mind was going round and round, never able to settle in the slot marked Chop or Fish.

The experience of denting a Ford Transit van, and being dented in her turn, wrenched Sheila out of her generation. It foreshortened her sense of priorities, so that she found anything short of physical trauma relatively hard to get worked up about. For this reason she became a more indulgent parent. Let them smoke, let them fool around, so long as they look both ways before they cross the road: that was more or less her attitude. Yet survival also made her feel worthless.

Cynthia's illness didn't let up. She and her husband and son came to stay in Anglesey during the summer after the accident. Sheila insisted on being ready for this, but it couldn't be anything but a strain on her, even before Cynthia walked unseeing into a sliding glass door and broke one of the glass bones in her arm. She was taken to the Caernarvon and Anglesey Hospital, the C and A, known locally (alas) as the Cremations and Amputations, where the bell-pull by her bed intended to summon the nurses made no sound.

Later that summer Sheila, out walking with Bill in Rhosneigr village and despairing of expressing her feelings of inadequacy, knowing that it was terrible ingratitude for recipients of miraculous reprieves from death or brain-death not to love their lives, broke away from him and tried to throw herself in front of a car. She discovered that road accidents don't always come when they're called, any more than children do. The car was going at no great pace, and swerved without even coming close. Sheila ran down to the beach, but Bill followed after her and in due course they returned together to the house.

It was medically suggested that what Sheila's brain needed, to shake it out of the depression that seemed to have followed from so much transcription, was a course of electric shock treatment. Obediently she paid weekly visits to Queen Square, where the attempt was made to expel her low feelings with high voltage. The theory of ECT is simply stated: there isn't one. It is no more than a practice, one devised to capitalise on a discovery made in the 1940s, that epileptics don't get depressed. Depressives, therefore, should be enabled to reap the benefits of epilepsy. Counterfeit fits were provoked originally by means of saline injections, before the superiority of electricity was established.

Sheila would come to herself piecemeal, in fuzzy instalments, and would make efforts to leave without an escort, though Bill or a son was invariably on the way to pick her up. Having her brain struck by tame lightning had the temporary effect of simplifying her mental operations, so that she had no idea, when she came round, that she was the sort of person that people looked after and cared for.

On the other hand her mind, even at its most smooth-running, had trouble entertaining such a cosy idea. This was in fact precisely the state of affairs that electro-convulsive therapy was in some way supposed to remedy.

ECT was a mixed success at best. Since it further scrambled Sheila's short-term memory over the period of the treatment, she could never know whether to believe Bill's assurances that she was getting better week by week, shock by shock. She didn't have much to go on. She knew her husband well enough to understand that he liked problems that could be solved quickly, and depressives who could be cheered up with a single dose of his energy. He didn't enjoy being patient except for short bursts. Her misery would end up undermining and exasperating him.

Cynthia Terry died in 1974, and in so doing fixed the certainty in Sheila's mind that the wrong woman had survived. Hadn't Cynthia loved life, as Sheila never quite managed to do? Sheila spent increasing amounts of mental time in a sort of agonising parallel universe, in which Cynthia stoutly recovered, while Bill in due time put aside his bereavement and married a Nice Ordinary Woman, who was good to Sheila's sons.

Thinking about the world better off without her, following through into the future her fantasy of family life soothed by her death, was both a temptation and a torture, an addiction. A perversion.

Only someone with a strong streak of self-abasement, a chronically lowered sense of self, could have wished on her children that thing from which she had so much suffered, a stepmother.

It was during this period that Sheila remarked to her least effusive son that she was glad *he* at least wasn't a sentimentalist, and would turn off her life-support without a second thought. She was quite taken aback when he reacted with dismay. There was no irony intended: she had meant it as a compliment.

If this was a time of interior collapse, it was also somehow a time of self-reconstruction. Sheila put into action a plan that predated her accident, and applied to be the chairman of a rent assessment panel. Her legal background qualified her for the job, which would be part-time – two days a week, say, plus the appropriate preparation. It was also a whole new area of work, with every possibility of the slowness and confusion she found in herself, her general inadequacy confirmed by the accident, being shown up. Perhaps it was best to know for sure, one way or the other.

Partly, too, she was urged on by irritation. If one more Gray's Inn acquaintance told her she was marvellous to have made such a recovery she was sure she would scream. What sort of achievement was it to come back from the dead, if all you were going to do with your ransomed life was sit around at idiot tea parties chattering about the marvels of modern science? She should go in for this ambitious new job, fall flat on her face and become properly acquainted with failure. Get it over with.

In fact she was a quietly spectacular success in the role. Her legal qualifications were indispensable, but what the job chiefly called for was patience and tact. The diffidence of Sheila's authority was underpinned by the fact that, after the accident, she was never altogether convinced of the accuracy of her arithmetic or her reading of the law. She was always open to correction or second thoughts.

The offices of the Assessment were in Newlands House, just across Mortimer Street, as it happens, from the Middlesex Hospital. The recovery that had got under way at the Middlesex, after its false start, was furthered by the bureaucracy on the other side of the street.

Sheila would be asked some weeks in advance whether she was free to work on a particular day, so she had a certain amount of control over her schedule. Successive Rent Acts narrowed the purview of the Panel, and Sheila sometimes had the feeling of being a smiling irrelevance. Nevertheless she enjoyed the work, with its starchy camaraderie: the duties expected of the chairman included buying drinks for the other panel members in a pub at lunchtime. The real rare pleasure of the job was being allowed into people's homes and being warmly invited to inspect them. Having people point out defects or improvements with a touching frankness and deference.

Every now and then a rent assessment panel was called upon to inspect premises occupied by someone self-neglecting or demented. On those occasions Sheila's mild poise was much remarked on by her fellow-members. No degree of disarray in living quarters shook her. No stench seemed able to make an impact. They complimented her on the seamlessness of her self-control, while she permitted herself a faint anosmic smile.

In the private life of her anosmia, Sheila didn't give up the use of perfume. She was still unwilling to do without the rituals of fragrance, reassurance that goes beyond the sensual. She successfully controlled the impulse to anoint herself more freely – the delusion that an extinct faculty might somehow be triggered by sheer excess of stimulus.

Still, she had a sense of frustration whenever a new perfume was launched. She didn't want to be trapped in the past by the subtle feminine carbon-dating of scent, stubbornly attached to her old faithfuls, Balmain's *Vent Vert*, Guerlain's *Chant d'Arôme*, when everyone else had moved on. A new advertising campaign would quicken her mental nostrils and make her curious, unless it was for an obviously inappropriate scent, something sultry or saccharine.

Sometimes she would buy the smallest possible bottle of something announced as fresh or citric, dab a tiny bit on, and then do what women without daughters or female intimates must do. Ask a man.

The men in her family would try with their snuffling male noses and their small vocabularies of sensation to inform her. Bill would say she smelled wonderful, but then he always said that, and his marriage-long inability to spot a new item of clothing unless it was pulled out of a smart carrier bag made him a suspect witness. Her boys were little better, struggling to be honest but baffled by even elementary principles of perfumery: that essences smell differently on different skins, that treble notes evanesce and bass ones linger.

The boys were more reliable when she held a vest or a pair of Bill's socks under their noses and asked whether these items needed washing. The doggy binary of fresh against stinky: that they could manage.

So why did she never have second thoughts about the son-heaviness of her family? The sonniness of Bill's temperament at least has a story to back it up – the fable of the four happy farming brothers. Sheila's falling in with the fable has no story of its own. And wouldn't it have been nice for her, if not at first then later, to have a gender ally in the home?

The only obvious possibility – and it is *thoroughly* obvious, as flat and pat as a newspaper think-piece – is that historically it was women who had damaged Sheila: Gladys by desertion, Lilian by imposition. It was men, historically, who had rescued her: Xavier Cremades (toast him in many tiny sherries), John Firth (toast him in tumblers of Scotch). Even, somehow, the toastmaster himself. Even Bill.

Bill was proud of Sheila's recovery, and liked to invite her down to Judges' Lodgings to show her off. Sheila didn't mind too much, except when she cancelled an evening class, took a train down to Bodmin or Norwich or Carlisle, and then had to sit at the dinner table and listen to Bill saying how wonderfully clever she was, how she was always studying something arty, linguistic or musical, if not all three.

Sheila received a lot of complimentary attention at these dinners, as on most formal occasions, but she had long since learned to neutralise it mentally. She reasoned that in an Ancient and Honourable Society like Gray's Inn, so closely tied to a hierarchical profession, deference was poured so freely over a High Court judge that some of it slopped on to his lady wife – just as tea sometimes spills from teacup to saucer. Bill lapped it up, but she felt she knew better. Nothing she heard was actually about her.

As a wife she realised that she had an obligation to be a good sport on these occasions, and didn't mind putting on the glad rags once in a while. She would even have her hair done, something she hated, before she left London. She was convinced that she had virtually no hair left, just as anorexic teenagers imagine themselves saddled with jodhpurs of cellulite. Sheila was a trichological anorexic, a trichorexic. She couldn't bear to see her hair in the mirror. If ever she mentioned her fears to Bill, of course, he only talked about his mother and her bloody Transformation. He seemed to be making out that what she feared was in some way a test of character – as if she needed any more of those. Something she wasn't allowed to mind.

There weren't all that many consolations of later life, or so Sheila found, but one unexpected one was that you could dress entirely for your own pleasure, now that nobody minded one way or the other. She liked the style of dress required by her work, which she interpreted as being *crisp* but not *cold*. It was no great effort to combine black and white, clean lines and the occasional flirty detail, so as to end up with ensembles that were professional but not unfriendly.

Even when she wasn't working she gravitated towards a style of dress that was somewhere between formal and informal. She favoured some third state between rigour and casualness, something neither chilly nor gushy. She had never suited either flatties or stilettos – for her it must always be a medium heel. Her clothes were never meant to intimidate anyone, but they played their part in helping her to stay in control of herself, whatever she felt like really.

The passing of time had not made her repent of the principles of dress she had laid down for herself as a young woman:

1. Navy makes my face look muddy.
2. I have Joan Crawford shoulders, so pads of any kind make me look as if I've forgotten to take the coat hanger out of my jacket.
3. My knees are vile and not to be seen by strangers.

After psoriasis came along, elbows were added to the knee embargo. Nobody else ever noticed the Joan Crawford shoulders, which proved to Sheila's satisfaction that she had learned how to draw attention away from them. She'd learned a thing or two.

There was never an item of clothing in the shops that she wanted as much as she had wanted a little gingham skirt she'd seen in a shop window after the war, blue with contrasting pockets, one red, one green, when she didn't have the necessary coupons. Otherwise she managed pretty well.

Sheila was brave enough to resume working for Moorfields on Monday mornings, despite the painful associations with her past, her personal Accident Black Spot invisibly marked on the road metal. In the late 1970s the Shaftesbury Avenue branch of the hospital closed down, and Sheila volunteered at Old Street instead.

Indefatigably she pushed the trolley of talking books, trying to wean people off trash, in an interlude of blindness that might even in this respect be merciful, without directly refusing them what they wanted. So if someone asked for a romance, Sheila would think, well, quite a lot of books are romances when you think about it. Surely listening to *Rebecca* had to be more enjoyable than the tired old clip-clop of something from the Cartland stable?

Her slimness, and the vigour with which she pushed the trolley, deceived some of the patients into thinking they were being served by a much younger woman. Sensing a lithe displacement of air, men would inhale appreciatively, and be greeted by a fresh and citric scent, difficult to place.

Sheila's flexibility and energy were notable – but then her Aunt Dot, at that time in her nineties, was proud of her sit-ups. Aunt Dot had been a dance teacher; she couldn't walk, but she could do sit-ups. Sheila went ice-skating regularly, at Queens Club in Queensway, at long last conquering her instinctive fear of going backwards on the ice. On summer holidays in Anglesey, she remained the family's water-skiing star, even getting the knack of the mono-ski.

She could have gone on water-skiing for hours, if it wasn't for the numbness in her fingers. All her life her extremities had been susceptible to cold, so that her fingers went white when she so much as washed a summer salad. Her system had no sense of proportion, and would interpret a sinkful of lettuce and tomatoes as the leading edge of an arctic tempest, requiring emergency measures, the hoarding of blood near the heart.

The principal indignity of the menopause, from her point of view, was having hot flushes that did nothing to warm her fingers and toes. At work when there were inspections to be done in weather that was less than balmy, she learned to use a little hand-warmer bought from a camping and survival shop. A tablet ignited at the beginning of the working day and laid carefully inside the little case would keep her hands functioning for hours. If the tablet ran out, she would have to spend ages bringing her fingers agonisingly back to life in warm water.

Eventually the tendency to numbness was diagnosed as Raynaud's Phenomenon, giving Sheila another support-group publication to subscribe to, along with the anguished bulletins from Compassion in World Farming and the encouraging updates in her psoriasis newsletter. Psoriasis was beginning to yield to science over this period, first to PUVA, a combination of sensitising pill and sun-ray lamp, and finally to the drug methotrexate, despite its whispered carcinogenic reputation. Sheila could adjust the dosage to keep lesions at bay.

Science was slower in getting to grips with depression. Whatever medication she was taking during these years, there was a part of Sheila that permanently identified with the abused calves shown in the Compassion in World Farming literature. Seeing herself as veal, atrociously blanched and tender.

While Bill lived in the present, almost to a fault, supremely confident that he was making provision for the years ahead, Sheila lived in the most dismal of futures, imagining eventualities that she felt she could do nothing to prevent. More than ever she felt there was a stroke in her head, waiting to pounce, and knowing her luck, she'd hang on for years unable to speak, trying to close her lopsided mouth round a soup spoon.

At the same time, her mind ran obsessively over the past, telling her that she had started with a good hand of cards but had somehow thrown them away, letting all her advantages come to nothing. The fault was not in the deal but in the play. If she could only think her way back to the exact point where she had gone wrong, she could . . . what? She would know, that was all, and perhaps she'd be able to live with the knowledge. She reached back mentally into the past, beyond the accident, as far as Lilian, but she could never quite fix the moment of failure.

The house in Anglesey, associated though it was with the heyday of motherhood, was becoming a problem and a burden. Sheila's sons gave no hint of reproductive ambition, and it wasn't that she was in any hurry to be a grandmother. But the logic of a holiday home by the sea fell down if there wasn't a breeding population of Mars-Joneses, a supply of small people to furnish the place appropriately with laughter and abandoned sandy swimsuits. She was afraid of the White House becoming a White Elephant.

Already there were times when she and Bill were there alone, and she looked with a sinking feeling from the chop on her dinner plate to the chop on his. How was it possible to have a sinking feeling when your feelings were a sink in the first place? She felt she was getting, not a holiday, but a prophecy of retirement. She noticed that sons didn't visit casually, spontaneously, but in pairs. Their visits had become dutiful, and perhaps there was even a system in operation, of co-ordinating phone calls to make sure that no son was ever there on his own with those uninteresting people, parents.

She told Bill that she didn't want to retire to Anglesey. He didn't disagree – out of season the island could be bleak – but Sheila wasn't able to make any positive suggestion about the years to come. It was retirement itself she dreaded, the dreary horror of her future.

In 1981 the decision was made to sell the White House, though to the extent that the debate over the house had been a debate about how to handle retirement, no progress had been made. Still, holidays for Sheila (on cruise ships to warm places with ruins and lectures) were now authentic exemptions from running a house, and that was certainly an improvement.

Bill invested the proceeds of the sale in stocks and shares, but in captivity the money could not be persuaded to breed, and slowly pined away. The market collapse in 1987 was only the clincher, after which the money lay on its back in the cage, stiff paws in the air.

A curious feature of Sheila's depression had always been that it contained no element of lethargy. She had plenty of energy, but it brought her no satisfaction. She was very struck by the term 'anhedonia', meaning the inability to experience pleasure, when she read that this had been the original title of the film *Annie Hall*, and determined to memorise it. From the time that she had been told that the learning of new words was the hardest task she could impose on a traumatised brain, she had become something of a bulimic of vocabulary.

How to combat anhedonia? One idea was to go to a therapist, specifically a Jungian, since this school of psychology seemed less obsessed with damage than most. She was estranged from her own vitality, that was what was the matter with her, and being united with your own vitality sounded like an orthodox Jungian goal. In practice, though, the sessions yielded little, and if her therapist was at one with his vitality he did a good job of concealing it.

Perhaps the mind and spirit could be reached through the body? She enrolled in a yoga class, feeling that she should take advantage of a flexibility unusual in a sixty-year-old. She had no difficulty with the exercises, but found the experience anything but transcendent. One particular thing she found unable to transcend was the fear that the individual mats used in the class, sometimes warm and damp from a previous session, were actively smelly. Not being able to verify her suspicions directly, and having an anosmic's natural horror of the undetectably unclean, she felt more than ever entrapped in her body and her negative emotions.

Early in 1985 Sheila realised that she had unaccountably fallen behind in her programme of screening for breast cancer. She was months late. When she duly arranged an appointment a lump was announced. She agreed to surgery, which revealed that the lump had indeed been a novice malignancy.

The men around her, simple souls, argued that if she really

wanted to be dead she would hardly have taken measures, however belated, to preserve herself. But Sheila was not so easily to be tricked into manifesting a life-wish. She knew perfectly well she would survive, worse luck; she just didn't want to be any more maimed than could be helped. Health was a lottery, and she was only interested in the jackpot. Nothing else would do.

Her life was no more than an old plate for her, but if she was going to be denied the satisfaction of going properly smash, she would choose to have the smallest possible number of cracks.

The surgery was successful and the disfigurement insignificant. She found she didn't think about it. Again, she had a short-term preoccupation, as she had in the Middlesex in 1973, when she had reached for her hard-won nose. Would she be able to continue taking methotrexate, or would psoriasis start to win all over again? That was what she wanted to know.

In the event there was no objection, as long as she continued with regular liver biopsies. She was punctilious with these appointments, at least, and never missed one.

If Sheila had few expectations of motherhood, she had none of grandmotherhood. It was only another form of retirement, really, a genetic redundancy notice. Yet when it came she took a pleasure in it that became in time intense. At last the family's notional Welshness came in handy: Sheila would be called Nain (pronounced Nine), Bill Taid (Tide), and these toddler-friendly monosyllables would give them an automatic advantage over Grandmothers and Grandfathers. Gray's Inn Walks proved an undiminished asset, and the playground in Coram's Fields re-emerged as a resource after thirty years. There was even some new equipment.

When she retired from rent assessment, after twenty years, she was given a party – something that even Sheila couldn't quite dismiss as an empty gesture, since no retiring chairman in her time had been honoured in this way.

Bill had retired in 1990, with an agenda of virtually torrential self-expression: he would perfect his neglected guitar-playing, memoirs and plays would pour from him. He had the titles ready. When a couple of years down the line Sheila shyly enquired what had become of all the creativity, he replied that he was catching up on a backlog that had built up during those long and stressful years at the Bar and on the bench. This as he explained it was a backlog of idleness, and would take an indefinite time to clear up.

He had remained in harness as long as he could, which means seventy-five in the case of High Court judges, so perhaps he too was dreading retirement, though he was not a man who could be made to own up to dreading anything, on either side of the grave.

Husband and wife had in common a religious background, but Bill was the one with the religious conviction, though he called it, unembarrassed, blind faith. He never seemed to pray, and was less than fanatical about church attendance. There were services in Gray's Inn Chapel during the short legal terms, and the Mars-Joneses usually attended, but there was a social element involved (seating was hierarchical, with designated places for Benchers, members of the Inn's governing body, and their spouses) and even a nutritional one, since lunch was laid on afterwards in Hall.

When there were children to be brought up, Bill and Sheila attended the City Temple in Holborn Viaduct, which was somewhat in the grain of Bill's native Congregationalism, but after the glory days of Dr Weatherhead and then Kenneth Slack things became a bit evangelical, and they discontinued the habit in the 1980s.

Sheila would often attend early morning communion in Gray's Inn, a sacrament poorly timed to attract Bill, but she was never impressed with the purity of her own heart, before or after Eucharist. Her motivations seemed to her in general horribly self-serving, and she would brood guiltily over sharp replies to testy questions which Bill had long since forgotten asking.

Sheila had more doubts than convictions, religiously, but

could not go to bed without spending time on her knees praying. She was unable to pray in any other position. But then it was the same with teeth: Bill rarely brushed but expected dental salvation, while Sheila wrestled nightly with floss, cutting-edge floss technology, international interdental products available only from John Bell & Croyden in Wigmore Street, since her teeth were too closely set to allow proper access to standard equipment. And still she lived in fear of the hell of dentures.

There was no retirement age for helpers at Moorfields, thank God, and there was also the possibility of new voluntary work. Sheila offered her services (and the benefit of her legal training) to a charitable organisation called Access to Justice, conveniently located in High Holborn. Which got her out of the house another half-day a week.

Over the years, Sheila's discreet death-wish held out against a whole series of medication regimes. When her GP asked her how she was, she would find herself saying she was all right. It saved trouble, and one of the words she had commited to memory after the accident – *endogenous*, as applied to her type of depression – made her think that medication wasn't really going to make a difference. She took the pills obediently, though sometimes when she felt woolly she would taper down the doses, until she reached the point of wanting nothing better than to feel woolly again.

She wasn't melodramatic about wanting to be dead, and she normally knew better than to blurt it out. Whenever she particularly liked a piece of music, she would say that she wanted it played at her funeral, but that was as far as it went, and she smiled when it was pointed out to her that her funeral was turning into a music festival lasting many days.

Still, in the early 1990s, when she was explaining why she had an irrational resistance to selling the car, she let something slip. Bill's decreasing mobility made taxis much more practical, after all. She could see the logic. Finally she admitted the basis of her affection for the vehicle. She had made the decision to keep Bill company while he was alive, but after that she was a free woman, and she was reasonably sure she could do the job with the car. She had no faith in pills, one way or the other.

The moment she had spoken she regretted the bafflement and pain she had caused, and guilt made her agree to see the doctor again. She managed to seem reasonably enthusiastic, even, doing her mime of hope, and this time, out of family loyalty, she didn't say she felt all right when the doctor asked how she was.

Once she came close to having her bluff called, when a son brought her a form of paper called a Living Will and suggested that she fill it in – if she was really so concerned about the possibility of being internally pulped by a stroke, but left living. It was a perfectly sensible suggestion, but then she lost the form in the flood tide of Bill's accumulated papers: financial reports, betting advice, wartime letters mysteriously resurrected from the filing cabinet, and despairing appeals from the Reader's Digest for payment regarding gardening books Bill denied ever having ordered. After that, she thought it would be kinder not to ask for another copy of the form; bad enough to be meekly suicidal without being vague as well.

If this made her seem insincere in her contemplation of last things, then that was just too bad. She was having to consider the possibility that she truly was a thing she did not admire, came close to despising: a survivor. To be a survivor was not an identity. It showed something close to bad taste, like being the last person to leave a party, when you were no particular friend of the host.

She had slim hopes of predeceasing Bill. The closest thing she had to true self-destructive behaviour was her continuing cigarette habit, but her consumption of tobacco had risen and fallen in a bell curve across the decades, since the days when smoking had been an aromatic declaration of independence. After her accident might have been a sensible time to stop, except that those who lose their sense of smell forfeit one of the positive motivations for kicking the habit. Carrying on with her smoking was one of the few faintly defiant aspects of her recovery.

By the early 1990s she was down to three Silk Cut Extra Mild a day. It was less of a crime against herself than a homoeopathic tincture of nicotine. Sons would tease her by telling her not to forget to smoke. Saying goodnight, they would remind her that she still had one cigarette to get through before bedtime, to be sure not to skip it.

When she gave up at last, she was spared the dismal fate of being a person without vices by a sudden passion for plain chocolate digestive biscuits. Her most recent anti-depressant medication increased her appetite across the board, but this was different. It was the first time she had actively craved something sweet since her childhood love affair with treacle tart. She described her taste for the odd chocky bicky in terms of compulsive behaviour, as if she'd be throwing herself down the staircase of Kensington Palace next.

If this was a binge, it was a binge in extreme slow motion, impossible to spot amid the entrenched moderation of her habits. She showed no signs of swelling back up from her wiry size 8 (6 or even smaller in the puzzlingly inflated American sizing) to the buxom size 12 she had been the day she married.

This after all was a woman with a passion for strong Cheddar who for years restricted herself to the placebo cheese Edam, and that in small quantities, for fear of elevating her level of cholesterol. Perhaps the austere binge on biscuits was only a letting up of anhedonia in one particular area, a reacquaintance with the basics of pleasure as pleasure-lovers experience it.

Sheila's vision had clouded over during the 1980s, to the point where actors were fuzzy angels even from the front stalls of a theatre. She was told that she could have her cataracts removed more or less when she wanted, but she chose to wait until after retirement. She couldn't bear to give up even a day of work while she was still entitled to it. That way too she could have one thing to look forward to after being put out to grass.

She would be able to see in full, crisp detail the dreary paddock of her life.

There was a bad moment, during one operation, when she felt a flat click inside her head and heard the laser operator swear quietly to himself. He'd cracked the new lens that he was meant to be bonding into place. In the end, though, her vision settled down without any more surgery. She now had one eye calibrated for vision at a distance, the other one for close work, a bizarre-sounding arrangement when first it was put to her but perfectly practicable. For the first time since she was a child she was wearing neither glasses nor contacts, and she could not only watch the play but read the programme. It wasn't the perfect sight without glasses promised so long ago by that charlatan Bates, but it was good enough.

Difficult to pass up such an image of bifocal awareness, vision not perfect but adequate for objects both near and far. To take stock: Sheila in her seventies is a woman defined as depressive but tirelessly energetic. Only now has she given in to the practicality of a shopping trolley on her daily trips to Leather Lane. At last she makes that concession to the iconography of mumsiness, as she trots on narrow feet daily to the shops, to buy the robust cheese she now allows herself, the Mocha Italia coffee from the Continental Stores that reliably stings her palate.

If depressives were electronically tagged like criminals so that their doctors could better monitor their progress, it would seem to the tracking team that Sheila had mischievously passed off her tag on some very purposeful little person, someone who surged indomitably to the theatre, to Moorfields, to the Royal Academy or the Tate, to Coram's Fields, to Access to Justice. Depression in her case seems to be more a matter of energy frustrated than killed, energy ingrown like a toenail.

Playing with her grandchildren, a group in which the girls now outnumber the boys without any slackening in her interest, she seems absurdly spry. Uncoiling from a long-maintained crouch in the wardrobe where a four-year-old has failed to find her, she mimes a wince at the crepitus of her knees, and seems more than ever like a mediocre actress remembering she has been cast as an old woman. Indulging in a little stage business. It is a poor impersonation of a London senior citizen in the twentieth century.

Sheila has her hair tinted out of a sense of aesthetic preference rather than vanity, if that distinction is tenable, saying she'd be happy to go white but can't abide dirty grey. She sits by the telephone in the sitting room of No. 3, Gray's Inn Square, reading a novel boldly by daylight, but jumps infallibly whenever it rings (the phone, not the novel). From the fierceness of her reaction you would think that Alexander Graham Bell had only just invented the instrument. That he had installed the prototype in Sheila's sitting room, so as to start it up every now and then, to see if it worked.

Sheila's life has been rich as well as, for long periods, almost continuously unhappy, although the richness of it is not apparent to her. She has felt trapped, first by other people's choices and then by her own. Like any animal in a trap, she has gnawed at her own leg to get free – it's just that sometimes she has gnawed the wrong leg.

Every so often, her life has run into a wall, the wall of a separation (from a mother, a father, a floating husband, a nose, a job) or a collision (with a stepmother or a Ford Transit). Is it surprising that when a life runs into a wall it is changed? Not surprising. The surprising thing is actually the reverse: how much people bring, stuffed into their pockets, clenched between their teeth, over the wall and into the after life.

When Sheila married, she knew that sooner or later, Bill's nature being what it was, she would have to cough up children. That was always the phrasing she used, to 'cough them up'. She gave birth to Tim in 1953, Adam in 1954 and Matthew in 1957. I am the middle cough of her womb's coughing fit from the 1950s. I love my life, which isn't quite the same as saying that I expect happiness from it. One of Sheila's virtues as a mother was to have stopped telling us, quite early on, that everything was going to be all right.

Written for Virago's book *Sons and Mothers*, edited by Matthew and Victoria Glendinning, 1996

My Hero

My lover Michael Jelicich died in May, of Aids, aged twenty-six, cared for by his family in New Zealand. I knew when we met that he was very likely to be ill, which raised the stakes from the start and made it impossible to keep our relationship casual. The virus helped our intimacy along.

Michael was in this country on a two-year work permit, but he didn't displace native labour for long. After nine months, in early 1987, he became unable to work, and I supported him after that. Michael hated to spend money, and took pride in how little his dependence cost me.

He often said that he was happier in London with Aids than in Auckland without, a statement that shocks me as much as it did when he first made it. But perhaps I underestimate the unhappiness of gay men in small cities. Michael was not attracted to the bleach-blond surfie in Day-Glo shorts who was, he insisted, the only isotope of gay style so far thrown up by his home town.

Michael was not an aggressive wit, a serve-and-volley wit. His was a quieter game, based on an outstanding return of serve and on passing shots brilliantly disguised. I remember him convincing his mother, Beverley, on her visit to London last year, that people who wore National Health dentures found them embarrassing, since they had no division between the teeth, and amounted to a hoop of white, upper and lower.

Michael hoped to be a part of the first generation to live with Aids long-term. In New Zealand he had been somewhat New

Age in outlook, a little mystical. He became more and more of a rationalist as time went by, but never mocked his friends' hopes or fears. I remember him saying to someone whose T-cell count had fallen to 400, 'That *is* low', with only the faintest Victoria Wood inflection for my benefit (his own count then stood at nine).

It was one of Michael's achievements to disguise mortal fatigue with a relaxed manner, so that people could genuinely think he was laid-back, rather than dying. When he set his heart on something, though, he usually got his way – Christmas at a Norfolk inn, for instance, last year, though he had to ride pillion on a motorbike through driving rain to get there.

Michael had to leave the country soon afterwards, when his visa ran out. His unwise sexual orientation meant that finding someone he wanted to live with gave him no rights. He chose to go back to New Zealand in January, so as to enrol for university, but he was also keen to catch up with his family. His sister Robyn was sixteen, and had been fourteen when he had seen her last.

He was uneasy, too, about the prospect of being nursed by me. Even when a bug called *Cryptosporidium* made him vomit in mid-bout of diarrhoea, he hadn't let me clear up. Now a cancer lesion in his mouth called for radiotherapy which would be debilitating, and he was more comfortable being looked after by Beverley.

Our household was also a little precarious. The flat I had bought in Highbury was small for us, what with Michael unable to work and me working from home. Having worked only as a hairdresser, he didn't realise that sometimes I only *looked* as though I was doing a crossword, and was inwardly refining some masterly phrase or other.

In any case Michael found what I wrote by and large tedious. Our relationship was not physically passionate, for a number of reasons including my fear and his exhaustion, but he could at least assure me that he didn't love me for my mind.

From Auckland he sent me audio tapes, until the inflammation of his mouth made speaking too difficult, and then he dug out his old typewriter. A central section of his pretty beard fell out, which greatly distressed him. Beverley fed him his favourite fruit sponges and crumbles, then mobilised her liquidiser so he could take everything in through a straw.

Michael was by New Zealand standards a veteran of Aids, and made his voice heard. He was proud of getting the standard dose of one particular drug raised from 50mg to 150, after his researches told him that the relapse rates were much lower on a higher dose.

The wonderful day arrived when he could eat toast again, but soon afterwards he came down with meningitis. He was able to tell me on the phone from hospital that in his dark glasses he felt like Roy Orbison. He discouraged me from coming out to see him until he had left hospital; normally he won that sort of bet.

I still listen to Michael's voice on his tapes and marvel at the mixture of sweetness and dryness, qualities incompatible in a wine but not in a person, or not in this one.

Michael would have been amused by the idea of being my hero, but he might have approved in a general way. He resented the assumption that Aids was tragic largely because it cut short so many glittering careers. Nothing died with Michael except a few thousand expert haircuts – and of course the happiness he had from his friends, and returned to them.

Independent Magazine, 1989. It was a privilege to get an obituary published for someone who had never been in the papers.